Fighting with Napoleon's Light Infantry

Fighting with Napoleon's Light Infantry

The Memoirs of Captain Vincent Bertrand 1805-1815

Dr Neil Sanghvi

Pen & Sword
MILITARY

AN IMPRINT OF PEN & SWORD BOOKS LTD.
YORKSHIRE – PHILADELPHIA

First published in Great Britain in 2024 by
Pen & Sword Military
An imprint of
Pen & Sword Books Ltd
Yorkshire - Philadelphia

Copyright © Neil Sanghvi, 2024

ISBN 978 1 39908 022 4

The right of Neil Sanghvi to be identified as the Author of this work has been asserted by him in accordance with the Copyright, Designs and Patents Act 1988.

A CIP catalogue record for this book is available from the British Library.

All rights reserved. No part of this book may be reproduced or transmitted in any form or by any means, electronic or mechanical, including photocopying, recording or by any information storage and retrieval system, without permission from the Publisher in writing.

Typeset in INDIA by IMPEC eSolutions
Printed and bound in England by CPI (UK) Ltd.

Pen & Sword Books Ltd. incorporates the Imprints of Pen & Sword Archaeology, Atlas, Aviation, Battleground, Discovery, Family History, History, Maritime, Military, Naval, Politics, Railways, Select, Transport, True Crime, Fiction, Frontline Books, Leo Cooper, Praetorian Press, Seaforth Publishing, Wharncliffe and White Owl.

For a complete list of Pen & Sword titles please contact

PEN & SWORD BOOKS LIMITED
47 Church Street, Barnsley, South Yorkshire, S70 2AS, England
E-mail: enquiries@pen-and-sword.co.uk
Website: www.pen-and-sword.co.uk

or

PEN AND SWORD BOOKS
1950 Lawrence Rd, Havertown, PA 19083, USA
E-mail: uspen-and-sword@casematepublishers.com
Website: www.penandswordbooks.com

Contents

List of Plates	vi
Preface	vii
Foreword	ix
Introduction	xiv
Brief History of the *7ème Régiment d'Infanterie Légère* 1805–1815: History, Training, and Identity	xx
Translator's Note	xxvii
Table of French and British Ranks during the Napoleonic Wars	xxviii

Chapter 1	1805 & 1806: Bertrand Joins the *7ème Léger* and the Battle of Jena	1
Chapter 2	1807: Napoleon's Polish Campaign	13
Chapter 3	1808: Garrison Duty in French-occupied Prussia	30
Chapter 4	1809: The Campaign against Austria: Echmühl and Wagram	36
Chapter 5	1810 & 1811	52
Chapter 6	1812: The Russian Campaign	59
Chapter 7	1813: Dresden, Kulm and Peterswald	105
Chapter 8	1814: Return to France and Garrison Duty at Huningue	136
Chapter 9	1815: Service with the Army of the Rhine, Disbandment, and Home to Nîsmes	156

Notes	178

List of Plates

1. *The Evening after Jena* (14 October, 1806), by Édouard Detaille.
2. *Napoléon on the Battlefield of Eylau* (7-8 February, 1807), by Antoine Jean Gros.
3. *Napoléon on the Battlefield of Eylau* (7-8 February, 1807), by Antoine Jean Gros.
4. Corporal of a French light infantry regiment (chasseur company), 1807-1812.
5. Carabinier of a French Light infantry regiment (Carabinier company), 1813-15.
6. *Death of Général Gudin at the battle of Valontina*, (19 August, 1812), by Zvonimir Grbasic.
7. *Marshal Ney supporting the Rear-Guard during the Retreat from Moscow*, (1812), by Adolphe Yvon (1817-1893)
8. *Charge of the Russian Cuirassiers at Kulm*, (30 August, 1813), by Vasiliy Fiodorovich Timm (1820-1895)
9. Officers of a French light infantry regiment in walking-out dress and service dress, 1813-15.
10. Carabiniers of a French light infantry regiment (Carabinier. company), 1813-15.

Preface

In tracing my memories, I did not have any pretensions of writing a military history from 1805 to 1815. I simply wanted to note down more or less day by day, my impressions, what I was able to do, what I saw done, and relive my life as a soldier of the *Grande Armée* on the battlefields of this memorable era. These memories are, as far as I know, far from being a literary work, but they can sometimes seem interesting and endearing. In any case, for me they have no other merit than to serve as a monument and a legacy to my two grandsons.

Paris, 26th May, 1861.
Vincent Bertrand, *7ème Régiment d'Infanterie Légère*,
Officer of the *Légion d'Honneur*, retired Captain.

Foreword

In his memoirs, my maternal grandfather Captain Bertrand modestly recounts his life of fatigue, misery and glory from 1805 to 1815. There are no brilliant and marvellous adventures, only the sincere account of what he saw and did, during these ten years, either on the battlefields, or in the cantonments in Austria, in Germany, in Poland, or finally in the painful stages of his captivity. Everything is enhanced with anecdotes that are gallant, burlesque or dramatic. Called to arms through conscription, he was directed from Nîsmes, his hometown, to the depot of the *7ème Régiment Légère* (7th Light Infantry Regiment), in Huningue, where he arrived on 16th November, 1805. He did not leave this regiment, composed almost exclusively of sons of the department of Gard, until 1815. He even refused, in the meantime, the great favour of entering the *Chasseurs à Pied* of the Imperial Guard, not wanting to be separated from his military family. The young Bertrand was of medium height, lean, active, of an ardent and energetic temperament, and fond of pleasure and danger. In a short time, he became an alert, vigorous, resourceful voltigeur, with unfailing bravery and composure. This would enable him to emerge with honour from many dangerous or delicate situations. With the military spirit fast growing within him, he began to resonate with all the great passions of this time: *la Patrie*, the regimental flag, and the Emperor Napoléon. He would join the ardent worship of this trilogy to that of his Catholic faith until his last day, as an old man. In the last days of November, 1805, the young soldier crossed the Rhine and left France, which he would not see again until 1813. He did his military training while covering stages of ten hours on average through Württemberg and Swabia. His detachment then joined the *7ème Léger* (in Heudelet's division of Augereau's *7ème Corps d'armée*), which was responsible for holding the line of the Isaar. In 1806, after the Peace of Pressburg, the *7ème Léger* would be confined to the north of Frankfurt-am-Main.

In October, the author received his baptism of fire at Saalfeld and Jena. He confessed to having displayed reckless bravery in the latter battle. In December, he took part in all the combats along the Narew and Wkra rivers. In 1807, he was at Eylau and Friedland, not to mention the many engagements against the Russian rear guards. At Eylau the *7ème Léger* was decimated and passed shortly after to Gudin's division of the 3rd Corps under Marshal Davout, to which it was assigned until 1813. The anecdotes relating to the Tilsit camp are picturesque and original. In 1808, he was in cantonments on the Vistula, then in Berlin, Brandenburg, Silesia, Saxony, and Hanover. In March 1809, war broke out towards the Danube. On April 19th, 20th, and 21st, Davout's corps of 30,000 men, with the Danube on their backs, fought off 100,000 Austrians between Ratisbon and Abensberg, pinning them down and holding them down by means of daring and skill, thereby allowing the Emperor Napoléon to carry out his manoeuvre on Landshut. During these three agonizing days, Montbrun's light cavalry division, aided by two battalions of the *7ème Léger*, heroically held and covered Davout's left flank. The author belonged to one of these two battalions, which also fought on at Eckmühl on April 22nd. The *7ème Léger* then participated in the siege of Pressbourg before returning to Wagram where Bertrand received his first injury: a musket shot to the right thigh. In 1810 and 1811, he and his regiment were in cantonments in Hanover, Westphalia, and Holland. He was promoted to *caporal* (corporal) in April 1810, and *sergent* (sergeant) in March, 1812. During the march on Moscow *sergent* Bertrand took his share of glory at Smolensk, Valoutina, and Borodino. During this last battle, in front of the Russian-held great redoubt, all the officers of his carabinier company became casualties. *Sergent* Bertrand, although wounded, took command and saved his unit from disaster. In the evening, at the bivouac, he received, from his equals and his subordinates, a curious certificate on this subject. In addition, he was nominated for the decoration of *chevalier* of the *Légion d'Honneur* by Gérard, the Division-general (*Général de division*) to whose command the *7ème Léger* was assigned. In the retreat, the *7ème Léger* almost always served in the rear guard. Bertrand would fight at Malojaroslawetz, Wiasma, Krasnoë, Berezina, Ponary, Kowno, and was one of the few of the regiment who whom the cold, hunger, and enemy fire spared enough to continue fighting. His story of the burning of Moscow and the human tragedy during the retreat is grand in its simplicity, and shows what the indomitable energy of a man can achieve, when joined to the loyalty and discipline shown towards the regimental flag. On 31st December, 1812, the *7ème Léger* entered Thorn with just 47 officers, 34 non-commissioned officers and 111 ordinary soldiers. When the regiment had crossed the Niemen, in June, 1812 it had numbered 146 officers, 196 non-commissioned officers and 3,000 soldiers!

In January 1813, *sergent* Bertrand was appointed company sergeant-major (*sergent-major*). Unfortunately, during the marches back to France, he fell seriously ill. Desperate not to abandon his regiment, he dragged himself from hospital to hospital, only escaping death thanks to his moral strength, and finally returned, in May, to Huningue. His joy at finding himself once more with the regimental flag was undermined by bitterness when he saw his comrades and even some of his subordinates promoted to officers. Nevertheless, he was appointed adjutant warrant-officer (*adjutant sous-officier*) on 14th June, 1813. At this time the *7ème Léger* was part of *Général* Philippon's division (assigned to the *1er Corps d'armée*), first under *Général* Vandamme, then Mouton, Count of Lobau). After the victory of Dresden, Bertrand receives the cross of *chevalier* of the *Légion d'Honneur* from the hands of the Emperor himself, with his appointment dating from 19th September. He miraculously escaped the disaster at Kulm on 13th August, 1813 but on 14th September, his battalion was completely destroyed in a rearguard action at Peterswald. Wounded by three sabre blows in the arm, two lance thrusts in the neck, a pistol shot near the face, and trampled by Russian horses, he was captured by the enemy. He was sent, step by step, to Transylvania after his wounds had healed. He would not see France again until August, 1814.

During the Hundred Days, the *7ème Léger* was part of the Army of the Rhine, in *Général* Legrand's division, attached to *Général* Rapp's *Corps d'armée*. *Adjutant sous-officier* Bertrand participated in all the combats that occurred in lower Alsace, on the Queich, in Seltz, in Surbourg and in front of Strasbourg. These skirmishes continued until 10th July, 1815, three weeks after the battle of Waterloo. At this time, *Adjutant sous-officier* Bertrand was promoted to Second Lieutenant (*Sous-lieutenant*) by *Général* Rapp and he witnessed *sergent* Dalouzy's astonishing adventure. Dismissed from the army on 1st November, 1815, he was sent on two months' leave with semestered pay. He then returned to Nîsmes, in the midst of the White Terror, at night, as a bourgeois civilian. During the following days, he was spared neither threats nor insults. Enrolled in the Legion of Gard on 1st December, 1815, he was definitively dismissed on 20th February, 1816, since the government of Louis XVIII did not recognise his claim to the grade of *Sous-lieutenant*. In March 1816, he resumed service as a fusilier in the 1st Infantry Regiment of the Royal Guard, and did not regain his rank of *Sous-lieutenant* until 1825. He was promoted to *Lieutenant* in the same unit by a Royal Ordinance of 1st August, 1830, dated at Rambouillet. He then transferred to the *43ème Régiment d'Infanterie*, becoming a *Capitaine* (Captain) in 1836.

He retired in 1839, residing at Paris. In 1848, at the age of 63, he valiantly led the 6th Company of the 3rd Battalion of the 11th Legion of the National Guard of the Seine during the bloody days of June. On 23rd August he received the Officer's cross of the *Légion d'Honneur* from the Government of the Republic. *Capitaine* Bertrand did not leave the uniform until he was 70 years old. This soldier, who had never known alcohol or tobacco, was still strong enough to go on foot, at the head of his company, from the Place Saint-Sulpice, Champ-de-Mars, for a review of the National Guard. His old age was consecrated, with the most absolute self-sacrifice, to his two grandsons, both orphans. He had the joy of seeing them enter the military academy of Saint-Cyr together, but the supreme happiness of seeing them wearing the officer's epaulette was refused to him because he died in 1864, at the age of 79, a few months before they left school. He lived a life full of honour, loyalty and devotion. Conforming to his frequently expressed wish, I devoted my earliest free-time in my retirement to reproducing his notes, classifying them in chronological order and religiously respecting their spirit. I only took the liberty of attaching a few footnotes (Original editor's note) in order to specify certain dates, or particular situations.

Chaland de la Guillanche, retired *Colonel* of Infantry
Shamrock House, Saint-Servan, 15th December, 1906.[1]

Introduction

Upon finishing the *Memoirs of Captain Vincent Bertrand*, the keen reader of the Napoleonic memoir genre would probably agree that Colonel de la Guillanche's foreword does not do his grandfather full justice in terms of his heroism. Vincent Bertrand was, during his service during the Napoleonic Wars, first an ordinary soldier, and then a non-commissioned officer (*sous-officier*) of various grades. In each he was a near-model infantryman, demonstrating character, discipline and patience, as well as dedication to his regiment and its values and standards. The non-combatants he saved, the esteem he earned from his comrades in battle, and the comfort he gave to a fellow convalescent on the brink of death, would all indicate he was a hero to some, and an admirable soldier to all. If he had any flaw, it was his desire to look after his stomach when the circumstances permitted it, and he was punished by his superiors accordingly when caught.

An army is only as useful as the force it projects, quantitively and qualitatively. Whilst officers at all levels lead and direct an army's labours, an army derives its strength and stamina from its soldiers and non-commissioned officers. The armies of Napoleon and his marshals contained the fullest range of human materiel. This was attributable to the ever increasing size of late eighteenth and early nineteenth century armies, the emerging imperfections of the Napoleonic conscription process, and the large number of men per company, battalion and regiment. Campaigning in a greater diversity of countries and climates, and against a greater variety of foes than any other army at the time, brought out the qualities and flaws of each of these men. This in turn impacted the army's *esprit de corps* from subdivision and company to regiment and *Corps d'armée*. Consequently, whilst the course of Napoleon's campaigns and the themes of French military service will quickly become familiar to readers of Napoleonic memoirs, each one will differ in how its author experienced those campaigns and themes. There will always be something surprising for the reader to discover, or something recognizable to cross-reference with existing memoirs. As for Bertrand's service record and his conduct, the French army relied on thousands of model soldiers like him to maintain its core strength over hundreds of leagues of marching. When others left the flag from sickness, weakness, foraging, or desertion, the officers of the *pelotons* and battalions could count on Bertrand's kind to arrive in good order and hold their position until the rest caught up and followed their example.

Consequently, the memoirs of Vincent Bertrand do not need anyone to tout them as exceptional or distinctive just so that they may stand out among others. It is sufficient that they add to and enhance our expanding knowledge of military experience in the *Grande Armée*, and that they do so in a well-paced and engaging manner. Furthermore, his memoirs are full of details to be absorbed in subsequent readings, thereby extending their value. As such, they rank among the best written by the ordinary soldiers of Napoleon's infantry, as opposed to those written by officers. From the latter we can demand more in terms of style and content, by virtue of their superior education and access to a greater variety of reference material. However, officers' memoirs also tend to suffer from the habit of turning into general campaign narratives as they rise through the officer grades, thereby losing the personal touch found earlier in their memoirs, or in those of ordinary soldiers. Bertrand continues to describe his face to face encounters, especially during the campaigns of 1813 and 1815, which can be somewhat rushed in other memoirs. Of particular interest in these later campaigns are the low-level skirmishes and pursuits Bertrand describes, a rare eyewitness account to the disaster at Kulm, and the extraordinary Dalouzy incident in 1815, when a non-commissioned officer took it upon himself to represent the needs of the Army of the Rhine to the hostile Bourbon government.

Serving his light infantry company with enthusiasm and steadiness in combat from 1805 onwards, it was only in 1812 that Bertrand distinguished himself in battle, at Borodino. As the senior *sergent*, he gave orders to his company when all other officers and *sous-officiers* were incapacitated. Afterwards, he would account for several enemies personally with his musket and bayonet, as well as carrying out his duties in organizing and administering the ordinary soldiers in his unit. Off the battlefield, he demonstrated much bravery and kindness to the victims of war, such as rescuing an exhausted Prussian child who was hiding in a burning castle. Before the battle of Eylau, he encountered a Polish woman trapped between a stove and a wall, and going into labour. Bertrand was able to bring an old woman to her, who acted as a midwife. Both these acts were recognized by his officers, but they only served to establish his heroic character off the battlefield. Such bravery was already in abundance among the French rank and file, having been encouraged by the diverse duties in the camps along north France from 1803 to 1805, and later described in various memoirs of Frenchmen from Spain to Russia, and from Naples to the Baltic. More remarkable perhaps, was when the entire regiment rallied to assist a *cantinière* as she went into labour during the retreat from Moscow. Lacking surgical instruments, the soldiers of the *7ème Léger* donated their precious linen to the surgeon delivering her baby, whilst Bertrand stole a blanket from an artillery horse to keep her warm. He was aware that this was a sinful act, but nevertheless felt justified in saving two human lives. A few days later, at the crossing of the Bérézina, he was unable to leave the ranks to assist the wife and child of one his colleagues, to his heart-wrenching regret. A far more grisly incident happened a few weeks later, when Bertrand found himself trapped in a crowded cellar with the exits blocked, with many occupants crushed to death or drowned in the alcohol that had pooled from smashed bottles. It was only by working with a fellow *sous-officier* that they were able to escape, saving each other in the process.

Through these tribulations it was the promise of promotion and the anticipation of receiving the *Légion d'Honneur* that motivated Bertrand to survive and carry out his duty. Until the Russian campaign it would seem that his promotion within the *sous-officier* grades was stalled by his weakness for seeking out higher-quality dining than what was officially available to his comrades. These included disobeying orders to remain in camp in 1806 by visiting a Berlin restaurant; bayoneting a loaf of munition bread under the eyes of an irate *Général* Oudinot; ordering a feast when he was supposed to guard the Museum of Antiques in Vienna in 1809; and remaining at a restaurant in Magdeburg in 1810 once all public places were ordered shut after 10pm. The consequences, though amusing, usually ended with imprisonment in the guard house for several days, and the entry of such punishments into the offender's service record.[1] Whilst perfectly understandable that a French soldier of the period would take any opportunity to make his situation more comfortable, it would seem that Bertrand crossed the line between strict observance of military discipline and deserved indulgence too often. Unlike his early mentor Lacour, Bertrand set a poor example for subordinates to follow during these early years. He therefore made a less suitable candidate for promotion, especially when there was no shortage of brave, disciplined soldiers in the early days of the Empire. At any rate, the fine dining of Bertrand and his comrades contributed not only to their nutrition, but also in topping up their morale, which could be said to have provided an edge in fighting spirit over their enemies, and even their contemporaries in other French units. Their *joie de vivre* can be compared to that of the *vélite* Bugeaud, an officer-candidate of the same age and also serving in the 1805 and 1806 campaigns, who found his two years of marching in the ranks to be unbearable. Unlike Bertrand, who loved his regiment but had no such guarantee of attaining officer status, only the promise of promotion kept Bugeaud from leaving the army altogether.[2]

Much more serious than breaking curfew was the marauding expedition that Bertrand joined after the 1806 campaign. In addition to being unauthorized and detrimental to local relations, it threatened the very lives of the French soldiers who sought to vary their diet. Attempts to obtain unauthorized food and drink provoked an angry response from angry Prussian peasants. Pursued to a nearby farmhouse, the marauders were only rescued by the approach of a French officer commanding a detachment of troops. The punishment for the marauders, decided in this case to be death, was only reprieved by the declaration of peace between France and Prussia. Bertrand's brushes with military discipline provide an interesting insight into how effective control of French troops was when occupying conquered territories.

Interestingly, even when promoted to *sergent* around January 1812, occasional infractions, such as the hurling of a potato at his German host's head, only earned him minor punishments, rather than a reduction in rank. By September 1812, He was the eldest *sergent* in his company. Although it is not clear when he was promoted to *sergent*, the time frame suggests that the other three *sergents* at the time of his promotion had even less time to adjust to their new role as non-commissioned officers. After his capture in 1813, he spent a year in Austrian territory with various commissioned officers, whose collective example of gentlemanly behaviour under adversity persuaded him to emulate their example. By the time he was released in 1814 however, Napoléon had abdicated and the royalist Restoration had taken place. *Sous-officiers* of humble origins such as Bertrand were precisely the sort of people the new regime intended to keep in their place, as had been the status quo before the Revolution.

Bertrand was fortunate to have avoided the White Terror, being warned by his brother of this anti-Napoleonic backlash in which several ex-Napoleonic personnel were murdered and many more persecuted by local populations. He was also fortunate in restarting his career as an infantry officer as early as 1825, when Louis XVIII had been replaced by the even more reactionary and despotic Charles X. Retiring from active service aged 70, Bertrand was living proof of the saying 'old soldiers never die.' He was also the founder of a military family, whose offspring would begin their careers as officers rather than ordinary soldiers. This must be considered a remarkable success and legacy for Bertrand, at a time when French peasants and bourgeois wished each successive generation to climb further up their chosen profession than their ancestors.

Dr Neil Sanghvi,
Oxford, 2023

Brief History of the *7ème Régiment d'Infanterie Légère* 1805–1815: History, Training, and Identity

Regimental History

The regiment that Bertrand knew and loved was formed in 1796, as the *7ème Demi-Brigade d'Infanterie Légère*.[1] The new *7ème Léger* was formed out of the old *20ème Bataillon d'Infanterie Légère*, and multiple volunteer battalions including those from the *Demi-Brigade de Aurois*, and the *Demi-Brigade de la Sarthe*.[2] In 1803, the regiment received its new title of *7ème Régiment d'Infanterie Légère*, which would remain until its disbandment and reorganization as the *Légion du Jura* in August, 1815.

Serving with *Général* Bonaparte's Army of Italy during the campaign of 1796, the *7ème Léger* participated in the siege of Mantua and the battle of Castiglione. In 1798, one of the regiment's three combat battalions embarked aboard the squadron that carried Bonaparte's Army of the Orient for his expedition to Egypt. This battalion of the *7ème Léger* was detached to Malta, which was garrisoned by the French en route to Egypt. It was decided to occupy this island to deny it as a base for the Royal Navy and the British army, who might use it as a staging post for a landing in Egypt. When the garrison of Malta surrendered in 1800, the battalion and two carabinier companies drawn from the other two battalions were repatriated to France.[3] The three battalions then served with the Army of Liguria in Italy during the War of the Second Coalition, with Bertrand's mentor, Lacour, earning a silver musket at the battle of Marengo.[4] It was also from this campaign that Bertrand proudly received his cast-off infantry coat.[5]

In 1802, the third battalion embarked on the expedition to the island of San Domingue in the West Indies to put down the rebellion of former slaves, where it was later incorporated into another unit. In 1803, the remaining two battalions of the *7ème Léger* were at Toulon, and later Bayonne, for an anticipated expedition to Portugal. It was then expanded to a four battalion regiment, incorporating the recently disbanded *20ème Demi-Brigade d'Infanterie Léger*.[6] In 1804, it was part of Marshal Augereau's *7ème Corps d'armée* at Brest, where it prepared for the abortive invasion of England. The first and second battalions were at Brest itself, whilst the third and fourth were Rennes.[7] In September 1805, Napoleon decided to call off the invasion of England and instead march east towards Bavaria and Austria, where the Austrian and Russian armies were mobilizing. It was his intention to forestall the planned invasion of France by the allies, and defeat them whilst they were still in their own territory. Camped at the westernmost extremity of France, Augereau's *7ème* had the furthest distance to reach the Rhine river of all the seven *Corps d'armée* that comprised the *Grande Armée*. Always marching behind the rest of the *Grande Armée*, it covered approximately 1,000km from Brest to Basel. Meanwhile, the other *Corps d'armée* had surrounded the Austrian General Mack's army at Ulm and forced it to surrender on 20th October. They then marched deeper into Austrian territory, entering Vienna on 12th November. By 14th November, Augereau's 12,000-strong *7ème Corps*, including the *7ème Léger*, had surrounded the Austrian General Jelacic's division of 4,000 men in the Voralberg, on the

Austro-Swiss border.⁸ Augereau had prevented Jelacic from covering any attempt by the Austrian Archduke John to march his army from Italy towards the main Austro-Russian army, which was assembling in the vicinity of Austerlitz. By the time Napoléon had won the battle of Austerlitz, which took place on 2nd December, Augereau's *7ème Corps* had relocated from the Voralberg to Ulm, but was still 700km west of the main theatre of operations.⁹ In late December, the *7ème Léger* was moved to Munich, Bavaria, where the detachment Bertrand was part of arrived as reinforcements. At this point Bertrand's own narration of the *7ème Léger*'s campaigns across central Europe, into Russia and back to France can take over.¹⁰

Training and Tactics

The French infantry during the period in which Bertrand served was composed of regiments of line infantry (*Infanterie de la Ligne*), and regiments of light infantry (*Infanterie Légère*), as well as elite Imperial Guard regiments drawn from both line and light units. Standard battle tactics revolved around the principle of 'manoeuvre to fire', rather than 'fire to manoeuvre'. This required the precise handling of large numbers of men and the deployment of close-order formations. This was to maximize the number of muskets that could fire per unit of space, to deliver a cohesive bayonet charge, and to harness the collective morale of the constituent soldiers.¹¹ When more flexible tactics were required, French infantry could also operate as loose bands (*en bande*), capable of working their way freely over difficult terrain without the restrictions of cadenced marching. They could also operate as skirmishers (*en tirailleur*), moving in pairs and spread out over a greater distance to reduce the chances of being hit by enemy fire.¹²

Brief History of the *7ème Régiment d'Infanterie Légère* 1805–1815   xxiii

The light infantry nominally received more training in skirmishing, reflecting its role in the late seventeenth to mid-eighteenth centuries as irregulars attached to the regular units of the line. By the Napoleonic Wars, both line and light infantry were largely considered to be equally adept at fighting in battle formations, as bands, and in skirmishing.[13] Indeed, their official training was the same, this being three 'Schools' designed to teach a soldier how to manoeuvre and fire in the battle line. The first, the 'School of the Soldier', taught the recruit how to stand, march and operate his musket alone. The second, the 'School of the *Peloton*', built upon this for a *peloton*, this being the basic fighting formation of approximately 90 men (and after 1808, 120 men), marching and fighting in three ranks.[14] In his memoirs, Bertrand mentions passing through these two schools as a recruit, but perhaps surprisingly, not the third. The third was the 'School of the Battalion' in which eight (and after 1808, six) *pelotons* formed a battalion. This was the smallest tactical unit that was large enough to be effective on the battlefield, and thus of direct interest to the generals commanding larger organizations. However, the number of men required for the 'School' meant that it was not always possible for a single depot to have enough recruits to train for it, especially with the combat battalions being on campaign in wartime.[15] It was nevertheless essential for both line and light infantry combat battalions to be proficient in deploying into marching columns, attack columns, the battle line, and the square formation. Consequently a smaller version of the battalion must have been attempted, possibly by combining infantry recruits from the regiments of nearby depots, or using men carrying flags as markers for skeleton *pelotons*. Alternatively, depot *pelotons* returning from service aboard the fleet as marines might make up the numbers.[16]

Beyond the three 'Schools', fixed in the Ministry of War's 1791 *Rules concerning the exercise and manoeuvres of the Infantry*,[17] and repeated in subsequent editions and unofficial manuals,[18] there was little other standardized training, and no 'School of the skirmisher.' There were, however, several not officially sanctioned manuals on skirmishing tactics and the operations of light troops at the advance posts. These were written by senior commanders for the units assigned to them, on their own initiative. Such works include those of Colonel Guyard, or Generals Morand and Duhesme, which were then published for a commercial audience if they found favour with a suitably distinguished patron.[19] However, these were more concerned with the roles that light infantry were expected to perform, and the procedures that were developed for officers to follow, rather than the actual training of the ordinary soldier like Bertrand. Consequently, it would seem that in practice, light infantry regiments were only distinguished by the frequency with which they were assigned these roles, and even then only if they actually acquired sufficient practice and skill to be better at it than their line counterparts. An indication that this may have been the case is the fact that light infantry regiments served in an army's advance guard more frequently than those of the line, as any campaign history or order of battle will suggest. Beyond this, we must rely on memoirs of light and line infantrymen which detail the daily operations of the troops, and compare them in terms of frequency, capability and efficacy where possible. Certainly Bertrand and the *7ème Léger* were regularly involved in the scouting, patrols, reconnaissances and pathfinding that light infantry was expected to provide, as well as skirmishing with enemy advance posts. Only the voltigeurs, of which each line and light battalion possessed a *peloton*, were considered elite skirmishers, with their soldiers being selected from the other *pelotons* for their physical ability, marksmanship and determination. These may well be regarded as dedicated light infantry, but this only highlights the similarities between the majority of the personnel in the light and line regiments.

The Regiment and its 'Flag'

Unlike the British infantry battalions, those of the French regularly served together on campaign, as a full regiment of two, three, four and even five battalions. A brigade usually consisted of two regiments of two battalions each, but the larger regiments formed a brigade all of their own. Consequently, the regiment was an important tactical unit, being able to deploy its battalions along a large front both in length and depth, and to detach battalions along multiple axis of manoeuvre to achieve different local objectives.[20] To the ordinary French soldier, however, his regiment was much more. As Bertrand regularly professed, it was his emotional and spiritual home, and the unit to which he gave his loyalty, pride and dedication. It offered the greatest permanency and cohesion in terms of personnel, identity and conditions of service. In particular, the 'Flag', or Eagle which Bertrand longed for when separated from the *7ème Léger*, represented the regiment in all its honour, traditions and glory. In 1804, the various flags of the former *demi-brigades* were replaced by a bronze gilded eagle mounted on a plinth and pole, to which a standardized red, white and blue flag was attached. In 1807, they were withdrawn altogether from light infantry regiments in the field, due to the impracticality of defending them when multiple battalions were tasked with light infantry duties.[21] Some light infantry regiments complied, whilst others retained them.[22] Interestingly, Bertrand clearly describes the eagle of the fourth battalion of the *7ème Léger* as having been damaged by a cannonball at Eylau in 1807, and serving as a rallying point during the retreat from Moscow in 1812. Perhaps more than any other infantry memoir, Bertrand emphasizes the true power of the eagles. They were more than just a visual rallying point during the confusion of battle or retreat; they were part of the values and standards that he learned when joining the *7ème Léger*, and part of the language he used when describing the call to duty he and his comrades felt every time they were separated from it.

Dr Neil Sanghvi

Translator's Note

In translating this memoir, I have taken every effort to preserve Bertrand's style and intent. Consequently, I have chosen to preserve as much French terminology as possible, especially where the names of military units and ranks are concerned. This has the advantage of allowing the reader to recognize the significance of units and ranks in the French military hierarchy when cross-referencing them with future memoirs translated by my hand, or with material still in the original French. For reference, please see below for a table comparing French Napoleonic ranks to their contemporary British counterparts. Where necessary I have added my own footnotes to provide further context to the 21st-century English-speaking reader. I have endeavoured to keep these footnotes according to the style required by the History Faculty of the University of Oxford. This is to provide consistency with any academic works or future memoirs that I may publish, and to give full credit to authors whose works have been cited in my footnotes. To distinguish my footnotes from those of the original editor and Bertrand's grandson, Chaland de Guillanche, each footnote is succeeded by (Translator's note) or (Original editor's note) respectively.

Table of French and British Ranks during the Napoleonic Wars

Other ranks (soldiers, corporals and non-commissioned officers)

French rank	British equivalent	Command	Role
soldat	Private	N.A.	Combat, labour
caporal	Corporal	*escouade* (12–15 men)	Combat, administrative
caporal-fourrier	Company clerk	N.A. *peloton*-level duties	Administrative
sergent	Sergeant	section (24–30 men)	Combat, administrative
sergent-major	Company Sergeant-major	N.A. *peloton*-level duties	Discipline, police.[1] administrative
adjudant sous-officier (*adjudant*)[2]	Regimental Sergeant-major	N.A. battalion level duties	Discipline, police, administrative, training of other ranks

[1] Police refers to the French military concept of keeping an orderly camp or bivouac, with designated areas for various facilities, a daily routine, and a roster for fatigue duties.

[2] According to Bertrand, the *adjudant sous-officier* was considered to be the most junior grade of officer, according to custom, and with some corresponding privileges, such as being included with commissioned officers as prisoners of war. Officially, it was still a non-commissioned rank.

Commissioned officer grades

French rank	British equivalent	Command	Role
Sous-lieutenant	Ensign/2nd Lieutenant	Subdivision (48–60 men)	Combat subaltern, supervises other ranks
Lieutenant	Lieutenant	Subdivision (48–60 men)	Combat subaltern, supervises other ranks
Capitaine	Captain	*Peloton* (90–120 men)	Combat, administrative
Adjudant-officier	Adjutant	N.A.	Administrative, training of officers
Chef de bataillon	Major	Battalion	Combat, administrative
Major	Lieutenant-Colonel	Regimental Depot	Administrative, second in command to the *Colonel*.
Colonel	Colonel	Regiment	Commands two or more battalions
Général de brigade	Brigadier-General	Brigade	Commands two or more regiments
Général de division	Major-General	Division	Commands two or more brigades
Maréchal de France (Marshal)	N.A	*Corps d'armée*	Commands two or more divisions

Chapter 1

1805 & 1806: Bertrand Joins the *7ème Léger* and the Battle of Jena

On the 16th November, 1805, I turned 20. I was at the depot of the *7ème Régiment d'Infanterie Légère* at Huningue, and was conscripted into the regiment.[1] Known as the *7ème Léger*, it was assigned to the brigade of Sarrazin, of *Général* Maurice-Mathieu's Division, in Marshal Augereau's *7ème Corps d'armée*.[2] Though saddened somewhat from saying goodbye to my mother and full of memories of Nîsmes, my hometown, I was nevertheless received cordially by the old soldiers of my company. They were veterans of our victories in Germany, Switzerland, Italy, and Egypt. My bed-mate was called Lacour.[3] He had a silver musket won at the battle of Marengo.[4] His weapon carried the following inscription: 'For capturing two cannon on the 14th June, 1800, at the battle of Marengo.' Lacour was assigned as my instructor, instilling in me the principles of the French army as well as the School of the Soldier;[5]

1) Obey your superiors.
2) Be brave on the field of battle.
3) Defeat the enemies of France.
4) Protect, in all countries and all circumstances, the children, women and the elderly.
5) Never lose sight of the flag; it is the rallying point, and the glory of France.
6) Never desert.

One of the lessons ended with him declaring 'in a few days we will beat the Austrians for the twentieth time. you will be near me, and I will show you how the musket priming burns the backs of these enraged rustics'.[6] I received a coat that was practically worn to the lining, and 20 centimetres too long; it was a glorious relic of the battles along the Adige or Mincio rivers in Italy. I was very proud of this uniform, and with it went a cartridge pouch of coastal troops, without the wooden cartridge holder inside, suspended from a shoulder-belt that was once black but now nearly multicoloured, a shako whose visor was attached with three staples, and an ancient musket manufactured at Charleville in 1771, whose priming pan could barely hold half the required priming powder. The bayonet alone was beyond reproach.

Departure for the combat battalions of the regiment

As our detachment crossed the river Rhine they cried 'Vive l'Empereur!' But I shed two tears onto my shoulder-belt, at the thought of my mother and myself. The first stage of the march was ten hours long, and conducted through driving rain. We were quartered in a village, and I was billeted upon a poor weaver, who could not even offer us bales of straw to lie on or feed his three children. Exhausted and soaking wet, we fell back on a hostel where for 2 kreutzers or 1.80 francs, we found hard bread, butter, cheese, and beer. Coffee was unavailable, but Lacour replaced it with heated brandy, which went to my head because I was unaccustomed to alcohol. Reclining sadly on our straw bales, we heard the sound of violins. I persuaded my comrade that it was better to dance than to sleep, and we went to the 'ball'. Having had four months of dance lessons before I joined the regiment, the quadrille and the waltz held no secrets for me. I overcame my timidity and made signs and gestures that I wished to dance, and I waltzed until the morning with many young girls, some with blonde hair, some with brown.

In the morning, the drums called for us gallant foot-sloggers, hussars, and artillerymen to form column, as the time to say goodbye had arrived. Before we set out for Augsburg, we left a few sous for the weaver's children.[7] We arrived at Augsburg in the evening.[8] After the treaty of Pressburg was signed, the *7ème Léger* went into cantonments at Munich. The Bavarian population received us cordially, seeing us as liberators from the Austrian yoke. I was billeted upon a doctor. By now I was an admirer of Napoleon, and decided to travel to Paris. For some time my soul had been following Bonaparte's star; I felt great admiration for his victory, and pride at being one of his soldiers.

In February 1806, the regiment received orders to move to Frankfort-sur-le-Main.[9] We looked back on the last ball fondly, since it gave us a chance to dance with and fully appreciate the beautiful Bavarian girls. By contrast, the young people of this part of Germany kept interrupting their invitations to dance, to drink and smoke. In these cases we invited the better-looking girls to dance with.

After three days of marching, my company was in a cantonment at a village whose entire population consisted of Huguenots chased from France by the Edict of Nantes.[10] All the men, women and children came to meet us, offering us beer and brandy, carrying our knapsacks, arguing over who was going to lodge who, and giving us the pleasure of speaking French. I was billeted upon the schoolmaster, named Godard, and whose family came from my region in France. Treated like one of their own in their house, it was not long before I fell to the charms of their eldest daughter. Her name was Isabelle, whose talents with the harp gave me such sweet enjoyment. I wished to learn music, but my heart beat too strongly for a measure, and as a loyal soldier, I had to give up on the advice of my host, who identified my difficulty as taking my lessons in German. A sudden order to depart separated me forever from my harpist. Our new cantonments, below the river Lahn, was 15 leagues away.[11] I wanted to write and return to see her, but Lacour made me see the folly of doing so, and reminded me of the principles of the army. A posting that was agreeable had turned into one of frustration.

I was a good swimmer, and took to bathing daily in the river Lahn, within sight of the castle where our brigade commander, *Général* Sarrazin, was quartered. The owner of this castle, a baron, had two daughters who, having seen me, asked that I teach them to swim. The *Général*'s aide-de-camp suggested it to me, and I accepted eagerly. On the 20th of July, 1806, I began my lessons under the watch of the *Capitaine*, who sat in a small rowing boat, having first built a cabin for the young girls and one for myself. I was soon lodged in the castle itself, and allowed to dine at the family's table. My two students made rapid progress. We launched ourselves into the full river, escorted by the gallant aide-de-camp in his boat. After each swim, which lasted one hour, we returned to our cabins, and I changed into my uniform, of blue breeches, coat, and forage cap, and went to the castle for refreshments. The girls then mounted their horses with the *Capitaine*, who, later, would marry the eldest, called Theresa.

The Prussian campaign of 1806

I left the castle and returned to the bivouac on September, 1806. As we passed through Frankfort-sur-le-Main on the 28th, we received equipment for the coming campaign, such cauldrons, pails, and mess tins. At the skirmish at Saalfield, Prince Louis of Prussia was killed by *sergent* Guindet of the *10ème Hussards*, who was decorated for his action by the Emperor.[12] The Prince's body was being transported to the church at Saalfield and my company was assigned to watch over the coffin of this young man who died gloriously on the field of honour. The funeral bier was improvised hastily, and was without a lid, and I could look at its contents at my leisure. He had a single wound; a deep sabre thrust beneath his heart. This figure, which lacked the pallor of death, kept the animated look of combat. He wore a brilliant hussar uniform, and his sabre lay next to him, with the Prussian coat of arms inscribed upon it. My company passed the night in the church. The Prince's aide-de-camp and his first gentleman of the chamber were admitted, weeping hot tears. We were perfectly happy to render assistance to this aide-de-camp, and he wished to give me money in gratitude. I expressed surprise, and he begged me to accept a pipe which had belonged to his grandfather, who had been killed at the battle of Rossbach during the time of Frederick the Great.[13] He said to me he was from Potsdam, and begged me, estimating that we would soon reach that town, to give the news of the Prince's death to his family. After the battle of Jena, my corps passed through Potsdam, but I was never able to leave the ranks to attend his family. The pipe he gave me was stolen, much later, in Silesia, and much to my regret. A chasseur of the *7ème Léger* named Delmas, came up with a verse which the whole army chanted the next day:

It was the Prince Ferdinand
Who thought he was a giant
Such was his hubris.
A hussar (quite rightly)

Said to him 'you may not pass'
Or else I'll send you quickly to your death,
To your maker, to your maker.

Three days after, on the 13th October, at the town of Jena, the *7ème Corps d'armée* was formed into the order of battle.[14] Bivouacs were established, and those units not on duty were dispersed, according to custom, in multiple directions to forage for supplies. This mission was usually given to the best marchers, of which I was one. I arrived with some chasseurs from my company at an abandoned chateau, which had already been pillaged by the Prussians and filled with French troops. It was the very picture of waste and disorder. Being on the second floor with a comrade, sword in hand but without the intention to fight, I arrived at a servant's room and noticed, under the bed, the soles of two shoes. I wanted to draw them towards me with my sabre. A cry was heard, and as I stooped I saw a child trembling thoroughly, trying to press herself between the bed and the wall. I tried to reassure her. We put our sabres back in their scabbards. It was a wasted effort as she remained as still as death. As night fell, the number of foraging parties increased, and we could not leave her to an uncertain fate. After our efforts, we prised the bed away and removed the girl with decency and care. She fainted. We pushed past the crowd, intending to leave her at a village some distance from the castle. But the curious followed us, amazed that we were carrying a corpse. They insulted and threatened us. The poor child, revived by the fresh air, and seeing herself surrounded by such figures, began struggling. Finally, an officer of Marshal Davout's headquarters arrived, who at first wished to arrest us, but after we explained the situation to him, commended us. Speaking in German, he questioned her, and, with the assistance of two other soldiers, we took her to her family, in the village. Halfway there, we noticed a great glow; a fire had burned down half the castle she had sought refuge in.

Arriving in the village, we found the place entirely occupied by ambulances, and the inhabitants turned out of the homes. Our young protegée, seeing her parents' house invaded, lost her head; despair seized this frail creature, we not knowing what to do. However we went to the pastor's house, which was serving as a headquarters. She threw herself into the arms of this religious official; he turned out to be her uncle. Happy at this reunion, we re-joined our company in the middle of the night and could all the better justify our long absence since the staff officer of Marshal Davout's headquarters had already visited our *Colonel*.

Battle of Jena, 14 October 1806

The following day, the 14th October, a cannonade at dawn announced to us that the fighting had begun. My battalion, in skirmish order, faced Prussian cavalry.[15] It was my second baptism of fire, but I was next to Lacour and in the midst of old soldiers. Suddenly some enemy cavalry pinned us and threatened our position. My comrades, calm and firm as rocks, said to me, 'Cadet, aim at the breast straps of these Prussian horsemen. They want some music, but we will make them dance.' I was, I dare say, brave to the point of impudence. After we returned fire, the skirmishers returned to the regiment and reformed into battalion formation. *Général* Heudelet saw how critical our situation was, and ordered us to form square, into which formation we barely had time to throw ourselves. The enemy cavalry charged around the immobile infantry square, which held like a block of granite. Then they withdrew to regroup, and the voltigeur company was sent forward in skirmish order, shouting 'Use the bayonet!' However, one of the sides of the square opened fire, and the voltigeurs returned to the battalion to avoid being hit by their own comrades. The enemy, encouraged by this development, made a determined charge, and were met with musket fire from all four sides of the square. Horsemen and horses were falling at our feet, and the charge descended into disorder. Then the carabinier and voltigeur companies of the battalion advanced forward, pursuing the fleeing cavalry at the point of the bayonet, and taking dismounted horsemen prisoners.

On the 17th October, after a long forced march in pursuit of Blucher's troops, the regiment bivouacked in the middle of the night.[16] The forward posts were established, shelters made, and as was customary, foraging parties sent out. We followed a small river, which led to a large town, about half an hour's march from the bivouac. We were dispersed about eight or ten per house, when suddenly the tocsin rang out, and the inhabitants attacked us. We only had sabres for weapons. We barricaded ourselves, with musket balls raining upon our position. We were obliged to leave the ground floor and move to the first. We resolved to sell our lives dearly. One assailant climbed to the first floor, and was shot. We heard the screams of our comrades caught in the street, some of whom managed to escape by running to the flag.[17] A battalion took up its arms and marched into the town. At its approach those who were attacking us or were in the streets disappeared. We were able to rejoin the regiment, which we found formed up in battle order at the entrance to the town. The *Général de brigade* immediately installed his command there. The next day, our comrades, who were victims of the madness of civilians who refused to follow the rules of war, were avenged. The *Général* forbade us to enter the homes of the residents or to give them any trouble, then billeted the *24ème de Ligne* upon them instead of us.

Entry into Berlin, October 1806

On entering Berlin, on the 26th of October 1806, it was forbidden to leave the unit without authorization. I left nevertheless left with some comrades to have a good meal, but before we could rejoin our regiment, we were placed under arrest by some officers and *sous-officiers*, and punished with guard duty for eight hours. On my return, I received a lively reproach from my comrade Lacour. We were in cantonments between Berlin and Charlottenberg.[18]

The *7ème Léger* was at a revue held by the Emperor on the 6th November 1806, and the following day we set out on the route to the Vistula. We were welcomed as brothers at Varsouvie. My company was ordered to guard the baggage teams and ambulances, near a town. I took advantage during the two day stay to visit it and take some relaxation. The regiment crossed the river Vistula, in the middle of the night, downstream of Varsovie, and in flimsy boats. The *7ème Corps d'armée* bivouacked on the right bank. During the night, an alarm and the galloping of the headquarters' horses caused panic among the servants and *cantinières*. We ran to our arms, and all the commanders, including Marshal Augereau himself, were at their posts. Our brigade general personally led some cavalrymen and a company of voltigeurs. He scouted the area, but it became apparent that it was a false alarm during which the French and Russian outposts took up their arms. We were able to have a few hours of sleep afterwards, and in the morning, we amused ourselves at the sight of our comrades who had slept downwind of the bivouac fires, and who were covered in black soot. This was because we had used pinewood for fuel, which was particularly resinous.

Bridgehead at the river Wkra, 24 December, 1806

The regiment, on detached duty from the division, was advancing rapidly, when in several minutes Russian musket balls began to wreak havoc on our formation.[19] Our voltigeurs were deployed as a skirmish screen, whilst the regiment supported them, in column.[20] We entered a wood which the Russians were defending. Our drums beat the charge and we drove them off with the points of our bayonets. As we left the woods, we found ourselves on the right bank of the river Wkra. The Russians had established themselves on the left bank for at least several days, since they had burned the bridge and placed artillery batteries behind earthworks.[21] The Marshal ordered us to re-establish the bridge and cross it in the night. A battalion of my regiment was entrusted with finding a crossing elsewhere, and a call went out for swimmers among the soldiers. I was among the first to volunteer to be part of this detachment. We numbered 150 swimmers, and were directed by officers from the corps headquarters, including the husband of the girl I taught to swim at the river Lahn.[22] After half an hour of marching we stopped at a place which seemed suitable, there being a mill and two small boats on the other side. One of the officers of the headquarters asked me to scout out the mill, but the entire detachment wanted to be the first into the water. The officers allowed only two *sergents* and a drummer to accompany me, the rest taking up positions in order to follow us. Wearing only our breeches, we reached the opposite side in a few strokes. The mill being occupied only by two older women, we returned with the boats. The rest of the detachment swam over and headed for the bridge, where musketry and cannon fire was raging.[23] The Russians spotted us, and turned their cannon fire on our position, and launched two or three companies of infantry against us. The detachment, covered by some skirmishers, found itself heavily engaged. Marshal Augereau, having heard the fighting and realizing that our situation was critical, given our small number, later made us say that we crossed the bridge instead.[24] At that moment in fact, under a rain of canister shot, the workers were still laying planks on the bridge supports which the Russians had not enough time to burn before our arrival. Hearing the drums beat the charge, we threw ourselves headlong at the enemy, and we arrived at the same time, as a column of infantry that by now had crossed the newly built bridge, before the Russian defences. These Russians, despite a stubborn defence, were ejected at the point of the bayonet.

As they retreated, they abandoned their artillery, but left a rearguard of two battalions of infantry in a fortified mill, which allowed a few cannon to escape. This mill was stormed by our infantry in a hand to hand fight when, to my horror, a fire broke out on all sides. We were seeking an escape route from the fire, when the cries of women and children reached our ears. We ran in that direction, and saw a stable, the roof of which had already been half consumed by flames. It contained two women and three children. One of us attempted to brave the danger to save them, but unfortunately he took a step in the wrong direction, and perished in the furnace. When it was my turn, I entered the stable with the help of god, as my source of my courage. The thick black smoke forced me to retreat, but I noticed a small side door through which I forced myself to re-enter. One of the women immediately clung to me, and I took her outside with the child she was carrying and the one she was holding by the hand. Leaving her infants outside, she returned to the blaze. I rushed after her, but she reached the other woman and her child before me, and saved them. This is how providence enabled me to do some good during this fire, where the cries of the wounded, abandoned to the flames and the night, left a sinister impression. I had a great deal of trouble finding my musket and my company afterwards.

Bertrand ruins the soup

The Mamelukes, engaged against the Russian rearguard, used their yatagans in a frightful manner; moreover, it was the only time they had the opportunity to charge during this campaign.[25] Their presence made us think that the Emperor was nearby, and we nearly burst with joy.[26] We arrived at the place we were to meet in the night-time, and placed our out-posts, collected fuel, and lit fires. I found, some distance away, in a large farm, set on fire by the Russians, two horses and two oxen, which were half burnt. Using my *sabre-briquet* (the light infantry carried a small sword, almost straight and very sharp), I cut a large slice of meat from the oxen, which I announced on my return to the joy of the bivouac. It went straight into our cauldron as soon as my comrades lay their eyes on it. Alas! We forgot to remove the skin, and when we wanted to try the resultant soup in the middle of the night, we found a greyish bitter bouillon in our spoons. It was a bitter blow for stomachs running on empty after two days' worth of combat, which had not seen a crust of ration bread since Varsovie. You can judge what blessings we launched in the direction of the poor cook.

Despite our skinny condition we still had to fight the Russians the next day, the 26th of December, at Golymin. During this battle Marshal Lannes pushed them back at Pulstuck (Pultusk). In this way we celebrated Christmas with three days of fighting.

Chapter 2

1807: Napoleon's Polish Campaign

We were in cantonments on the outskirts of Osterode, where the Imperial Headquarters was established.[1] The army took a brief rest, of which there was great need. Up to that moment, in the middle of a harsh winter, only the Imperial Guard had been issued greatcoats. The rest of us had to use cloth taken from captured Russian stores. Each company received two sheets of cloth of the same colour; ours were white. Our tailor had had his thigh fractured by a bullet, so we had to cut and sew the greatcoats ourselves, which we called 'sentry boxes', as they were so ineffective at keeping the cold out. Mine was the most skilful and I received compliments from the *Capitaine*, an old soldier who had fought at Marengo. We also had to make gaiters and breeches ourselves; we could not count on the regiment's master-artisans to make these items, as they had stayed at the *7ème Léger*'s depot, in France.

Action against the Russian rearguard, 4 February, 1807

On the 1st of February, 1807, we left our so-called cantonments to march towards Eylau. On the 4th, we encountered an enemy rearguard attempting to block our path. After two hours of relentless fighting, we were finally masters of a village which had changed hands again and again.[2] In the middle of musket fire and cannon balls, some unfortunate women, carrying or holding infants, panicked and ran everywhere; some of them fell dead to the musket fire and cannon balls. It was horrible. My battalion was designated to occupy the village, already half destroyed. We set out, Lacour and myself, *sabre-briquets* in our hands, in search of provisions.

Arriving at a small building, next to a mill, we heard crying from a weak voice, and we discovered, on the ground floor, between a large stove and the wall, a young woman spread out on the straw, with traces of blood on her feet. Seeing us holding sabres and with faces animated and blackened by combat, the poor creature thought her final hour had come. She clasped her hands in a gesture of prayer, and asked for grace. We wanted to rescue her and tried to lift her but she opposed it. Having lowered myself I noticed a child frozen with the imprint of death, and understood her reason for refusing our assistance. This poor woman, seized with fright during the fight for the mill, which the Russians had valiantly defended, had gone into labour.

'We cannot leave her,' I said to Lacour, and I began to take the child to remove it. But, taking my hand, she showed me what was hindering me. With the grace of God, and the courage of this woman, I managed to complete the delivery. Lacour came back with some comrades carrying a mattress, which we slid under her. A German-speaking corporal asked her what she needed, but she could only sob. However, as she was shaking with fever, I gave her a glass of water with sugar that I possessed. We were nevertheless ashamed at our helplessness before the sufferings of this woman, thinking that at any moment we could be forced to abandon her. She succeeded in making us understand her desire and need to have a female with her. I left immediately and noticed an old woman in a neighbouring field. I ran to her and indicated, by signs, to follow me. Speaking in broken sentences, she fell to my knees, and begged for mercy. After arguing, I put her on my shoulders, and like Paris carrying Helen of Troy, I was on my way to the mill. The poor old woman was nearly unconscious from fear; along the way my comrades greeted me with questions of the most picturesque kind. Two officers wanted to stop me, but I continued and deposited the old woman at the feet of the baby. This baby, thanks to her, received all the care that was required to keep it alive. The two officers, surveying this scene, understood my well-intentioned actions without explanation.

When I returned to the bivouac, my *Chef de bataillon*, my *Capitaine*, and several officers, having heard of the affair and laughing at the 'kidnapping,' warmly congratulated me. The *Chef de bataillon* made a report to the *Général*, of which nothing came, but we considered it sufficient reward to have acted in a charitable and Christian manner. One of the regiment's *cantinières* received an order to drive this young lady, who was a miller, to the neighbouring town, in her wagon, to reunite her with her family. I like to think that this young woman would have maintained a good memory of us French soldiers.

The Battle of Eylau, 7–8 February, 1807

Four days later, during the bloody battle of Eylau, the *7ème Corps d'armée*, of which I was part, suffered the most, out of all the army. The divisions of Desjardins and Heudelet were deployed between the village of Rothenen and the town of Eylau, at intervals, in the first two lines. At 1000 hours, they advanced toward the Russian position, passing between Rothenen and the cemetery, in closed columns. Once they had passed, they deployed into battle formation. The 1st brigade of each division deployed, and the 2nd brigades behind in squares. As they advanced, a burst of snow obscured their direction of march, causing them to move left, and leaving a large space on the right. At this moment, no less than 72 Russian cannon rained down vast amounts of cannon balls, which in less than 15 minutes annihilated these two divisions. My regiment, the *7ème Régiment d'Infanterie Légère*, was formed up on the right of the first ligne of Heudelet's division. We had reformed, when the Russian cavalry charged into us. After a brief but courageous resistance we were forced back to the cemetery, yielding ground all the while, but without being driven off it entirely.

During the night of this sad victory only *sergent* Lagasse, the corporals, and 17 other chasseurs were present in my company.[3] In the middle of the night I slept on the battlefield, in front of our funereal bivouac, until I felt a hand place itself on my shoulder. My first movement was to take hold of my sabre, but I saw it was a Russian soldier who had dragged himself up to us, his thigh being crushed by a cannonball, and only being held on by a few skin flaps. I left immediately to find a surgeon, because of the two surgeons on the regiment's establishment, one had been killed, and the other was with the ambulances. I had the good fortune to meet with the surgeon-major of the *24ème Régiment de Ligne*, who was busy attending to a senior artillery officer. He went to inspect the wound and declared that there was nothing he could do, because the poor fellow was not strong enough to endure an amputation of a leg. This poor Russian soldier, whom we cared for as best we could, died very peacefully, lying on the snow, which was stained with his blood, holding my hand, which he did not let go of until the final moment. What a sobering sight! The horror of this was worsened by the large snowflakes which fell, with a frost of 18 degrees.

We passed the night wandering about with corpses in our midst, in search of our missing friends. I wanted to find a childhood friend whom I know had been struck when the hail of Russian canister shot had broken our square. I was at first deceived by the movement that the regiment had made to the right at nightfall, but it had in fact returned to the front of the church of Eylau, where during the long hours of the battle the Russian cannon balls had decimated our ranks. It was here that I found my friend, his face against the ground, horribly mutilated, but still holding his musket, bravely killed whilst facing the enemy. I took his frozen hand and squeezed it with mine, but, hearing the drums beating the rally, it was with a heavy heart that I said my final goodbye, and returned to the bivouac. The following day of the 9th February, 1807, we passed over the battlefield. We were thus able to secure the wounded, and as much as possible, bury the dead. My friend was not forgotten and he was buried with his musket in his hand. My white greatcoat, which I had made with such care, was severely mistreated by musket balls; nevertheless it would continue to serve me for a long time.

After Eylau, the remnants of Augereau's *7ème Corps d'armée* were attached to the *1er* and *3ème Corps*, and my regiment, the *7ème Léger*, was assigned to *Général* Gudin's division in the latter, commanded by Marshal Davout.[4] For four months we carried out advance post duties that were as annoying as they were dangerous. We received some provisions, from distant Thorn and Varsovie, but for the majority of the time, we were reduced to organizing foraging parties. The Russians were doing the same, and we sometimes met in the same village. We had to fire our muskets at them, and rarely did we come back without having to regret hitting some of our victims.

The inhabitants had hidden everything they owned in the forests, from food and drink, to clothing and personal articles. They were either in holes in the ground, or at the bottom of the ponds.[5] Also, our detachments always included men carrying their arms on their backs, and those without arms carried canvas bags, picks, shovels, and ramrods from our muskets. We called these last the 'probers'. It was their job, in effect, to probe the ground, whether plain or forest, to discover buried crates or barrels.[6] As soon as the ramrod encountered some resistance, the picks and shovels went to work, and in this way we found crates of flour, lard, salted meat, dried vegetables, and potatoes. All clothing and personal effects, except for linen underclothing, was carefully respected, because the Emperor had given the strictest orders on that subject. One day, I was acting as a 'prober'. My ramrod struck a wooden board under the ground, the others quickly dug up the earth, losing very little time, because several of our advance-posts had been taken by Russian patrols. The lid of the crate was lifted, revealing the body of an old woman who had not been buried for long. Seized with fright, we immediately heaped earth over this poor dead person, so that she could rest in peace for eternity.

The day after this macabre discovery, running through the forest, we reached the edge of one of the many ponds found in Poland. After probing it with long poles we brought a barrel up to the surface. Great joy! But it kept drifting away from us. After an hour, misery and hunger performed prodigies, and we brought it back to the shore, without a boat of any kind. Our sabres breached the circles, the moat fell, and to our celestial joy, we found ham, lard, and smoked sausages. We returned to probing the pond, but without further success. However, convinced that this pond hid other riches, three of us, despite the rigours of the month of March, threw ourselves into the water and discovered mooring cables attached to strong ropes. Immediately three other swimmers threw themselves into the pond, and we had the supreme satisfaction of bringing up large pots that had airtight seals, and sturdy crates. They contained butter, fat, jugs of *eau de vie* and rum, bottles of Sauterne wine and wines from the Rhine region, flour, and dried or salted vegetables.

That night, the company had a feast on a scale we had not known for a long time, and the *Capitaine* having put all the provisions in a safe place, the following day we made a distribution with all possible care and economy. But that source of provisions was soon exhausted and the radius within which we could search contained nothing else.[7] Meanwhile, the Russians were reinforcing their lines, and we could no longer expand our search into the countryside. Since this lack of food was joined to the considerable annoyances of service at the advance-posts, and as we were spending 15 to 18 hours in every 24 under arms, with even the closest posts being an hour's march from our camp, you can appreciate our miserable situation. Moreover, those mounting guard arrived at their posts two hours before daybreak, but this last fatigue was compensated by the result obtained. Because these grand guards were doubled when the Russians attacked at dawn, they weren't quick to congratulate themselves at how well we received them.

The rare distributions of bread coming from Thorn and Varsovie was, despite all the efforts of the Emperor, insufficient, and we had to resort to digging up potatoes, cut in half or quartered, and buried in the earth like seeds. After having taken all the food from the poor peasants, we would take away their hope of their harvest. But we were driven to it by the harsh necessity of hunger. I could not think without admiration at the resignation, full of grandeur, and the devotion of the unfortunate Polish nation, whose resources we exhausted, and who, in the middle of the misery caused by our presence, stayed at our side, as loyal and faithful friends.

During this period, forming part of an advance post, I was doing duty as a sentry, from 0000 hours to 0100. The *caporal* showed me the direction of the enemy and told me to fire my musket at anything that came from that direction. About half an hour later, I heard marching in this direction. I doubled my attention, not wanting, by unnecessarily firing my musket, to invite the mockery of my comrades, all veterans who had fought in the Revolutionary campaigns under Moreau and Bonaparte. The noise increased, I marched resolutely towards it, but I had barely moved 10 paces when a great mass leaped out and knocked me down violently, with me on one side, and my musket on the other. The sentinel who was between the small post and myself also encountered the same mass and cried out 'To Arms!' Then I noticed that it was a very large deer. But the small post believed they were under attack, and took up their muskets. An officer, a *caporal* and four soldiers went to see the cause of the alarm, and I found myself looking for my musket so I could have in my hands something to defend myself. I was overwhelmed with questions I could not answer, but we soon knew the truth. We laughed at length, but a patrol was nevertheless sent as close as possible to the Russian lines, which like us had been put on alert. That cursed deer, who had been at least as scared as me! We spent the rest of the night on our feet, carrying our muskets. It was the talk of the company for a long time.

Skirmish against a Russian rearguard on the 9th June, 1807[8]

Towards the end of May we left our camp without regret and marched to Heilsberg. On the 9th June, 1807, after a rough day of marching, as night fell, we approached a wood, when suddenly a Russian battery opened fire and the rounds from its cannon thinned our ranks. The regiment's three companies of voltigeurs went into action, the rest of the companies followed, but the artillery attached to our advance guard was stuck in the rear and could not support us. Consequently, we were unable to gain any ground, when suddenly the sky was obscured, and a terrible thunderstorm broke out; the lightning flashes succeeded one after, the thunder growled, the Russian cannon replied, and to these devilish sounds we charged towards the wood, which we took. These convulsions of nature, this din among the heavens and of war, accompanied by the cries of the wounded, and the howls of the living, created a horrific image that lingers before my eyes, even though this affair of outposts was of little importance and was frequent enough during this period. My bayonet was warped along its length by a lightning bolt.

Battle of Heilsberg, 10 June, 1807

My battalion, deployed as skirmishers, was advancing, as they had at Jena, with our first dash forward resulting in a group, of which I was part, becoming separated from the rest of the battalion. One sergeant, four voltigeurs and myself, a chasseur, were surrounded by Russian Cossacks who were deafening in their shouts of 'Urrah'. Not at all frightened by the pistol shots they fired as they fluttered by, we kept them at a distance with our bayonets, but our position began to become untenable, with the battalion withdrawing toward the regiment, when a unit of French hussars under *Général* Pajol came up and dispersed the Cossacks.[9] We slept on the battlefield and the following day we left the bivouac. We marched through a torrential rain when we heard a distant noise that we knew all too well. It was the Emperor! The columns of troops stopped and deployed into battle order. He passed by, on horseback, at the walk, in front of the troops. Water poured from his bicorn hat, down-turned by the rain, onto his grey greatcoat, which was itself covered in mud up to the shoulders. The drums beat on the field, the music and fanfares of victory and glory could be heard, and feelings of joy and enthusiasm beat in all our hearts. The Emperor noticed a drummer of our regiment with his head bandaged by a handkerchief soaked in blood. He asked him what caused the injury, and this drummer, whom we called 'the Egyptian' because he had participated in that campaign, answered 'Sire, yesterday, when beating the charge, I had an ear unhooked by a Russian ball.'

The Emperor, seeing that the drummer had the *Légion d'Honneur* on his chest, and on his drum belt the drumsticks of honour won at Marengo, said to the *Colonel* of the *7ème Légère*, 'This brave man was with me in Italy, send him to me'.[10] A little after we arrived at the plateau of Eylau and bivouacked around a monument raised to the glory of the *14ème regiment de ligne*, in the middle of the remnants of that unit's abandoned weapons, already rusty, and the tattered uniforms of French and Russian soldiers; never had so many brave men lain beneath the earth.[11] At dawn, the drums and music joyously announced our departure, chased by funereal visions. On 13th June, my regiment formed the advance guard of a probing attack into a forest. I noticed *Général* Oudinot who, at that moment, commanded a division comprised of grenadier and voltigeur companies taken from each regiment of infantry. He was on foot, with one of his aides-de-camp, guarding a huge pile of bread. For some time my knapsack had been deprived of this precious foodstuff, and as we had fixed bayonets to advance towards the enemy, I approached. The *Général* shouted, ordered, threatened, but without being intimidated I speared a piece of bread of a reasonable size. Then, with the musket on my shoulder, I legged it.[12] The *Général* tried in vain to catch me in his riding boots, and despite the aide-de-camp the others imitated me and made a breach in the bread pile that was quite irreparable.

The following day of the 14th June, the battle of Friedland occurred. On the 15th, the remnants of the Russian army retreated towards Tilsit. We pursued them in a lively manner and took many cannon and prisoners. At the end of the month we arrived at the river Niemen, where the Russians had burned the bridge after crossing it.[13]

The camp at Tilsit, July, 1807

Our camp at Tilsit, composed of barracks, was the grandest and the most beautiful that we had seen, as much by its regularity as by its embellishments. On the day of the famous interview between Napoleon and Alexander I, we marched over the Niemen in full dress to go to the Russian bivouacs. In my enthusiasm I took the hand of a Russian grenadier, and we spoke without understanding each other, when a big devil of a Kalmuck, armed with a type of bow, approached me, his knife in hand, and tried to cut off my buttons. I pushed him away, but several others came back at the charge. I had to give in and leave them three buttons. As soon as they got them they ran away, beaming with joy. Having found one of their commanders who spoke a little French, I complained about this treatment. He explained to me that they believed my buttons, being highly polished, were made of silver and that they were allowed to take them. He offered to recover them and give them 20 blows of the knout. I declined, saying that in the French army corporal punishment had been discontinued, and was not much surprised to learn, much later, that these brutes belonged to the Russian Imperial Guard.[14]

On 8th July, Napoleon received Alexander in a house in Tilsit. On the 12th, the King of Prussia and his beautiful Queen were his guests. I was part of the piquet on that side of the Niemen, at the place where they landed, and I could watch them at my leisure. Some days later there was a grand review and manoeuvres. The Emperor offered his imperial and royal guests, as well as the marshals and generals of the two armies, a lunch in a tent erected in the centre of our camp and in front of the line of standards.[15] After the meal, the two Emperors, the King of Prussia, and their suites, visited our camp. The right side of each regiment was adorned with lawn ornaments; pebble mosaics of many colours, forming verses appropriate to the occasion; and poles garlanded in national colours. Finally, in each *corps* was the regimental flag, still hot with the glory of Friedland, floating above a bust of the Emperor, crowned with laurel, oak and olive leaves. The King of Prussia said to Napoleon: 'Sire, you make superb military camps, but ruins of villages.' We had, in fact, devastated those within three leagues all around our installations. These august personages, arriving at the kitchen line, expressed surprise at seeing it surrounded by a grassy embankment and admired the works. They stopped at my company, where I was busy cooking, and chance would have it that my cauldron was uncovered. The Emperor Alexander, having laid eyes upon it, said, 'here is a stew that looks good'. Napoleon demanded a spoon, I presented mine to him, who tasted it and gave it to Alexander, who did the same and gave it to the King of Prussia. It passed through the hands of the Russian generals, then Marshal Davout, *Général* Gudin, and the rest of the suite. Everyone found my cooking to be excellent. As they moved away, Alexander said 'the officers of my Guard don't have it better'. My *Colonel* was beaming with joy. The following day an aide-de-camp of Alexander came to bring him 100 ducats from the foreign sovereigns, for the company, which came to about 15 francs per soldier or *sous-officier*. This aide-de-camp asked to see me and said 'the Emperor my master has charged me with complimenting you on the care you take on feeding your comrades'. They called me 'the valet of the monarchs' for a long time after.

Bertrand joins a marauding party

We did not content ourselves with the distributions of rations we received in camp and sometimes went marauding. One day, at the beginning of July, eight chasseurs from my company left, and followed the left bank of the Niemen in the direction of Konigsberg. After three hours of marching, we met up with other marauders of all units, who like us were looking for something better to feed their cauldrons. We then numbered about 20 or 25, a third of us without arms of any kind, the others having only sabres. It is worth repeating that, in the light infantry of which I was part, the *demi-espadon* was as I have already said, formidable in our hands.[16] This is because half the soldiers and other ranks in each company were masters at arms, *prévôts*, or sharp shooters.[17] I was myself a qualified *prévôt*, having trained before my entry into the regiment, thanks to the solicitude of my dear mother. Having agreed to stick together through good and bad times, we resumed our march and met a surgeon from our army who was going to the hospital at Konigsberg. He was called Wagner and joined us. Having turned to the left and moved cross-country, we arrived after an hour of marching, at a large farm, closed and barricaded. We climbed the walls to open the gate. We found only three old people whom we frightened somewhat, but whom we did not take notice of. Everyone got to work; one killed a sheep; another heated the oven, a third prepared the flour, I churned the butter. Soon the mutton was in the casseroles, the bread was cooked, and we prepared to sit down at the table, before returning to the camp with all the provisions we had collected. But we had neglected the most elementary of military precautions. We had neither watched the inhabitants, nor the surrounding area. A reconnaissance would have immediately revealed, behind a small wood, the fairly large village of Bernsdorff. The inhabitants were Prussian, and therefore naturally hostile, and exasperated by the evils of war. This would have put us on our guard. Our recklessness would cost us dear. In effect, the three old people had gone to the village to protest our presence in the farm. Immediately, the inhabitants, numbering about a hundred, and armed with muskets, sabres, pistols, pitchforks, scythes, etc., led by the burgomaster, had marched on the farm. They arrived just when we were going to return to camp loaded with our loot. Fortunately they did not have the courage to attack us immediately, because then they would have surprised and massacred us. They simply surrounded the walls without any attempt at concealment. Noticing them, we rushed to our sabres, shut and barricaded the gates, then we named the surgeon as the commander of the 'detachment'. He accepted and we promised him our obedience. Next we adopted posts about the farm which we had designated as such. In the meantime the peasants opened fire and wounded one of our men with a musket ball in the arm, then climbed the wall on the side that was most accessible. We ran to that side, and they disappeared, only to begin multiple assaults from different sides. The surgeon, who was from Alsace, put a white handkerchief on the tip of his sabre, and came out to negotiate. He was rejected, but returned to the 'charge', saying to our assailants that we were 50 strong, well disposed to mount a sortie, and that we could not all be killed in doing so. It would only take one of us to reach our camp, for the infantry and artillery to come to avenge us, requisition everything, and then burn the village. The peasants, slightly scared, agreed to let us go, but on the condition that we would leave at the farm, not only all the property that we were preparing to take away, but also our sabres.

We could not accept this last dishonour, and deciding to conquer or die, we formed two companies under the command of the surgeon. Those lacking sabres, carried pitchforks and other tools and we opened the gate. At the moment when our sortie marched out we heard a drum beat the *pas accéléré*.[18] We could not believe this unexpected salvation, and some of us suspected it to be a trap laid by the peasants. I climbed aboard a cart, blocking the gate, onto the wall, and noticed a fairly strong French detachment, under arms and with an officer at its head, followed by a group without arms. We put the surgeon Wagner at our head, whilst our 'detachment' cried 'Vive L'Empereur! Vive L'Empereur!'

The officer who commanded was a *Lieutenant* of the *21ème d'Infanterie de Ligne*. After hearing of our adventure, he praised our resistance. He told us that he was charged with taking the sick and wounded to Königsberg via the Niemen, and that he had left a transport boat under guard to go to the village to stay the night with all of his convoy. After a brief halt, he left us some armed soldiers and carried on to Bernsdorff, where he found neither the burgomaster nor any inhabitants, and only some old men and some women, the rest having fled in panic. He lodged himself according to military custom, and established a correspondence post with the farm. As for us, the rest of the night was spent looking for wagons and loading them with provisions. At dawn we left the farm, at the same time as the *Lieutenant*'s detachment left Bernsdorff, and travelling on his boats, we arrived at our camp at the moment when the 'Diane' was being played. I presented myself to my *Capitaine* with the wagon loaded with bread, flour, lard, salted butter, dried vegetables, four sheep, poultry, etc., and handed him a certificate signed by the *Lieutenant* establishing our good conduct. Nothing helped, we had been reported missing during the daily roll call, and that evening we had to leave the ranks and be placed under guard until a decision was made. The report from the *Capitaine* went up the chain of command to *Général* Gudin, who after more information, left it to the *Colonel* to decide our punishment. This was fixed at eight hours under camp guard. Our poor comrade, who was wounded in the arm, was evacuated to Königsberg; he returned to us, fully healed, three months after, at the camp at Thorn. The day of our entry into the camp guard, *Général* Gudin was visiting the posts, and questioning the punished men. When he arrived at us, he was followed by an aide-de-camp, the *Colonel*, and our *Capitaine*. He wanted to see the defenders of the farm and asked which of us was the eldest. It was me, and I expected to bear the full brunt of his wrath.

'Did you,' he said to me, 'have permission to leave the camp?'

'No, my *Général*.'

'Did you know that you would be punished severely for your unauthorized absence?'

'Yes, my *Général*, but we had the firm resolution to be present for the evening roll call, carrying with us some provisions for our company, which we had been prevented from doing, as you are aware, to our immense regret. We do not wish to remain prisoners or martyrs to the Prussian peasants, and we acted as on the day of Friedland.'

'I approve your energy and courageous conduct, but you have committed no lesser fault than forgetting the very first rule of the soldier.'

Our *Capitaine* might have pleaded our case by highlighting our good service records and prior good behaviour during the recent battle of Heilsberg, but the *Général* was inflexible. Fortunately, four days later, all disciplinary punishments were waived at the signing of the Treaty of Tilsit.

Some time after, Gudin's division was directed to Thorn, where we built our camp. The August heat was particularly strong. The meat rations, despite the greatest care taken by the butchers in our regiment, was often spoiled, resulting in many soldiers falling ill, and consequently the town hospital was overwhelmed. The ranks cheered up considerably when we received the order to depart, which had the same effect as a victory on us. We left this fatal camp in December, 1807.

Chapter 3

1808: Garrison Duty in French-occupied Prussia

At our new cantonment, my company occupied a large but poor village on the outskirts of Wlockaweck, a small town in Poland along the Vistula. This village yielded few resources and few pleasures. Fortunately, our supplies, which came to the town, were regular. I saw that, in Poland, the seigneur owns the land and villages, and the peasants nothing. I do not wish to criticize the first, whose noble pride has something grand and magnanimous in it, nor the second one, because both had given France irrefutable proofs of their perseverance, their courage, and their loyalty. Our *corps d'armée* soon after left for Berlin, where we arrived after several days of marching. Half of us were with the inhabitants, the other half in the barracks. I was lodged with three of my comrades in the house of Monsieur Schmidt who, at the start, lacked the goodwill needed to receive us. But afterwards he became more hospitable and invited us to his daughter's wedding, as well as the ball which took place after. We also danced every day at the Frederick ball.

We were reunited, twice a day, with our arms and baggage, with orders that once received, we could not leave anything behind in our lodgings. The first three times these orders were fulfilled to the letter, but then each time someone left something behind to lighten the load in the haversack. One morning, at the roll call, the order was renewed, then the rally was beaten on the drums, and the battalion went to the assembly point as the day before. This time however, we formed up into companies and we set off with drums beating. My division left by the Potsdam gate, never to return to Berlin. I can only imagine the disappointment felt by those who left their belongings behind! For my part, I particularly regretted leaving behind a piece of percale cotton, with which I had intended to make a shirt.

My *corps d'armée* took up cantonments in Brandenburg, encircling Krossen on the river Elbe. My company was directed to the large village of Palczig, which possessed a castle owned by a baron. We arrived there on a Sunday, and made ourselves comfortable as soon as we had taken care of our weapons and clothing. We undertook to offer a ball, with the permission of the village burgomeister, and the authorization of our superiors. We invited all the young people in the region and their families to where we were lodged. We had plenty of ladies who danced, and as we had a well-stocked coffer, we bought brandy and sugar with which to make punch that the women of this region were fond of. On one side of the dance hall there was a partition where the men could drink beer and smoke. Everything went as we wished. Around midnight the music of the region replaced the waltzes which we preferred. So we left, and everyone returned home content.

Bertrand acts as a second to a young Prussian officer in a duel

During the four months that we stayed in the village we had a ball not only every Sunday, but also on Mondays and Thursdays. We thus made up for three months of bivouacs during the Prussian and Polish campaigns. The baron, as the seigneur of the village, had a nephew, a young man of good manners. He was a cavalry officer in the Prussian army, named Pauli Hoffman. His regiment had suffered greatly at Jena; for his part the young man had suffered two wounds and, seeing the state of chaos that the Prussian army was in, he was at home at the château, thinking he could heal better there than at a hospital. He sometimes came to see us in our dance hall. It was a barn belonging to his uncle. Inside we practised our skill at arms and held dances, the only occupations for a soldier of that time other than service and combat. One day, after eagerly accepting my invitation, and after leaving the range, he wanted to drive me back to my lodging. Speaking fairly good French, he reminded me of our victories, particularly Friedland. We should, he said, be proud to have such a great soldier for our Emperor, and such a genius, far above Alexander the Great. He finished by declaring that if he had not been Prussian he would rather have been French. I did not know what to think of these words but his frankness seemed so sincere to me, that I attached myself to him. He presented me to his uncle, who gave me the best welcome, and offered to continue with the fencing lessons that he had already been receiving. I obtained the necessary authorization from my master at arms and found foils, gloves, masks and breast plates at the château.

So here I am teaching my enemy a lesson, who I could have killed at Jena. After a month he showed considerable improvement. One day, after having vigorously proven the co-ordination of his hand and eye, he asked me the favour of presenting him to our skill at arms sessions and our dance hall, which I did. The following day, he offered refreshments to our masters at arms, *prévots* and several students, which were very well served and during which all went well. In addition to my lessons at the château, he began to attend our skill at arms sessions, practising with our stronger students, and was welcomed by all. Unfortunately he was brutally provoked by one of our students, who was a bad head. The poor young man, seeing that no one in the room dared to speak up for him, but having been provoked again with great violence, could not back down. Arriving at the ground where the duel was to take place, the four witnesses (I was Hoffman's second) still tried to make our comrade listen to reason, but that individual did not wish to hear. The fencing foils had their protective tips removed, were crossed, and the duel began.[1] After 20 minutes of fine thrusts and parries, seeing the arms of the two duellists flex, I put my own sword between them. The witnesses took advantage of this respite to try to get the aggressor to admit he was wrong. Unfortunately for him, he remained deaf to our advice and entreaties. The fight resumed in a fierce manner, and without inflicting a scratch. All of a sudden our comrade turned pale, his legs began to stumble, and he fell into my arms, with a serious wound. The sword thrust had penetrated under his armpit. He was carried to our lodging, and was immediately evacuated to the hospital at Züllichau where he found the regiment's headquarters. He suffered from his wound for a long time, and after his recovery, he developed a shortening of nerves for which he had to receive treatment.

As for myself and the other witnesses, despite the explanations we gave to our officer, who was lodged at the château, we were punished with five days in the guard house by the *Colonel*. The baron drove his nephew to Krossen himself. Three days after, this young officer came in a wagon to see me at the guard house where I was taking my punishment. He told me of his deep regret for what had happened, and his concern for what might happen to us. Touched by his efforts I assured him that the imprisonment was the full extent of the punishment, and that he should immediately return to his uncle at Krossen. I never saw him again. Five days after we left for Silesia, the most beautiful and prosperous province in Prussia. We saw Glogau, Breslau and Schweidnitz, the three historic sites on the Austrian frontier.² This last town was designated our garrison.

Several days after our arrival, a comrade and I were in a brasserie, when a fresh faced, good looking fellow offered us some tobacco and asked permission to sit at our table. We allowed him to do so, and he spoke passable French. He began by expanding on the fatigues and miseries of the soldier when on campaign, next he grew bold enough to propose to us, using sweet language and fine promises, to desert. Noticing our indifference, he doubled his audacity and showed us his purse, which was quite full of thalers. It was too much to bear! We took him to the guard house, and the *Colonel* ordered that he be sent under escort to the General Headquarters, where he was to receive his rewards for being an Austrian recruiter.³

Bertrand and his comrades put on a theatre

Since we wished to put on a comedy, we decided in a meeting, to involve a comrade called Delmas, whose education and rare intelligence we were familiar with. With the permission of our superiors, and the burgomeister's help in obtaining a fairly large room, we set to work. Those soldiers who were joiners, carpenters and painters by trade constructed the theatre, and those who were tailors created the costumes. We made helmets, cuirasses, lances etc., from wood or cardboard, as props for tragedies. At the town bookseller we found the works of Molière, Voltaire, Beaumarchais and Désaugiers; we started our renditions with *Mérope*, by Voltaire.⁴ One of our comrades, from Alsace, had made several posters by hand which were placarded in different parts of the town. The printed entry tickets were available to the locals for a minimal fee, whilst our officers, *sous-officiers,* and soldiers were of course admitted for free. The soldiers attended in their companies. Our troupe, consisting of 15 actors, included two young farriers, a drummer and a musician, who played the female roles.[5] The orchestra was provided by the regimental band. We received considerable applause at our first performance. On the third performance the room was filled with the all the distinguished inhabitants of the town, and their reaction was beyond all our expectations. The *Général* and *Colonel* congratulated our director and all those who collaborated. We then performed the 'Triumvirat' and the 'Prodigal Son', both by Voltaire. Of our earnings, half went to cover our costs, the other half was transmitted to the burgomeister for the town's poor. Consequently the inhabitants said that the French were soldiers, actors, and benefactors. Our fame had spread 10 leagues in every direction when, to our great displeasure, we were sent to the Kingdom of Westphalia, and had to leave our balls, performances, and the kind Silesian ladies, the objects of our passions.

Chapter 4

1809: The Campaign against Austria: Echmühl and Wagram

Around the middle of January, 1809, the sounds of war began to be heard. Pitt, our implacable and fierce enemy, again used English gold to influence the Aulic Council against the victors of Austerlitz.¹ We went to give the Austrians their fourth lesson.² In the first days of February we marched from Schweidnitz to Magdebourg, and then onto Cassel, which was the residence of King Jérôme.³ This prince had organized his army and had the idea of uniting the French and Westphalian soldiers and *sous-officiers* by means of a banquet. Held on 8th February, 1809, I had to my right a gigantic sergeant of Westphalian cuirassiers, who never ceased to eat, drink beer, and smoke. We got on well immediately, and I poured him drink after drink. Seeing a plate of asparagus in front of him, he asked me how to eat it, not knowing how. With the greatest seriousness I bit into the white part; he immediately imitated me and tried to chew and pull, without success! But having noticed one of his neighbours, who was more of a connoisseur, eat only the green part, he became furious at my joke to the point of striking me. Fortunately, his sergeant-major, a distinguished young man, to whom I confessed in a light-hearted manner, calmed down my adversary and observed to him that quarrels of this sort were not settled with fists, but on the duelling ground, and that French soldiers were well versed in duelling.⁴ For my part, I declared to my colossus that if I thought I was offending him I would have abstained, but if he still was not satisfied, I was at his disposal to take it to the duelling ground. He packed up and the matter was closed. We stayed in these provisional cantonments during the entire month of February. In March, pushed by the other divisions, we marched on Halberstadt, always towards Westphalia.[5] On the 25th March, the entire *corps d'armée* of Marshal Davout was concentrated from Bamburg to Bayreuth and its outskirts, and an order was given at 0400 to leave at 0500 for Nurnberg, the first town of Bavaria. It was there that a concentration of the army was effected, and the Emperor passed the night there. The following day we began the campaign with a skirmish as the advance guard, and nothing could stop us. We passed Ratisbon on the 18th April, and on the 19th we had our first serious engagement there. This combat reminded the Austrians that they had the veterans of Austerlitz, Jena and Friedland on their heels. On the 20th, 21st and 22nd April the enemy was beaten everywhere we encountered them, and the Archduke Charles withdrew towards Bohemia with the remnants of his army. I am proud to say that I was at Eckmühl, with the *3ème Corps d'armée*, which checked a large part of the Austrian army. The shock was sharp and the battle fiercely fought. For my part, acting as a skirmisher, I had to face two Austrians at the same time. My bayonet made one of them bite the dust and the other, having his musket broken, remained at my disposal. Unfortunately this prisoner made his escape later in the action. Our intrepid Marshal, Davout, was created Prince of Echmühl for this feat of arms. As Napoleon was constantly within our midst, victory could not desert us; and nothing could slow down the flight of our eagles.

On 8th May, 1809, we saw the mountain and château of Diernstein on the right bank of the Danube, where Richard the Lionheart had been kept prisoner.[6] The *corps* of Marshal Mortier avoided disaster not far from there in 1805, due to the hesitation of the Russians.[7] We were lodged at St-Pölten. The following day we arrived at Mölk, where we found a Dominican convent on a high plateau.[8] My company had been designated as its safeguard, which we were all ecstatic to hear. We had not had a moment of rest since the opening of the campaign, having fought and marched all day and night. We had climbed halfway up the road when we encountered the Superior of the convent with several of his monks and the staff officer in charge of billeting us there. The *Capitaine* formed up the company and placed us on the march, drums beating, preceded by the monks, marching in step. It was a truly amusing spectacle. As soon as the outposts were placed and the entrances secured, we were taken to a refectory, where our stomachs were as happy as they were surprised to find some good and plentiful fare. Our officers received the same treatment after being assured that we were comfortable. I have never seen a monastery so large, wealthy and well ordered. We pressed the monks with questions, and one of them, who spoke French, opened his heart to me. He was called Brother Joseph and, during his free time, he told me the following:

'I was born at Besançon, the eleventh child of a family which emigrated, during the sad days of the Terror, in 1792. I followed them out of obedience and unwillingly left my country, which I regret with all the force of my soul, and I have the most ardent desire to see it again, even if I was to die an hour after. But I would not definitely be able to return, having made my vows in this house, where I occupy a superior position. Besides, I am too old and have given all my patrimony to this community. My father was a *capitaine* of cavalry in the Royal army, and he continued to serve in the Austrian army in the same grade. He was killed by a French cannonball during a sortie by the garrison of Mantua, when that place was under siege by Bonaparte.⁹ Ah, Napoléon, the greatest captain of the century, whom I would like see! My mother wanted me to serve in the Austrian army, or to become a priest. The first seemed to me to be dishonourable, while the second did not require me to fight against my countrymen. I lost my mother soon after receiving holy orders. I wanted, at that moment, to renounce the cassock and return to France, but, on the advice of Monseigneur the bishop, I became a Dominican, and I inherited a modest fortune which my parents had saved from a shipwreck. The first years were the most painful. I worked hard, and in recompense I went on mission to Rome. After my return I was nominated brother-treasurer in the Order. After being the object of jealousy and bad humour among my brothers, due to this nomination, I began to see them as my best friends.'

Another time, father Joseph presented brother Antoine to me, who was German. This one declared that if he was not German he would like to have been French, so much was his admiration of the genius of Napoleon and his victories. He had, furthermore, spent most of his studies at Dijon. The lateness of the night separated us, and all night I dreamt of this story and all that I had seen. The following morning, from the Angelus, brother Joseph brought me a notebook and prayerbook.[10]

'Please,' he told me, 'accept these two souvenirs from me, which come from France. Promise me to look after them, and I will be happy knowing that they will once again see France.' I was very touched, and gave him my word of honour that I would fulfil his wish. The clock signalled that it was time for prayers, and for my part, I responded to the call to muster with my company. We were relieved two hours after, but I could not obtain permission to say my farewell and take a letter from him for Besançon. I never saw him again. After the campaign, seeing that my *corps d'armée* remained in Germany, I sent the prayerbook to my dear mother at Nîsmes. As for the notebook, it did not leave me until the day when I was taken prisoner by the Russians, in 1813. I was stripped of my possessions by them.

Two days after, on the 10th May 1809, we entered Vienna. My division (commanded by *Général* Gudin), was detached towards Prince Eugène's *4ème Corps d'armée*, which was coming from Italy. We linked up with them at Raab.[11] Next we went to besiege Pressburg, which was of little strategic importance. During this siege, I was on duty at the advance posts one day, when a *Général* who was making his rounds approached me and asked if I had seen the Austrian sentry who had been posted opposite me. On my response that I had, he said to me, 'this sentry annoys me: we must make him disappear immediately – open fire'. I obeyed and saw him fall. The *Général* expressed his satisfaction, but for some time after I felt guilty that I had perhaps killed a soldier who had done me no harm, and probably wished me no harm either. Nevertheless, I had followed the first military rule: obedience!

We occupied, for the moment, an island along the Danube in front of Pressburg, which we christened 'the Island of Midges'.[12] These pests proved very inconvenient. When I was on guard, it so happened that I was questioned by a *Colonel* of the General Headquarters during his rounds. I presented arms, and during our conversation, which seemed rather long, one of those wretched mosquitoes landed on my face. I did not have the means to defend myself from its bites, apart from the contortions of my eyes, lips, and every muscle, nerve, and fibre that I had at my disposal. It was far from subtle, and the *Colonel* must have had a unique idea regarding the elasticity of my face. We were unable to sleep because of these insects, but as vineyards were plentiful in the area, and there was no shortage of wine, I followed the example of Diogenes, and slept in a barrel.[13]

What a mistake! The mosquitoes came, in column, to find me. I blocked the opening of the barrel with one of the large canvas bags which we used in the bivouacs, and slipped inside. However, part of my legs stuck out. Difficult though it may be to believe, the darts of these enemies were able to pierce the leather of my shoes. Weary of this war, we took it in turns to sleep, with a comrade hunting down the mosquitoes with a branch. The officers and soldiers alike soon adopted this method.

It being the feast of Corpus Christi on the 24th June, the *7ème Léger* rested and had nothing to fear from the enemy. Our superiors, taking part in the religious meditations, authorized us to celebrate with a grand party. We had a huge pyre, at the top of which was the sign of the redemption, decorated with foliage, announced with solemnity. Immediately the flames spread among the pyre, and at this happy sign we called into existence the Supreme Being, the benefactor and provider of all things here below. The local peasants, believing there was a fire, rushed forwards. Once they were reassured, they became our friends and being good Catholics, they shared in our joy.

The day passed without incident, and during the night, the peasants returned home and we went to our bivouacs. On the 3rd July, we were replaced by the Italian *4ème Corps d'armée*, which continued the siege of Pressburg instead of us. We passed through Vienna on the 4th July, and the Emperor reviewed us on the right bank of the Danube. Immediately after, we took the island of Lobau, where my division was placed in the first line on the left bank of another branch of the Rhine. We had barely arrived, when we were overwhelmed with a violent thunderstorm. As we were on the low ground, we had to pass the night with water up to our legs. We received shells from the Austrian artillery and the bridgeheads on the left bank, fortunately without too much damage.

Battle of Wagram, 5 and 6 July, 1809

On the 5th July, in the early morning, we crossed the bridges. The Austrians were beaten and forced to withdraw after a vigorous resistance. The whole day was spent conducting skirmishes against the enemy rearguard.[14] The two armies assembled during the night, and our division was in the first line. It was forbidden to light fires. We passed this night standing, with our muskets resting by our feet. I suffered from a fever brought on by our stay in the water the night before.

At daybreak on the 6th July, the cannons announced a great battle which would be called Wagram. The *7ème Léger* was situated in front of an enemy artillery battery, and suffered heavily from canister shot, over the course of an hour.[15] At the middle of the day the Emperor passed in front of our lines. We felt happy, and redoubled our strength, on seeing him. He spoke to Marshal Davout. Soon after, the order to charge was heard; the Austrian battery which had been thinning our ranks was taken, and nearly all the artillerymen were either killed or mortally wounded by our bayonets. We took position at Neusiedel: on the plateau of Wagram the battle was raging.[16] Once again the Emperor appeared in front of us, at a moment when cannon shot and canister balls rained down, and we trembled at the thought that he might come to harm. Never until then, had I burned through so many cartridges, and my musket was so burnt that it could no longer serve me.

Towards four hours into the battle, we were pursuing a column of Hungarians when I received a ball in the fat of my right thigh.

My wound was not dangerous, and I complained all the less when the Hungarians lay down their arms. The battle was won by nightfall, and my *corps d'armée* rallied itself and took a roll call. The *7ème Léger* had lost 800 to 1,000 men, the majority of whom were dead. My company had been reduced to a third of its effective strength in the morning. My *Capitaine* was seriously wounded when we attacked the artillery battery. Among the dead was my bed-mate Lacour, to my profound chagrin. He was a soldier of valour, and a good man, to whom I was attached from the bottom of my heart. The Surgeon-major was able to extract the ball from my thigh without having to send me to the ambulances, which were already crowded. I stayed with my company, where I knew I would be well looked after.

Those still standing with the flag left to find provisions, that is to say, to maraud. They came back loaded with provisions of all kinds, from the village of Wagram, or nearby. They even drove barrels of wine to the bivouac. Unfortunately, everyone whose turn it had been to carry the cooking pots, of which two were in my subdivision, were either killed or wounded.[17] We didn't have a single cooking utensil. However, we killed a sheep and put the legs on a spit. To achieve this, we had put sticks about 1.5m long into the ground at a certain angle, over the fireside. Each leg was suspended over the fire by tying some string to it and the stick. From its weight and position, it turned quite naturally. But we still had not found a container with which to cook the rest of the animal. Fortunately, not too far from our bivouac, was that of *Général* Bordessoulle's, who commanded a brigade of cuirassiers.[18] This brigade was placed in column behind the infantry, like the rest of its division. It was waiting for the moment to sweep aside all before it, but had suffered from a murderous canister fire in the previous hour. These 'steel vests', as we called the cuirassiers, could not take revenge until we had opened the way with our musket fire and our bayonets.[19] As we were near the ground on which the cuirassiers had endured the volleys of canister fire, I thought that there must be many helmets and cuirasses left behind. I found one such cuirass for myself, and brought it to the bivouac. We fixed two split sticks at their ends, and with two of us holding this new-fangled pot over the fire, were able to cook the rest of our sheep, with a generous quantity of butter. All the while we thought about the hero who had worn this armour, and had repulsed and beaten the enemy, only to have received his death on the field of honour.

At the moment when this substantial meal was being shared out into our mess tins, *Général* Bordesoulle entered our bivouac with his aides-de-camp. 'What are you cooking there, my braves?' He asked. 'My *Général*,' I replied, 'It is Austrian sheep.' We gave him a mess tin with a generous portion, and he and his aides made themselves comfortable, as they did honour to our roast and our wine.[20] After dining well, he thanked us and went to tell our *Colonel* of their windfall. 'It's a good thing,' added the *Général*, 'to make war alongside such fellows.'

'They are the children of the Midi region,' our *Colonel* replied, 'I have fought in Italy with men from this region, and I am always well looked after by them.' The *Colonel*, charged with returning his thanks to us, said 'I thank you, for the reception you gave the *Général*. Your conduct in this regard and during this battle shows what you are and what you will be. It is far from finished, and I am proud to be your commander.'

'*Colonel*, we are happy to have fought under your orders on this memorable day,' A *sergent* replied, and the more happy to see you with us, safe and sound. You will always find us ready to obey you and march to do what needs to be done.'[21]

Bertrand is sent to the hospital

During the night, we resumed our pursuit of the enemy rearguard, and we took some cannon and prisoners from them. Our direction was towards Nikolsburg and Znaïm. A relentless skirmish broke out in this place, among the vines.[22] That evening, there was a ceasefire and an armistice. The *4ème Corps d'armée* went towards Brünn, the capital of Moravia, and the *7ème Léger* was designated to occupy the town only, where we found Marshal Davout and his headquarters. What a pleasure it was for us, after four months of bivouacking, to sleep in the beds of a barracks! I suffered from a severe haemorrhaging during this period of rest. I was sent to the hospital, where all the treatments that were tried failed; ice, even sinapism.[23] I continued to lose blood through the nose, the mouth, and sometimes the ears. Feeling my strength diminish, I only had my morale to support me, that most excellent of doctors, which never failed me in the greatest of dangers. Nevertheless, I had come close to death, and I regretted having to die in a hospital bed. I thought it would be preferable to fall, some days after, on the field of honour, like so many braves who had paid for victory with their lives.

In the meantime, Baron Larrey, the Surgeon-General of the *Grande Armée*, visited the hospital, after hearing reports of my case from the doctors and surgeons there. He asked me if I knew how to swim. I replied in the affirmative, and he advised me to throw myself in a great lake situated on the edge of the town. I drove there, supported by two infirmaries. Two of my comrades were there ahead of me. I did not hesitate to let the water flow around me up to my shoulders, being suspended under the armpits by a bed sheet held by my two friends. I only stayed a short time in the water, and drove back into the hospital. I slept with a restored warmth. I still lost a little blood each day, but I felt an improvement. The doctor continued to prescribe baths as soon as my strength would allow, provided I remained no longer than 10 minutes in the water, and continued to move. After the second bath I found myself extremely weak and could only drink a cold broth with fat. On the third day of this treatment the bleeding ceased, but for a long time I was unable to ingest any hot food, until I was fully recovered. This annoying affliction continued until I was 50 years old.

The Emperor came to Brünn. He entered, with Marshal Davout on his left, in full dress, as well as all the generals in his suite. The Emperor wore, as he always did, his grey greatcoat. All the soldiers cheered him. An innumerable crowd filled the streets, eager to see the great captain, but confused Marshal Davout with Napoleon. He preferred to ride to Davout's left, his hat off his head, and his eyes fixed on the illustrious commander of our *corps d'armée*. I made a remark to an inhabitant of Brünn about this error, which had lasted for almost an hour.[24]

After the Emperor reviewed Davout's *corps d'armée* we left Brünn, to occupy camps along the route to Austerlitz. Four companies, one of which was mine, went to the village of that name. Napoleon assembled about 25,000 men and we re-enacted a small version of this famous battle on the same ground.[25] The inhabitants of Vienna, Pressburg and Olmutz came to watch out of curiosity. They must have thought that, despite English gold and the hatred of Pitt, the sworn enemy of France in all her glory, we had for the fourth time beaten the coalition and broken the pride of Austria.[26]

The following day, we took the route to Vienna. We arrived there after a long day of marching, through driving rain, and covered in mud up to our shoulders. My squad, with the *caporal*

1809: The Campaign against Austria: Echmühl and Wagram 47

at its head, had its billet in the Léopoldstatt district, at the house of an old man with a respectable figure. We were assigned a large room on the ground floor and immediately after, according to the first duty of the soldier, we began to clean our effects, equipment and weapons. One asked that he have his gaiters washed, another for a thread and needle, a third for soap, and a fourth for tobacco! The servants were bewildered. The lodging arrangement required the host to feed us until further notice, and we were served a plentiful and comforting meal. Seeing that we were reasonable, the staff of the house were reassured, and made us look good during the ten days that we stayed there. Nevertheless, from the master to the last servant, all invoked the saints of paradise in their desire to see us leave.

October 1809

Several among us had well-filled purses. For my part I had a fair number of assignats, paper money, because in this period coin was unknown in Austria. I decided therefore, to dine at a good restaurant which was in the vicinity. We returned to our lodging, content, when suddenly were assailed by the townspeople who manoeuvred themselves to strike at our shoulders. Surprised, we took the first blows, but placing our *sabre-briquets* in our hands, we beat down the Germans, whose sticks and hats remained on the ground, until the approach of a patrol (who were French of course).[27] The brave *sergent* who commanded us went to the post house with the Germans. My bed-mate and I legged it, but seeing that that others, held on account of their sabre belts, could not get away, we returned to the scene of the crime. At the post house, the real aggressors were put in prison, but the officer in charge made us pass the night in the company of the guards, to ensure that there would be no further incident, when in fact we would have returned to our cantonment. Our *Colonel* gave us eight days in the guard room for leaving our lodging, thanks to a report from our *caporal*, and despite that of the officer in charge of the post house. It would have been appropriate to reduce our punishment to four days.

According to a clause in the Peace Treaty, the fortifications of Vienna which faced towards Bavaria had to be dismantled.[28] The Governor-General of Vienna ordered all the French infantry and artillery under arms. Our weapons were loaded in the presence of an immense and menacing population, we set fire to the mines and ramparts, several centuries old, which then collapsed. I was, for my part, watching the part of the surrounding wall that leant against the Imperial Palace, a part that had to be respected. The force of the explosion knocked me down to one side, and my musket to another. Some days after, an insane young man called Staps tried to assassinate the Emperor at a review of the Guard at Schönbrunn Palace. He paid for his crime with his life.[29]

Our stay in Vienna lasted a month, and I remained unhappy amidst the various distractions that I found there. One day I was going to a ball with a young and beautiful person, the daughter of an Austrian sergeant-major, who was a prisoner in France. She only granted me this great favour after many solicitations, and I was delighted, because I knew that she danced the waltz perfectly. The ball was attended by a number of French soldiers and young men who were native to Austria. The ball had been going on for two hours, towards nine in the evening, when a violent brawl broke out between the French and Austrians. The waltz ended, the lanterns were broken, the chandelier shattered, and in the darkness everyone was shouting and striking in all directions. The women let out heart-breaking cries, and I made every effort to protect my gracious waltzing partner, and tried to lead her towards one of the exits. I found them to be crowded, the flight redoubled, I felt a blow and was separated from her. Although I found her a little time after, I had lost all hope of saving her when I noticed an open window. The accolades of a good deed gave me Herculean strength; I took her under my arm, climbed onto a bench with my precious bundle, and lifting my protégée up, I was able to help her over and into the garden. For my part, I returned to the battle, but at its height a piquet of infantry surrounded the room. Remembering my recent encounter, I made no resistance, but grew tired of being surrounded by these 15 soldiers who could hardly contain 40 of us, since their muskets and equipment served to encumber them. In view of my docility, no one distrusted me, but as soon as they set off for the headquarters, I took flight, pumping my legs as fast as I could to my lodging. On the way I learned that my dancing partner had been taken to one of her relatives.

The next day, I stood guard with three of my comrades and a *caporal* at the Museum of Antiques. This post was not subject to the usual rounds of our superiors, because it was under the direction of the museum curator. We consequently decided to have some fun. We ordered a hearty dinner from a neighbouring restaurant and washed it down with the best wines from France. The clerk and concierge, whom we invited, drank and smoked like Germans, so that they rolled under the table and we spent part of the night in good and frank revelry.

The next morning, our guests from the night before were sick and in bed, but we ordered a full lunch from the same restaurant. Unfortunately, after this lunch our poor 'postmaster,' the *caporal*, already a little indisposed, became ill to the point of losing control of his head and legs. We had to abandon our post and help our leader. So we sent for a carriage, but there came instead an old cart from another century, pulled by two equally ancient nags. We piled in our arms and equipment. Unfortunately, the barrels of our muskets poked out from between the doors. A staff captain encountered our motley crew and arrested us to obtain an explanation. According to his report, and the investigation made by order of our *Colonel*, the *caporal* lost his rank and was placed under close arrest with the regiment. We got away with 24 hours in the police room. This sad end to a joyous night made me reflect deeply, and I promised myself, when it was my turn to be the one in charge, I would never have such weakness.

December, 1809

I went the following Sunday, with some comrades, to visit the palace of Schönbrunn, which looked a lot like the one at Saint-Cloud, and contained a museum of natural history and a menagerie. I saw, among the many visitors, my dancing partner in the company of two of friends. I saw that she had seen me and that my gaze had made her lower her eyes. Despite my great desire, my shyness prevented me from going over. At the end, comforted by the advice of my comrades, I regained my courage and planted myself, shako in hand, in front of these three women. I asked permission to congratulate Miss Maria on her speedy recovery. I saw that they did not understand the little German I had, and I was very embarrassed by my situation, which turned to ridicule, when one of the two ladies congratulated me, in very good French, on my fine conduct at the ball, and thanked me for saving her niece. I modestly refused this praise, saying that I had the character and reputation of the French in mind, regarded in Vienna as the soul of chivalry. She then told me, to my great astonishment, that she was from Lyon. When the troops of the National Convention had seized Lyon in 1793, all the honest people, who had become suspects in the eyes of the ruthless representatives of the people, were brought before the Revolutionary tribunal and only left to go to their death. Her husband was denounced, but was able to flee. She, left with two children, lost them and was on the point of dying of grief and misery. No one dared to help her, the Terror was so great. She had the audacity to present herself to the Committee of Public Safety, to ask for a pass to reach Chambéry where she had learned that her husband had taken refuge. Either out of pity, or because of the very large influx of similar requests, it was granted to her. From Chambéry they had to flee before the Republican army which was invading Savoy. They settled in Vienna, where they found positions in a large family, he as the master tutor, and she as a teacher under him. She invited me to visit them, which I did the next day.

But seeing as my heart was taken, and reflecting that a soldier in the field owes everything to his flag, I did not return to this house. When, a few days later, we left Vienna, I wrote a letter to the aunt as respectful as it was affectionate, in which I sent Miss Maria my best wishes. I thought I acted in this matter with gallantry.

Chapter 5

1810 & 1811

On 31st December, 1809, my division left Vienna. The *7ème Régiment d'Infanterie Légère* was quartered in the village of Ebersdorff, six leagues from the Austrian capital. Before entering the cantonment, our *Capitaine* formed the company up in a circle and read out the regulations approved by the French and Austrian authorities, which made it known what the inhabitants had to provide us for food and for sleeping. My bedmate and I found ourselves poorly lodged by the locals. The village being large, and many houses unoccupied, we made inquiries and learned from our hosts, who were jealous of the burgomaster, that he had forgotten about a relative's farm when assigning the tickets requiring the recipients to lodge the French troops.

The *Capitaine* received our complaint and did his duty by obtaining authorization from the burgomaster to send us to this farm. At first our new host seemed to us to be in a very bad temper. However, seeing that we exacted only what was strictly due, and that we surrounded his wife with care and consideration, his mood improved and he even took me fishing at a nearby pond. Our cheerfulness gave rise to the idea of having a ball the following Sunday.

After obtaining the authorization of our *Capitaine* and the permission of the burgomaster, we rented the large hall of the village inn, paid in advance, and hired the musicians. A deputation from our company went to visit the parents, who granted us their daughters as dancing partners. Everything was ready when, at the Sunday sermon, the parish priest began to rant against the ball, as well as the scandalous promise of the parents. He then ordered them to go back on their word, to the great excitement of all. However, as our host was the priest's brother-in-law, my bed-mate and I went to see this pitiless priest, and I made such an eloquent speech to him that he gave us back our dancers and our violins.

March, 1810

Soon after, we were directed to Braunau, where I saw the Austrian Archduchess Marie-Louise on her journey to France, to share the first throne in the world.[1] From there we went to Magdeburg, a place of war, which had a large garrison.[2] We had to send back a battalion of Corsican *chasseurs*, due to the many brawls that quickly led to duels, because we had very little sympathy for this unit. A Frenchman from Metz, Mr. Gardel, had set up a restaurant which was very fashionable, and we gathered there for a fraternal and patriotic banquet. Weapons taken as trophies and national flags, embroidered with the names of the victories in which our regiment had taken its part, all instilled in us a sense of joy. We sang *Le Beau Dunois, Rolland, La Sentinelle*, etc. until midnight. At this moment the most reasonable remarked that it was necessary to return to the cantonment. The service at Magdeburg was, in fact, very hard, and the discipline very strict. All cafes and public establishments were to be closed at ten o'clock. Unfortunately we did not listen to the voice of duty. M. Gardel, closing all his doors, consented to let us pass into a room in the ground floor overlooking a courtyard. We were playing billiards there when a *sergent* of our regiment, on patrol and hearing the noise we made, had the door opened by a servant who was oblivious to the situation, and entered our room. Immediately we turned off the lights and everyone sought their salvation in flight. I went up the stairs of the house four at a time, behind a friend. He, arriving at the attic, grabbed a rope used to lift the fodder and let himself slip into the void. He fell into a courtyard where people, bewildered, took him for a thief. He ended up being thrown into the street, to his great satisfaction. As for me, I walked down a dark corridor, hands stretched out, until a door gave way. I found myself in a room where a human form was lying in a pallet bed. I quickly hid my sabre and shako and, lifting the sheets, I slipped in besides the occupant. I recognized that she was an old woman, and she opened her mouth to cry. I put my hand over her mouth.

The *sergent*, rigorous in his search of curfew-breakers, entered the room. Upon seeing two people sleeping in bed, he immediately withdrew. After the patrol left, I apologised to the poor woman, mute with horror, and went downstairs, where I was greeted with bursts of laughter. I was covered in duvet feathers. I returned safely to the cantonment, but five of our merry band had been recognized and apprehended. They received fifteen days' imprisonment in the city's citadel. Four days later, we left Magdeburg to go to Hanover, where we celebrated the birth of the King of Rome with great solemnity. The Emperor, from the great solicitude he had for the army, had established a school for infantry and artillery in this city, with the intention of perfecting the incomplete training of young soldiers sent to the occupying army. It was, in fact, very difficult for less fortunate parents to pay for this instruction before their sons left for their regiments, and even more so to pay for a replacement, whose price was very high. Having at this moment the rank of a *caporal*, I was admitted to this school and placed under the direction of *Lieutenant* Marcel, a child of Paris. I worked hard, especially in the artillery drills, of which I was very fond of. However, our departure took away all my hopes for the future. It was during our stay in Hanover that a *Lieutenant* joined our company, from the *3ème Régiment de Hussards*.[3] He was the son of Marshal Moncey. Although I was only a *caporal-fourrier*, he was kind enough to take an interest in me. He offered to arrange my transfer to the *2ème Régiment de Chasseurs à Pied* in the Old Guard, even though I hadn't accumulated the necessary service time. I declined this great honour, preferring to stay with *7ème Régiment d'Infanterie Légère*, my military family, with whom I had already made four campaigns, where I was known and was on the verge of becoming a *sous-officier*. The threat of a British landing in Holland required the reinforcement of Imperial troops, which, after the abdication of King Louis Bonaparte, had been absorbed into metropolitan France.

My regiment was sent there, but we only stayed there for a short time, and instead joined the garrison at Bremen. On our arrival in this city, I was ordered to occupy the police station. This post was inhabited by the 100 so-called soldiers of the Free City, along with their families. Instead of finding a guard under arms in front of this post, we were surrounded by these unfortunate people, their wives and their children, each lamenting that they were driven from their homes. But, as we declared that we were content with the room on the ground floor which served as a post office, the cries of this poor crowd were immediately calmed.

Goods imported from England were to be burnt, according to the continental blockade, and my battalion was ordered for this service. The wagons brought these goods to a vast area near the city, which soon formed the site of a huge pyre. But the crowd, coming from the city and the surroundings, that our battalion could hardly contain, threw themselves on this flaming heap to loot it, and they forced us to bring reinforcements to complete the destruction of these riches. The next day, my regiment did everything we could to prevent this display from re-occurring. We escorted the wagons, muskets loaded, with cannons pulled by drag ropes to the area and their fuses lit. When we arrived at the grounds, our three battalions formed a square, with the cannons at the angles. The destruction took place without incident, in spite of English agents, who scattered fistfuls of gold to create difficulties for us in accomplishing this task. This destruction was repeated for four days, until all the English products in the stores were wiped out. The loss was said to be two millions a day for England. They were quality goods, from rich fabrics to watches and jewellery. Various sentiments arose among those who witnessed these burnings. Some of us thought it would have been better to give these riches to the military. The locals said it would have been better to distribute them to the poor. But it was the Emperor's order that settled it. We learned that the same had been done at Lübeck and Hamburg.

After the first reception, which had been gloomy, the inhabitants of Bremen took us in friendship thanks to our sensible practices and our good behaviour. Very few of them requested that we be assigned a new billet after the first ten days, as our commanders had allowed for, in co-operation with the civilian authorities. I was staying with a rich shipowner who treated us with kindness and affection. When my battalion was sent to cantonments outside the city, we parted from him with great difficulty. My section was housed in a large village on the right bank of the river Aller. As always, our first care was to install a weapons room and a dance hall, which allowed me to waltz with Mlle. Georgette Schmidt, the daughter of my host. A few days after our first ball, I was sent three leagues from this cantonment, to replace a *caporal* who had been punished with imprisonment. I was sorry to be separated from my dancing partner.

In the meantime, winter surprised us, with all the rigours to be expected in northern Germany. The flooded plains were covered with thick ice. The rest of the year, the men, women and children used the rivers and canals as we use roads and paths, using boats to travel to the city or local markets. In the winter however, skates took the place of boats, and the inhabitants thus always avoided the very long detours required by following the paths along the dikes. I constantly saw crowds of skaters pass by and admired their skill. I had the happiness, one day, to recognize among them the elegant silhouette of Mlle. Georgette, who had come to see her brother, who was married to the burgomaster's daughter in the area where I was in cantonments. The next day, which was a Sunday, as soon as I had reviewed my men and ordered the service, I threw myself on a sledge to go to Olgheim where the ball was taking place. Many of my comrades were there. I was introduced to Mlle. Georgette by her brother and had her as my dance partner throughout the ball. Our gallantry, our honesty, and the respect we showed, was in fact, sufficiently appreciated by the inhabitants, so that no fear mingled with their affectionate reception. I was brought back in a sleigh at three in the morning, and I paid no attention to the cold or the danger of this night, since I was at the side of an honest and agreeable young girl. The next day I decided to learn to skate and quickly became able to compare myself with the locals in this exercise. I participated in several races organized by the locals on the ice. The women sat in graceful sleds, and rivalled each other in elegance, wearing outfits festooned with furs. These were drawn by skaters, either with a handspike hooked onto one of the crossbars, or by holding the backrest with their hands. We rushed forward like this, intoxicated by the air and open space. At the end of the race there was a generous meal with plenty of drink, and then the waltz began. I was enough of a graceful skater to drive Mlle. Georgette's sleigh. Shortly after, she married the son of the burgomaster. I have been in correspondence with all these good people for a long time.

Chapter 6

1812: The Russian Campaign

This pleasant and healthy life was abruptly interrupted, at the beginning of January 1812, by the order to leave our cantonments within 24 hours and to march on Magdeburg, where we arrived at the end of March. Our armament and clothing were completed there, and in the last days of April we crossed the Elbe below the citadel.[1] In 48 hours we were out of King Jerome's former kingdom. The entire *1er Corps d'armée* under Marshal Davout marched in front, in direction of Thorn, where we found the Emperor. He reviewed our division, under *Général* Gudin, at Gombin camp.[2] That same evening we marched towards the Niemen.

My section (by now I was a *sergent*), was housed at a farm. As always, we were ordered to be satisfied, with the resources of our host for our meals, however modest they might be. I had enough trouble subsisting my thirty men, and promised myself to set an example of moderation. Unfortunately for my good resolutions, the farmer served us, all in all, three bowls full of bacon and potatoes. This sad dinner was already darkening the faces of my men, when I realized that the potatoes in the bowl in front of me were not cooked enough. I politely remarked on it to our host. The latter, believing that I did not understand German, replied in that language, with a sneer, that it was quite good enough for French people. I turned around and threw a potato at him, which stuck to his forehead. I immediately regretted this reaction, because of the authority of my rank. But my peasant, very coldly, keeping his potato on his forehead, went to complain to *Colonel* Rome.³ This officer, who at that moment was surrounded by all the officers of the regiment, could not help but burst out laughing, as did the entire group. Nevertheless, after investigation by my *Capitaine*, and in spite of the impertinence of this boor I received eight days of guard duty in the camp and had to go there immediately with weapons and baggage. I found some honourable company there, and that June night was calm and serene. At 0200 hours the *reveille* sounded, and at 0300 we were on the march.⁴

On the dawn of 24th June, 1812, we crossed the Niemen above Kowno.⁵ Some companies of voltigeurs had preceded us on the left bank, and had only burned a small number of cartridges establishing a bridgehead. On the 25th, a little before daybreak, *Général* Gudin, our divisional commander, visited the outposts and asked the officer on duty why this *sergent*, pointing to me, was there. The officer not being able to inform him, I did it myself, confessing it to be my fault. 'Ah! The devil', said the *Général*, 'another time be more careful. Come, return to your company, because today all the bravest must be there, and tell your *Capitaine* that I will lift your punishment.'⁶ We arrived in front of Wilna, towards the end of June, after having burned a few cartridges against the enemy rearguards.⁷ The rain had fallen in torrents all day, and destroyed the roads, so that the cavalry and artillery suffered fairly significant losses in horses.⁸ My *corps d'armée* did not enter the city, instead taking up a position in a lowland. The *7ème Léger* found itself placed, en masse by division, in the water and mud which came up to my ankle. I expected to spend the night, like many other times, with my musket in my hands, in this quagmire. However, the *Adjudant* told me that I had been assigned as an orderly to Marshal Davout. To my great satisfaction I had go to the right of the division and from there to

Marshal Davout's headquarters, in town. The house he occupied was between that of the Emperor and that of the Marshal Murat, King of Naples. I found myself in the company of *sous-officiers* of all arms. Everyone was looking to get away to find something to eat, but the aide-de-camp on duty was only giving leave to a few of us, and only after waiting in turn. I was looking for a corner to rest, having had a long and tiring walk of the day, when I saw a double door. I ventured to open it, finding two locals and two other occupants wearing turbans, sitting around a well-lit table enjoying a comfortable dinner. Servants, dressed in the livery of the Emperor, were serving them. I was amazed, not knowing whether to move forward or backward, but not yet knowing the march of retreat, I entered with my shako in hand.

'What are you looking for?' said one of the two turbanned diners.

'A place to rest, but I see that is not possible here, please excuse me.'

'If you are alone,' said a turbanned diner, whom I recognized to be Roustan, the Emperor's Mameluke valet, 'come in, for your division has been in the vanguard today and you must be very tired.' Then he made me sit down at his table. Although stunned by this lucky windfall, I valiantly planted my fork in a chicken wing followed by glazed ham, all washed down with the best wines. The second turbanned diner, Marshal Murat's Mameluke valet, brought in a square-shaped flask protected by a straw envelope. We drank to the Army, to the Emperor, and to his worthy companion, to the Imperial Prince, King Murat, then I stuffed my knapsack with provisions. At this moment, I heard the aide-de-camp call for the orderly of the *7ème Léger*. After thanking my hosts many times, I introduced myself to the aide-de-camp and received an urgent dispatch for *Général* Gudin.

I left immediately, and the regiment left the bivouac at 0200 hours to march on Minsk. The stage that we marched was lengthy and the avant-garde had a skirmish with the enemy along the way. All the villages we passed were deserted. Having left the road to Minsk, we travelled by forced marches, taking all the usual precautions prior to the eve of a great battle. But upon reaching the entrenched camp of Drissa, we found it had been evacuated. On the day we reached this camp, the avant-garde had had, as on the previous days, a fairly general, hot and long skirmish. In front of the battle site was a hillock with a rich chapel, belonging to a large abbey two leagues away. The Russians had established a battery on this hillock, which was removed after a fierce resistance from our adversaries. During the action, this chapel had been ransacked. As soon as we were masters of the position, and in accordance with the severe orders given by the Emperor on this subject, additional companies had been placed in this building. Those who had committed this impious sacrilege turned to a *chasseur* from my regiment, who was called the 'second-hand dealer,' and even 'the Jew', to sell off the stolen objects, and who usually bought and sold. There were second-hand dealers, so-called 'Jews', in all regiments. This *chasseur* had been my bed-mate: he was good, helpful, loved, and esteemed by all, having nothing of the sordid and rapacious reputation of Jews in general. The unfortunate man was weak enough to buy two sacred vessels from the looters.

Marshal Davout, having received complaints, gave the order to search the men of the *7ème Léger*, as the only regiment which had participated in this affair. The four battalions were immediately formed in line, with open ranks, and the soldiers' weapons on the ground, as well as their knapsacks open. The three officers of each company took a rank and inspected it. My poor comrade was thus discovered to have, at the very least, concealed the theft. The men put their knapsacks back on, shouldered their muskets, and closed ranks. The battalions were then formed into a square. A Council of War consisting of the officers then formed in the centre. The unfortunate *chasseur* was brought there, tried, condemned to death, and shot by the men of his company. The whole matter could not have lasted an hour. We barely had time to dig a pit at the foot of a large oak tree, before setting off again. In it lay the old soldier of Jena, Eylau, Friedland, Wagram, who not long before had fought valiantly. For a long time I had in my ears the cries of despair of this victim of military duty. At his request I had the painful task of informing his family in Toulouse of his sad end.

Leaving this place of pain and mourning we walked on Witepsk which we found deserted and where we only made a short stay in bivouac. After having received food there we took the road to Smolensk. On 16th August, 1812, the day before the battle of Smolensk, my battalion was sent to reconnoitre the Dnieper below this town. We had two guns with us and were commanded by a staff *Colonel*. After three hours of marching, our small vanguard was attacked by the cavalry. The voltigeur and carabinier companies were sent forward, first in square, then in skirmish order, and pushed back the enemy horsemen. We crossed over, at a run, broken ground over which our guns were not able to follow. At the end of a large ravine, we found no more riders and the river Dnieper in front of us. The Russians had passed it in small boats which *Colonel* Rome ordered us to use ourselves. Being the regiment's swimming instructor, I brought together my 20 instructors, to which 30 volunteers joined. Our weapons and effects remained in the care of the battalion, a battery was formed from our guns, and, at a given signal, we threw ourselves into the water. The enemy sent a few musket shots in our direction, but a round of canister from the guns put them to flight, and we were able to bring back 15 boats. One swimmer was killed and disappeared below the waves, whilst two were slightly injured in the head and neck. As the voltigeurs embarked, a staff officer brought the order to rally to the *corps d'armée*. We were not sorry because the day was ending, and night operations are painful. We walked for part of the night, meeting only poor isolated houses, and only re-joined the regiment, which had been able to rest and eat, when it was leaving its bivouac. We had been on our feet for 16 hours.

Capture of Smolensk, 17th August, 1812

At about nine o'clock in the morning we meet with troops of all arms emerging from multiple directions. Each took its place in the order of battle. The Emperor appeared, covered in dust from head to toe, followed by a group of *Généraux* and marshals. He moved ahead of them, then went to give his orders, to the right of a division. Marshal Ney dismounted near my company, took me by the arm and led me on a small hillock. He rested his telescope on my shoulder, watched the enemy positions for five minutes, then went to report to the Emperor. Almost immediately, a strong cannonade opened the battle to our right. Smolensk was surrounded by a rather high wall, crenellated and flanked by bastioned towers with dry ditches. There were two gates. A very deep and very dense ravine covered the whole front of the city. It is in this ravine that the Russians were waiting for us. We attacked by battalions, then by companies, as the very uneven ground disordered us. Our officers had few or no men with them, except the *Capitaine* who was followed by a half-section.

At one point, I found myself fourth in front of ten Russians; after burning a cartridge we charged with the bayonet, undaunted by the numbers. The Russians' guns opened fire too early, for in this jumble they hit their soldiers as well as us. We were slowly advancing in this hand-to-hand combat, when the cries of 'Forward' were heard, and the drums beat the charge. We took the lead and emerged from the ravine after pushing everything in front of us. The cannonade redoubled to our right, and we took cover at the foot of the walls, without suffering too much, from the cannon fire from towers and bastions. Marshal Davout exploited the breach in the Grand Bastion, and we followed him there and entered the city, as other troops entered by the neighbouring gate. We found Smolensk deserted, the Russians having set fire to it to cover their retreat. Such was the great battle in which the *7ème Léger* suffered many losses. I lost one of my good friends there, struck by a bullet in the forehead. As for me, all I had to regret was the pom-pom on my shako, cut by a projectile. We spent the day of the 18th August in the midst of smoking rubble and corpses of all sexes and all ages, no longer in human form. Of the holy city only the main buildings remained standing, among others a church which seemed remarkable to me, as much for its grandeur as for its oriental architecture, and which was full of the dead and dying. I was very surprised to see that this great city was intersected by a rapid and deep ravine.

Valontina, 19th August, 1812

On 19th August, we left these ruins, and crossed the Dnieper on a pontoon bridge, and marched onto Valontina. Shortly after, the cannon roared. An aide-de-camp came to transmit the order to open the cartridge boxes and to light the fuses.⁹ On a second order, we entered a forest at the run where *Général* Compans's division was grappling with the enemy. This division supported the left, and my division, commanded by *Général* Gudin, replaced it. As soon as our column head emerged from the woods, it was met with canister rounds from the Russian artillery.

We were at the foot of a steep and very high plateau, at the bottom of which flowed a stream 10 to 12 meters wide. The only bridge had been destroyed by the Russians, and it was necessary, under the bullets and the cannon balls, to cross this broad stream. Our commanders set an example by jumping into the water, the drums beat the charge, and the *7ème Léger* and *12ème de Ligne*, eight battalions in all, were soon on the other side. Two battalions of my regiment were launched in skirmish order across the entire front of the plateau, which was occupied by the enemy. We encountered an abatis which delayed us and forced us to take a long detour.[10] In the midst of these difficulties our brave *Général* Gudin fell near me, struck by a cannonball. Transported to Smolensk, he died there the same day.[11] Night fell, and yet the fierceness redoubled on both sides. Feeling that we had to make a supreme effort, we allowed ourselves to be carried away by the cry of 'Forward!' coming out of every mouth, and by the charge which beat furiously.

Finally, after a frightening melee, we captured the redoubt, which was our objective, after turning the artillery battery protecting its flank. The enemy retreated, but headed to the edge of a thick wood. Night was descending on this carnage when I heard *Colonel* Rome say: 'Soldiers of the *7ème Léger*, the Emperor wants to be master of this wood, he wants us to enter it.' Immediately, without further orders, the drums beat again, directing us to load our muskets. Some voice said, '*Colonel*, we have run out of cartridges'.

'You have your bayonets,' replied our *Colonel*. We entered the woods headlong. I was chasing an officer when two Russians tried to surprise me from behind. 'To you, Bertrand,' a comrade shouted to me, 'hold on, I'm running.' The two of us got rid of our two adversaries. I stabbed mine with a bayonet thrust that knocked his eye out of its orbit. This fight, which according to the Emperor was one of the most memorable, cost us great losses. From the stream to the crest of the plateau, the ground was covered with dead, dying and wounded. The Russians suffered even more than us. They definitely wanted me, because I had my shako pierced by two bullets. The next day, 20th August, 1812, the Emperor reviewed us on this glorious field watered with the blood of so many brave men.[12] As usual, he distributed rewards.[13] We then walked on Wiasma which we baptized 'the city of fish' because of their enormous quantity.[14] A *cantinier* had been arrested there by the *Gendarmerie* while he was looting a house.[15] He was brought before a Council of War, at which he was condemned to death. I saw it pass: he could scarcely support himself. The picket that led him to the place of execution having passed in front of the house where the Emperor was, he asked the cause of the noise he heard, and said that he granted the pardon of the convict. The unfortunate *cantinier*, already in the throes of death, felt such emotion that he stiffened in frightful convulsions. On 3rd September, 1812, we arrived in Ghjatliz, a small town regularly built, with houses made mostly of stone, which is rare in Russia. The fields were covered with cabbages. On the 4th of September, at about 0100 hours, we left this locality. Throughout the morning, we saw columns of all infantry and cavalry, as well as a numerous artillery pieces, arriving from all points of the horizon.

On the 5th September, we were in front of the Russian army. The day was spent conducting reconnaissance and assuming positions. On the 6th, two battalions of the *7ème Léger* were sent to search a large ravine near Borodino, where the cannon was roaring. They spent the day there. The enemy appeared and there were a few killed and wounded on both sides. Then we spent the night in the front line.

The Battle of La Moskowa (Borodino), 7 September, 1812

At dawn on the 7th September, each company commander assembled his men in a circle, and read the Emperor's proclamation. 'Soldiers, this is the battle you have longed for. Now the victory depends on you. It is necessary for us, it will give us abundant supplies, good cantonments and a speedy return to *la Patrie*. Behave as at Austerlitz, Friedland, Wittepsk, and Smolensk, and may posterity cite with pride your conduct on this day. Others will say of you: He was at this great battle on the plains of Moscow.' The reading finished, the cry of *Vive l'Empereur!* flew from every mouth, with enthusiasm emanating from each word. The cry of 'Forward!' was heard. We formed into line, and, hardly had we appeared on the plateau when the Russian cannon balls flew to our bayonets. As we advanced further, this artillery fire cleared our ranks. We were marching on the great redoubt from which we received a shower of canister, causing terrible pain among our ranks.[16] A cannon ball struck the head of my *Capitaine*, and killed or fatally wounded four men of the first rank. The *Lieutenant* replaced the *Capitaine*, but barely had this officer taken his new post when he was himself struck by a canister round which broke his thigh. At the same time the *Sous-lieutenant* had his foot smashed by a Biscayan (they both died as a result of their amputations).[17] The company's officers were *hors de combat*, and our *sergent-major* was absent. As the eldest *sergent*, I took command of the company, the carabinier company of the fourth battalion. We were at the foot of the redoubt. Two battalions of the *7ème Léger* seemed to me to be retreating in steps, whilst the other two were moving obliquely. At this moment, the *Colonel* ordered me not to move. I did not know the reasons for this order, while remaining very proud to command an elite company. My musket slung on my shoulder, facing the redoubt, and under the canister fire, I was talking to my comrades when suddenly a *peloton* of Russian dragoons emerged from the redoubt to the cries of 'Urrah!'[18] Surprised, I recommended my company to remain calm and ordered 'form a circle around me'. This was done with lightning speed. Without waiting for other commands my comrades began a rolling fire which made the cavalrymen, already almost on our bayonets, pay dearly for their audacity. They disappeared and, thanks to the calm and courage of my comrades, others came to our aid. The *7ème Léger* returned to the redoubt, but we still had to leave it. Until 2000, the cannonade shook the ground beneath our feet and the action continued fiercely. Finally, the enemy retreated and we remained masters of the battlefield around 2200. I had received a bullet at the foot of the redoubt which struck me in the shoulder, but only slightly wounded me, thanks to the strap of my knapsack.

In the evening, after the action, while we were waiting to take our post, a bullet took away my shako and killed a *sergent*, my compatriot. It wasn't long before we discovered my comrade's murderers. There were three of them, nestled in a large hole, in the centre of a small ravine. Justice was done by two bullets and the bayonet.[19] *Capitaine* Chevalier took command of the company which, that day, had lost 37 men killed, wounded or missing.

During the night, *Colonel* Rome was kind enough to address to me with some kind words about my conduct, in the presence of several officers. The next day he informed me that our *Général* Gérard, our division's commander, had proposed me for the cross of the Legion of Honour. The disasters of this campaign meant that I did not receive it until the following year. That same night, my comrades from the company, surrounding our flag, did me the honour of presenting me with a certificate stating what I had done during the battle. I was very sensitive to their memory and very grateful for their attachment to me, although I felt that I had simply done my duty as a soldier.[20]

We continued our march on Moscow, taking part in some skirmishes at the advance posts. The Russians were setting fire to everything in our path, even the growing crops, and already we were struggling for our subsistence. Finally, on 14th September, 1812, we saw the much-desired capital and the cry of 'Moscow!' was repeated twenty times, coming out of every mouth. This large city, with its oriental constructions and its many bell towers, struck the imagination. Part of the army crossed the city and moved forward.

The Emperor made his entry at the head of the Imperial Guard. The *1er Corps d'armée*, to which my regiment was assigned, remained in front of the city on the banks of the Moskowa.[21] Once the advance posts were established, my *Capitaine* designated me to look for food. Having chosen the men I could trust, I walked with them into the city. We were only armed with our sabres. But the only bridge was guarded by a picket, and the prohibition to enter Moscow was official. We had go down the stream in search of a ford, and had to cross to the other side with water up to our belt. We were at the entrance to the suburbs, where we met many other soldiers also in search of food. Moving away from our competitors I led my squad to an isolated house where I saw light.

We struck the door, called, threatened, and sent forth a summons, but no one answered. Finally I spoke in German, and explained what we were looking for, as well as reassuring my hidden interlocutor. Then, a woman's voice intervened in French. After much discussion the door opened, and the poor woman recoiled in terror before the faces of six warriors whose faces had been browned by four months of bivouacs and battles, and worn by so much fatigue and danger. I managed to reassure her once more, and asked to be introduced to the masters of the house. We were taken into a well-furnished living room where a family of ten appeared, ranging from grandparents to grandchildren. They were French, originally from Caen, and were now tulle makers in Moscow. We were received with open arms, and served a good dinner, washed down with French wines. We then asked for food for our comrades who were anxiously awaiting us. This excellent family gave us a cart on which we were placed bread, a large quantity of flour, pulses and a host of other provisions. After saying our goodbyes and expressing our gratitude we went up the bank and towards the bridge, in the middle of extraordinary congestion. Fearing that marauders less fortunate than us would attack us, and knowing that a hungry belly has no ears, I hid our cart in the brush at the edge of the water and arranged my men around, sword in hand. I then went to the bridge in person, where there was an advance post of the *16ème Léger* commanded by a *Capitaine* and a *Sous-lieutenant*. This officer immediately gave me a horseman and six armed infantrymen as an escort. I was thus able to rejoin the *7ème Léger* without incident, and rewarded our dear comrades of the *16ème Léger*, who returned to their post, delighted. My company turned our return into a cause for celebration. Everyone surrounded the cart with joy, and the rest of the night was spent in a fraternal banquet.

The Moscow fire, 18 September, 1812

On 16th September, in the morning, I went with two comrades to pay a visit to the good Norman family who had received us so well. Not only did we no longer find the house, but it was almost impossible for us to recognize its location. This house, whose inhabitants had been so hospitable and generous a few days ago, had burned down in the fire. Just as the *Capitaine* was about to order bread to be made with our flour, the division was ordered into Moscow itself. We crossed a part of the city where the fire was causing the most appalling devastation, to reach a still untouched quarter, where we were lodged in a Russian barracks.[22] The company's barracks consisted of a large room, with camp beds on the right and left. At the end was a huge stove, then a small room for the *sergent-major* to attend to his paperwork. Not far from our barracks were the palaces of the Russian nobility, open and abandoned. If we had had the benefit of hindsight, the harm would not have been great, and most of us would have been content with food, linen, and fine furs. However, seeing the flames move towards the palaces and the riches within, many thought that it was better to take what could be useful or flatter, before it disappeared.

In the cellars, in particular, we found many French wines, mainly Médocs and Champagne. I entered with one of my comrades, into a luxurious boudoir. Inside was a library of French books, and I allowed myself to take some of these volumes. Lifting a magnificent tapestry door we found ourselves in a gallery of paintings where we admired the Lebruns, Mignards, Bouchers and Davids. We then arrived in an office adorned with sumptuous furniture. All the keys, as if to entice us, were in the locks. But already we had to think of withdrawing. The sparks coming from a neighbouring hotel fell on the one in which we were. I took in a basket, a coffee maker, jams and bottles of liqueurs, whilst my friend had two large hams and cooked poultry into a bag. We had barely taken a few steps out of this palace, when flames broke through all of its windows, the panes bursting with a noise like that of that of two ranks of infantry firing a volley.[23] We no longer knew which direction to take to get back to our barracks, and we walked cautiously with a group of other soldiers, so as not to be caught in the vortex of fire that enveloped us. My basket, so well stocked, became a dangerous burden, and I did not hesitate to throw it away.

Suddenly we found ourselves in front of a group of arsonists, torches in one hand, a weapon in the other. We only had our sabres and several of our little group were unarmed. I took command, saying 'Close our ranks, for if we break up we are lost'. These infamous galley slaves, with repulsive faces, let loose by Rostopchin to destroy the city, rushed at us, uttering savage cries. We met them calmly and with energy. Seeing that they were trying to envelop us, we clung desperately to the walls spared by the fire. One of these bandits tried to burn my face with his torch, I got off with a few drops of hot resin on my hand. Our position was becoming critical, being obliged to fight off this horde of assassins and to guard against flaming brands falling on all sides, as well as zinc roofs, common in Moscow, which crumbled with a formidable crash. Finally, we reached a street where the fire burned less cruelly, and there were less brigands. We began to breathe more easily when a roof, crashed into our group. Two of us were thrown down, with rather serious injuries. Fortunately, the arsonists had given up continuing their pursuit, and we were able to help our wounded by quickly following the street. Shouts and gunshots are heard: after some hesitation, we decided to march towards the fire. It was well that we did, because, after crossing an inferno with difficulty, we arrived at a place in front of a church, which served as a guard post for the *Chasseurs à Pied* of the Imperial Guard. Already this post had taken a certain number of arsonists, into custody. These despicable convicts were brought to justice by shooting them on an island in the Moskowa river.

We finally returned to the barracks. The following days, no longer having to fear these madmen, we continued to obtain provisions in the rare hotels or houses spared by the fire and abandoned, so that the barracks was soon changed into a vast store of foodstuffs. I will not talk about the luxury items that were there. On the second day of the fire, on the night of 17th September to 18th September, we were at the advance posts, and I was sent by the postmaster to command a patrol of twelve men, to search the surroundings. We were barely on the march when, by the light of the houses we saw seven or eight arsonists laden with packages. I sent a few musket shots in their direction, and they rushed off at full speed. We charged them, and three of these brigands were brought back to the post. They had on them luxurious weapons, surgical instruments, jewels, precious stones and a number of gold Fredericks, amounting to a rather large sum. Most of the rich and abundant churches were left intact by the fire. The dregs of the population of Moscow and the surrounding area tried to tear the silver plaques from some of them. The Emperor had posts placed at the entrance to these monuments. Looking into one of these churches, I saw a crowd of unfortunate people of all ages, of all sexes, covered in rags, who had escaped the disaster, and were dying of hunger, in this holy place where the day before they found calm in prayer. This was the result of the monstrous determination of Rostopchin, to which his master was no stranger and who, in order to devastate the French army, made nearly 60,000 innocent victims among the population of Moscow. I read the following day or two after our departure from Moscow, on the road to Kaluga, the following inscription: 'Count Rostopchin, Governor of Moscow, and master of this castle, set fire to it himself, so that no French could lodge there.'

Our beautiful days of plenty were gone as quickly as they had come. Soon it was necessary to forage some distance away for provisions. The regiment organized a battalion made up of officers, *sous-officiers* and soldiers taken from all the companies, under the command of a *Chef de Bataillon* and assisted by a staff officer.[24] We were going in the direction covered by the troops of Prince Eugene and Marshal Murat, which were ahead of Moscow to the east. I was part of the first of these expeditions which, in the first days of October, led us to an immense and superb castle, after three hours march from Moscow. Nearby was a miserable village with straw roofs. The detachment of thirty men, of which I was part, entered into negotiations with the old servants who remained in this house, with the assistance of a Polish soldier. After placing posts to secure us from being surprised, the battalion was formed in the courtyard of the castle. Only the officers and the soldiers forming the fatigue detail for carrying the food entered this building. No object of any kind, apart from what was requisitioned as food, was removed, thanks to the very severe orders given on this subject.

We were able to bring the supplies back on a cart drawn by a miserable horse found in the village. We had found a good amount of provisions of all kinds, and we had even discovered flour and pulses in the poor houses of this hamlet. Being the eldest *sous-officier* of the detachment, I obtained permission to visit the princely palace, followed by the *Chef de bataillon* and the staff officer. What struck me most was a collection of armour, from the most ancient times to the present day, and I felt that those of the Moors of Spain were the best suited for combat, the most artistic, and finished the best. We left these splendours empty-handed. The next day, the 9th October, we returned to the regiment where we were joyfully received. The distribution of food took place immediately, with the surplus going to the store to add to the daily distributions, which so far consisted of potatoes and sauerkraut. We made barrels of this last commodity as provisions for the winter! From October 14th to 15th we were surprised by the first snows, which lasted, it is true, only two days. On October 15th the evacuation of Moscow began.[25] It was the start of the retreat, which was not to end until December 31 in Thorn, 78 days later.

Evacuation of Moscow, 17 October, 1812

The *7ème Léger* remained in town, along with the *1er Corps d'armée* and the Young Guard, under the command of Marshal Mortier, Duke of Treviso. On the night of 19th and 20th October, after blowing up the Kremlin, we set out for the holy city of Malojaroslawetz, 30 leagues from Moscow. After a few skirmishes, we took part in the battle of Malojaroslawetz on the 24th October. All honour is due to Prince Eugene who, with the *4ème Corps d'armée*'s 20,000 French and Italians defeated the 90,000 Russians of Kutuzov.[26] Only the elite companies of the *7ème Léger* fired their muskets, whilst the rest of the regiment manoeuvred all day. In the evening, we made our bivouac, on the road to Kalouga.

During the night, a horse belonging to a *cantinière* escaped, dragging along many others. There was a terrible panic, in the midst of which the generals themselves ran after their horses. The stacked muskets were overturned, and many men were wounded, or burned by falling into the bivouac fires. All the main guards and the first lines took up arms, the Russians in front of us did the same, and we had to spend the rest of the night with our muskets at our feet, our knapsacks on our backs, and without being able to enjoy even an hour of sleep which we needed so badly. On the 25th October, during the day, we returned to the road to Smolensk. The *1er Corps d'armée* formed the rearguard of the *Grande Armée* from this date.[27] The *7ème Léger* marched on the extreme left, a hard and perilous task.[28] On the 29th October, we passed over the battlefield of the Moskowa. A thousand remnants of weapons and equipment belonging to the two armies lay under our feet, as well as the remains of our fallen comrades here and there. The redoubts, although damaged, were still standing and reminded us of the alternative outcomes in this battle of giants. This one, we had taken with the bayonet, that one had repulsed us, etc. These were glorious but painful memories!

An hour after we crossed this field, the enemy attacked us in force. The *7ème Léger*, serving as the extreme rearguard, took up position at Koloskoi Abbey, which had served as an ambulance for the two armies during the battle of La Moskowa. This position cost us a few killed and wounded. The latter no longer resumed their posts at the regiment's standards, which, from that moment on, became the invariable rule. The abbey still contained a few wounded from the battle of Moskowa. They were also abandoned, although almost healed. When we left this position, we had Russian cannon firing at our heels, as well as the irregular, barbaric Cossacks, who united with the peasants to do us as much harm as possible. These, mounted on lamentable nags, were armed with a long stick, at the end of which they fixed a spearhead or a long nail. From that moment it was necessary to fight one against ten. A soldier from my regiment, seriously wounded in the head in our defence of the Koloskoy abbey, was walking alone to the left of the column formed by our division (of *Général* Gérard). Assaulted by three Cossacks, he was hit with several lance thrusts and fell. These savages wanted to take him away, but, as he had kept his sword, he rose up and presented his guard, wanting to resist until death. The atrociously unequal fight began. Fortunately the howls of the Cossacks reached his comrades who protected the column's flank. A *caporal* went back to rescue the injured. His musket misfired. He then launched himself with the bayonet and soon, assisted by the soldier he put out of action one of the Cossacks and made the other two prisoners. This heroic soldier was able to bear arms on our way out of Smolensk and was killed by a cannon ball on the 17th November at the battle of Krasnoë. On the 31st, we made these miserable Cossacks pay dearly for their audacity. That same day, our *Général* Gérard, commander of our division, would have remained in the hands of these savages, had it not been for the courage of a *carabinier* from my company. He was decorated in 1813 on the report of the *Général*. On the 1st November, 1812, we rallied with the rest of the division. On the 2nd November, approaching Wiasma, we found the enemy was already in position. We established our bivouac on the edge of a wood. Being in the rear of the division, we were the last to arrive. Beside us soldiers from the artillery train slept in shelters around a warm fire. Driven by hunger, which tortured me, I had the cruelty to take advantage of their cook's absence, to jump over the sleeping men and run away with one of their full pots, which comforted my comrades and me. We were getting ready to sleep when we were made to leave without the sound of drums or trumpets.

Rearguard action at Wiasma (Vyazma), 3 November, 1812[29]

In the daytime, we were saluted by Russian cannon fire. The battle lasted until nightfall and was fierce. The *7ème Léger* faced the Russian regular cavalry for part of the day. Two muskets broke in my hands that day; the first when loading it, and the second when cocking it. I suffered no other harm than a heavy concussion. At nightfall, the army crossed the very deep river flowing at the bottom of the town. The *7ème Léger*, was designated the rearguard, and covered the troops passing over the bridge. The enemy cavalry, threatened us, so the four battalions of the regiment were formed into a tight *column en masse* of divisions.[30] This was because our troops were already much weakened by our losses from the battle the day before, and the retreat from Moscow. Around nine o'clock in the evening, when, seated on our knapsacks, we were taking a well-earned rest, we were warned of the enemy attack by musket fire from our outposts, one of which was taken. It was the enemy cavalry. *Colonel* Rome ordered the head of the column to be drawn up, the last division of the formation turned around, the files on either side turned to the right and to the left, and we thus had a full and compact square, outside the regulations, but well suited to the circumstance. The four faces of the square immediately began to fire, and more than one Russian rider was killed under our bullets or on our bayonets. There were only a few men injured by pistol shots fired by their cavalry. Our *Colonel* received compliments from *Général* Gérard.

An hour later we approached the bridge. The first battalions of the regiment passed over it. My company, the carabinier company of the fourth battalion, received the order to defend the bank closest to the enemy until the column had completely crossed over. The *Captaine* of my company (son of the Marshal Moncey), sent me to reconnoitre upstream, along the river, with a few men of my choice. After 20 minutes of walking I received musket fire. I established myself at the edge of a wood to retaliate, and I dispatched a *caporal* to warn the *Captaine*. The entire company, and even everyone that had not yet crossed the bridge came to my rescue at the run. However, the enemy troops we made contact with, had disappeared, and we returned to the other bank. The night was already well advanced.

The following days, we were assailed by whirlwinds of snow, and an icy wind, with 16 to 20 degrees of frost. No more food, no more rest, neither day nor night. We were constantly attacked in front, pushed from behind and harassed on the river banks by the whole Russian army, aided by the Cossacks and uprising peasants. Most of those present with the flag were frozen or very numb and could no longer load their guns. Most of the time, we had no other means of salvation than to show them the bayonet. However, the smallest fight, in spite of our bravery, always cost us too much, because our ranks were thinning visibly. The cold was still increasing. On 12th November, we arrived in front of Smolensk. The Russians tried to dispute the passage. The few artillery pieces that we had been able to keep took the lead, and after two hours of an energetically contested struggle, we crossed the bridge, crowded with unfortunate wounded or frozen people. The next day, 13th November, the *Ier Corps*, with Marshal Davout in the lead, passed Smolensk in quite a number of places and took up a position beyond. My *Capitaine* sent me back to the town with two carabiniers to look for food. Thanks to the Emperor's foresight Smolensk had been stocked with provisions, clothing, linen and shoes. But, the employees of these stores had abandoned their post, and the crowd of wounded, frozen stragglers ahead of the column had, with the most inexpressible disorder, plundered all these resources. All these unfortunate people, without their regiments and without leaders, and mostly no longer being able to hold a musket, had rejected all discipline. They had only one thought which was to eat, or at least to warm up, and yet these same men had faced death on twenty battlefields! The temperature was 23 degrees of frost.

At the depot of Smolensk, 13th November, 1812

At Smolensk I was able to find 5 to 6 kilograms of flour and a few pieces of biscuit. Before bringing back to the company these few grains of life, a very poor resource for 60 men, my carabiniers and I had to put our *sabre-briquets* in our hands and defend these meagre provisions against those who, with the most frightful threats and their own weapons in hand, wanted to snatch them from us. Around our bivouacs were houses where officers and soldiers had sought shelter from the cold after lighting a fire inside. One of my good comrades had entered there. Foreseeing what was going to happen I begged him to come out. At my insistent prayer the officers and a few men came out, already numb with the heat and incapable of making a decision. He would not hear anything and was killed there. Soon, indeed, a crowd rushed on these houses, those who were there wanted to defend their rest, a horrible struggle ensued and the weak were ruthlessly crushed. I ran to the bivouac to report these atrocious scenes. Hardly had I arrived there when the flames devoured these houses with all those who were there. In the daytime we saw ruins and corpses. My elite carabinier company still had a good number of men. Our bivouac formed a post, detached from the remains of the regiment, where the *Colonel* and the officers were standing. For warmth we set fire to ambulance wagons, abandoned for lack of teams, and had a good night's sleep and happiness, not complete however, for we still had to defend ourselves, musket in hand, against the cursed Cossacks, but we were nonetheless cheerful around our good fire.

On 16th November we left Smolensk. During the previous night most of the horses had ended their suffering. After two hours of march, my regiment, which formed the head of the weak advance-guard, in a phalanx style formation, encountered the Russians, on horses on the road, with a large and well-supplied artillery train. We only had two artillery pieces against them, our muskets were difficult to load, and we were low on ammunition. The Marshal was in the lead, but we were losing men and the position was becoming critical. Even in this great peril, no one thought that we could surrender. The charge was beaten on the drums and with cries of 'Forward, long live the Emperor' we advanced with our bayonets, through the Russians, but we left behind us our wounded, leaders and comrades, to whom we said an eternal farewell.

Battle of Krasnoë, 17th November, 1812

The following evening, as we approached Krasnoë, we were strongly attacked in front and on our flanks by Russian cannon, regular cavalry and Cossacks, but soon we saw the Emperor at the head of the Imperial Guard. This sight tripled our courage and, after six hours of fierce combat we were masters of the city.

However, the victory had cost our division dearly. We bivouacked outside the city in 24 degrees of frost, on the battlefield. I had very carefully kept a little of the flour found in Smolensk in my knapsack. An artilleryman lent me a small pan on condition that he would have his share of the feast. I planned to make a pancake. For this purpose, I fixed the pan to a long stick, and having melted enough snow to obtain a little water, I made the dough and presented it to the fire. I waited with rapture for the baking process to finish, when suddenly we received cannon balls and canister from the enemy artillery. One of these projectiles took the pan and its contents away from me. I suffered no injury other than a very strong jerk in the right part of the body, but, in despair, I began to cry! Towards 0200 hours the cold increased again, and, through my sufferings, I saw the Emperor walking again, armed with a long stick, on the ground covered with ice and thick snow.

In the daylight, we resumed our march, abandoning our dead and our wounded. These suffered from the cruelties of the Cossacks, according to one of them who had been able to escape. We stayed at Orscha. The weather had warmed up and we received some food. Not being harassed by the enemy, many wounded and frozen were able to join us.[31] It was there that Marshal Ney reappeared, who had not been with us since Smolensk. The day before our departure from this town the intense cold resumed. The Emperor entrusted the rearguard to the remains of Davout's *1er Corps d'armée*.[32] The next day, my battalion was in position on the left bank of the Dnieper with the mission of containing a swarm of Cossacks as long as possible. We held off this mass, whose cries and cantering hardly frightened us, until the few cannons found at Orscha and the other troops had crossed the bridge. We crossed in our turn and the Marshal did not pass until after the last voltigeur of the battalion. Beyond the city the road was nothing but ice. We could no longer stand, and anyone who fell dragged the others. Many, not being able to get up due to the excruciating cold stayed behind and were at the mercy of our barbarian adversaries. We heard the cries of these unfortunate people sometimes very close to us, but we could not turn around to help them. We had to walk, always walk, to avoid the cannon and irreparable losses.

Crossing the Bérézina river near Borisov (Barysaw), 25th–29th November, 1812

On 27th November we arrived on the Bérézina river. The day was spent changing positions, and exchanging a few shots with the enemy. In the evening, the division established its bivouac fires on the edge of a large wood. We had large, old oak trees there to keep us warm, but nothing to eat. According to my habit, I went on a quest to explore the surroundings. A Jew was often found near the *cantinières*, who only sold his wares one-on-one and discreetly. I did not find anyone at that time. However, my lucky star made me meet a childhood friend whom I had not seen since Wagram. He was a *sergent-major* of the pioneers of the engineers, who worked on the construction of bridges.[33] After embracing him I told him of my distress. He immediately put a pancake in my hand, saying: 'It was cooked in tallow, you will find it good.' I found it delicious and did not fail to give a part of it to my right arm, *sergent* Durand. Just as I was getting ready to sleep in front of a good fire, I was told that one of our *cantinières*, Louise, was about to give birth and was in great pain. The whole regiment strove to help this unfortunate woman who found herself without food and shelter, under this icy sky. *Colonel* Rome set the example. Our surgeons, no longer having their equipment, abandoned in

Smolensk for lack of means of transport, received handkerchiefs, shirts, and whatever else we could give. I had noticed near us an artillery park belonging to the *corps* of Marshal Mortier. I ran there, and, seizing a blanket placed on the back of a horse, I rushed back to carry it to Louise. I had done a bad deed, but I knew God would forgive me for the motive. I arrived at the moment when our *cantinière* was giving birth, under an old oak tree, to a well-formed male child. I met him in 1818 as an *enfant de troupe* in the *Légion de l'Aube*.[34] So our brave Louise gave one more defender to *la Patrie* in one of the most critical moments in which the remnants of the *Grande Armée* could have been found.

The Marshal gave praise to us all, but in particular to the surgeons, for our generous conduct. On 28th November, a little before daylight, we come out of the woods and adopted our battle formation, with Russian cannon balls beginning to fall on us. The action began, and, strangely enough, we beat the Russians, taking cannon and prisoners. In the evening we marched towards the bridges, in column. The Emperor was already on the other bank, where the enemy had also been pushed back. On November 29th we presented ourselves at the entrance to the bridges, and at that moment I saw, with my own eyes, a spectacle of such horror that after fifty years my pen can still hardly reproduce it. It was a mass of unfortunate people, officers and soldiers of all arms, the wounded, employees, women and children, all prey to the cold and hunger. They could have crossed the bridge the day before, without incident, but nothing had been able to tear them from the fires around which they regained a little life. They were now rushing to cross the bridges. The corpses of those members of this lamentable crowd who had already succumbed during the night had been trampled underfoot by the cavalry and the artillery. We saw scattered heads, arms, legs, and bloodied mud!!

As we approached, all those who had retained a little moral courage wanted to join our ranks. But our officers, foreseeing what would happen if we gave in to our sense of humanity, gave their attention to saving all that had remained grouped around the flag; our salvation was at the end of our bayonets. As our column was very closely followed by this mass of victims, I heard myself called by my name and I saw in this sad crowd the wife of a *sous-officier* of the regiment, holding her child in her arms, who was dying. This sight gave me the most atrocious impression I have ever felt. I will always have before my eyes the expression on the face of this mother with distraught and pleading looks. But my duty as a soldier, while tearing my heart out, came before any feeling of commiseration. In any other circumstance I would have given my life to save this woman and her child. May God judge me!!! All these unhappy people remained in the power of the Russians.

At the entrance to the bridge, two horses cluttered the passage. Cries 'Let them be thrown into the water,' could be heard. Having learned that they belonged to senior officers, we did nothing, but the poor beasts were beaten with bayonets. Shortly after, my *Capitaine* ordered me to take the place of the guide on the left who had just received a bayonet in the thigh. To move from my position as replacement *sous-officier* position to the rear of the company, I started to run. One of *Général* Gérard's aides-de-camp, believing that I was fleeing, shouted at me 'Where are you going?' At the same time he began to strike me. As swift as he was, I deflected it, and I raised my weapon even faster, realizing his mistake. Finally we were on the bridge, but as the planks sagged on one side, we were walking on a very steep slope, and several of us fell into the water. I saw them pass over huge ice chunks, trying to reach the other side. Among them was the officer who disappeared under the waves as a result of the shock of another ice chunk. Others however, were more fortunate. The Marshal was at the end of the bridge, giving direction to each of the remaining troops as they reached the other bank. A staff officer indicated the position we were to occupy. With great difficulty we lit a fire, and, like so many other times, we called for those missing, sending our brave, lost comrades our regrets and memories. I then went to find the *Colonel* to tell him about the blows I had received. He was already informed and sent me, led by an *Adjutant*; near the aide-de-camp who, after having shown me all his regrets, shook my hand, saying: 'Let us forget, my old comrade, and close ranks, because we will need it for tomorrow.' This night of November 29th to 30th was very cruel for us. Our position was roughly parallel to the Bérézina, and we were in charge of some of the prisoners taken on the 28th. Towards midnight the cold increased. Our prisoners died or escaped, our small number preventing us from keeping them. Our fires, lit on the snow, melted it to the earth underneath, and we found ourselves as though at the bottom of a well. The sky, dark until this moment, cleared, and the icy north wind began to blow. It lifted the burning embers of sand from at the bottom of the fires, which fluttered up to our eyes like silver sparks. In the morning, many of us were blind. Those who had been spared by this burning sand led their blind comrades. For my part, having been only slightly affected, I was the conveyor of *Adjutant-Major* M. Rougeant. Two days later, all had regained their sight.

Early December, 1812

Our miseries increase still further!! Without shoes, without clothes, tortured by hunger, by a cold of 28 degrees, we could not count on a moment's rest, neither day nor night. Death was everywhere. We expected to fight every moment, while the cold paralyzed our hands. The small number of men who retained their arms could no longer take a cartridge, even from their pocket. Most of the muskets could not fire anyway. However, it was necessary at all times to bear in mind the hordes of Cossacks who served as our escort on our flanks and closely followed the rearguard *pelotons*. They only had the courage to assassinate the unfortunate stragglers overwhelmed by suffering, unable to use a weapon, and who no longer had the strength to follow. It was enough for the Marshal to say to the *Colonel* 'Chase away this pack,' for them to flee. Fifteen or twenty men sufficed to disperse them, and our bayonets had learned to do swift justice. On the 2nd December, 1812, we headed to Wilna. The betrayal of our Habsburg ally, Schwartzenberg, had handed over the city of Minsk to the Russians. We had hoped to receive clothes, food and rest there. On the evening of that day, when death had continued to harvest many of us, we thought we could enjoy a few moments of respite. The remains of the *1er Corps* took up position near a forest and efforts were made to light the fires. But the energy of those who had been able to stay in the ranks had begun to weaken, indiscipline ensued, and hardly anyone wanted to act. As a *sous-officier*, and being expected to set an example, I ordered several carabiniers of my company to follow me to fetch wood at the entrance of the forest. Some obeyed, and I forced one of those men who was turning a deaf ear to walk; fire alone, could save us. We entered the forest and found a big pile of logs, but they were covered with snow and almost stuck together, so we had great difficulty pulling them out. Garrigue, the carabinier who came with regret and grumbling, did not move. I forced him to work like us. This unfortunate one clung to a log that did not give way. He redoubled his efforts but his strength failed him, and he fell, seized by the cold. We come to his aid, but it was too late. His limbs were already stiff. He could barely articulate the words 'my mother, my mother, France, the Emperor,' and slipped into eternity. We were preparing to bring him back to the company, but an 'urrah' indicating the presence of Cossacks prevented us from fulfilling this duty, and we had to let our dear comrade sleep his last sleep where he had fallen. I had only done my duty as a soldier by forcing him to come with me, but it hurt me to tears. On 3rd December, we left this bivouac, leaving the dead and dying, as we did every day. The company, reduced to about thirty men, was sent, by order of *Général* Gérard, to reconnoitre the flank of the column, with the recommendation not to lose sight of it. But, as usual, *Capitaine* Moncey pushed too far, and we were attacked by three or four hundred Cossacks. The *Capitaine* said to us 'See, it's just a few Cossacks, let's be firm and calm.' We were hardly afraid of these barbarians who only knew how to shout, and we were heading for the flag, already far away, when we saw part of our enemies advancing to block our way. We entered a peasant's hut, in time to avoid the lance and sabre. We barricaded ourselves there, opened loopholes in the earthen walls and began to fire our muskets, albeit feebly. The column, hearing these sounds, stopped and sent us reinforcements. We were thus able to abandon our fortress, leave the forest, and rejoin the flag, with a few musket shots. The Cossacks had shown us again, in this circumstance, their usual courage. I had noticed, in a corner of the hut where we had fortified ourselves, a heap of seeds of an unknown species. As we passed very close again I entered the hut and saw, with inexpressible joy that this heap was intact. I filled my pockets with it and ate it greedily. Several comrades, with whom I had shared this happy discovery, also made an ample provision. It was unfortunately hempseed, I found it excellent and strong for my taste, but it resulted in dysentery which made me seriously ill. Despite this annoying inconvenience I could not make up my mind to get rid of what remained to me, because I considered that these seeds had saved my life. Besides, I found my succour there, for in the same day I was able to exchange part of it for four candles. In the evening, a cavalry officer offered me a piece of sugar for two of my candles, which I accepted. These candles restored my stomach to a boil and led me onto Wilna.[35]

Arrival at Wilna (Vilnius), 8th December, 1812

It was to our astonishment, that very day when I made these singular exchanges, to see comrades coming to meet us from this city, with white sword belts, shaven, well clothed, in good health, well-armed. They belonged to *Général* Marchand's division, which had not been in the campaign. The contrast between them and us was as bizarre as it was terrible. A few days later they were unrecognizable, but they at least showed they knew how to fight at Wilna and Kowno.

Until now God had protected me!! Possessing a dry and thin temperament, of a strong constitution, having been accustomed, from my childhood, to braving the cold, I had, except for a few ailments, never been ill. My mobile, alert and confident character had always maintained my moral strength at the height of the greatest perils, but, at this moment, I could not help but notice that I had remained the only *sous-officier* of the regiment with the flag. We were, moreover, so reduced in numbers that the officers had begun to stand guard as *sous-officiers* and soldiers a few days before, and continued thereafter. The night of 3rd–4th December was excruciatingly painful for us. We hoped, despite the 28 degrees of cold (a temperature unknown until then, according to the inhabitants of the country) to rest a little when we were attacked by Cossacks. The gleam of our bayonets put them to flight, but as the enemy infantry announced itself by its camp fires, we had to set out again and resume our retreat. On 4th December, when day broke, we were no more than a weak phalanx, grouped around our commanders. Despite all the goodwill of those present, who until now had observed all the rules of the discipline, it was no longer possible to demand that we march in order. Until we entered Wilna, we gave up fighting against the cold, the road being strewn with the dead and dying, especially cavalry. On 5th December, at Smorgoni, we learned of the Emperor's departure for France. It is claimed that from at this moment the army looked upon him with contempt. This is an infamous lie; I affirm on my honour that it did not happen. The Emperor remained for us, I will not say a God, because we recognized only one, but our Emperor, neither more, nor less. The evening before we entered Wilna, I served as an orderly near the Marshal, in a barn where we were to spend the night. I heard *Général* Gérard say to Marshal Davout, 'Monseigneur, you are here in the midst of your *Corps d'armée*. Seven months ago this 70,000 strong *corps* marched in front of this barn, inside of which it is fully present today.'

At around 0100 hours I also heard a staff officer tell the Marshal that it was 29 degrees cold. Here we are at the gates of Wilna, the capital of Lithuania, where, as in Smolensk, the stores of food and clothing had been looted in dreadful disorder.[36] We lost hope for a second time to comfort ourselves. Not only were we squeezed very closely by the enemy when we entered the city, but we had been preceded by Cossacks. It is true that prompt justice was done to these by the few depot troops that we met there.

Night, however, calmed down and the remnants of each *corps* was assigned a post. For our part, we were appointed a convent of Benedictine monks. Since Moscow we had not set foot in the most humble cottage, so it was a miracle that we were able to rest, that night, under the cloisters of the convent, around a good fire, and with the modest provisions that the religious had sent us, not being able to do for us all that their heart dictated to them. There was a severe prohibition to enter the interior and, moreover, all communications were inaccessible. The monks spent the whole night in songs and prayers at the foot of the altars. I will never forget the deep and almost supernatural impression these songs made on me, rising up to God, above so much suffering and horror, hovering over the agony of an army! This incredible happiness to have found, even for a moment, fire, shelter, food, help and consolation, would prove fatal to many of us.

The Russians, in fact, had received reinforcements the day before and attacked the town towards the end of the night. The call to arms sounded immediately, not drummed, because for a long time we had no more drums. Instead it was sounded by the only cornet left in the regiment.[37] At this ringing, we had to leave the convent, but more than half of us, despite being old soldiers of Italy and Egypt, remained deaf to the orders, and to the prayers of the commanders. This night of absolute rest around a good fire had finished destroying their courage and their energy. They felt a general numbness, a heaviness in the head which deprived them of the faculty of thinking. Dazed, and acting as though drunk, they tried to stand up, only to fall heavily. Only those who had known how to take their share of this beneficent night, with wise precautions of movement, were able to follow our commanders. We never saw those who remained. It was not yet daylight when we entered, our ranks swelled by the depot troops, in a street crowded with the sick, the frozen, the wounded. To make matters worse, a long line of sledges, piled up one on top of the other and each of which wanted to overtake the others, had come to a stop. In this horrible crowd we had to defend ourselves in front, in flank, in tail, not only against the Russian troops, but also against the inhabitants who were quite fierce. Our unfortunate sick and wounded, deprived of the sledges that they were to be carried on, could neither move forward nor backward. We, who had conserved our energy and our weapons, owed them protection and help. We did our best to fulfil our duty to them, but soon, outside the city, overcome by numbers and cold, we had to abandon them to their terrible fate. They were falling and exhaling near us on the frozen earth. Three men of my company perished in this manner. As for those who remained in the city, they were mercilessly slaughtered by the Jews! Our *Capitaine*, Moncey, had just left us, by an order.

Escaping from this hell, we found ourselves in front of the pass of Ponari, which presented a very steep slope, which the ice had turned into a true mirror.[38] The Russians had been waiting for us there since the day before. *Général* Gérard informed the *Colonels* that the pass must be forced. He and all our officers put themselves at the head of the remnants of the elite companies, with the rest of the column trailing behind us. We couldn't take a step without falling over others, and walked very slowly. Many of those who fell like this remained stretched out, after many efforts to get up. The Cossacks, dismounting, finished them off mercilessly.

Wanting to avoid attacking the pass head-on, we made an oblique movement to throw ourselves into a thicket, and we no longer heard the heart-rending cries of our slaughtered brothers in arms!! At the moment when we believed ourselves saved we receive the musketry of the Russian infantry, posted at the edge of a wood which we had to cross at all costs. Mad with despair, we rushed forward, aided by a weak reinforcement. The fight began in the woods, and after having driven back the enemy, we finally emerged beyond the disastrous parade on the road to Kowno. On this tragic mountain we left not only leaders and comrades but, fortunately also, the treasure wagons, filled with gold and silver, which the Russians, leaving their ranks, began to plunder. We took advantage of this to gain ground and rejoin the remnants which had preceded us. From Wilna to Kowno, we were involved in a series of fights and skirmishes, increasing the losses caused by the severe cold. No more regiments, no more ranks, everything was confused, and we marched pell-mell. Our uniforms were replaced by rags of all colours and of all kinds, and we carried the most bizzare of accoutrements. Three-quarters of this lamentable crowd were unarmed, with some suffering from frostbitten feet or hands. The unfortunate and wounded clung to those who were still able-bodied, and at the slightest alarm, threw themselves among us, under the shelter of our weapons, as if we were a citadel. They bothered us a lot, because the Marshal wanted to keep all those who could still carry a musket together, this being the only way to protect the disarmed mob. When we were obliged to take the lead, which often happened to us, we were forced to abandon our poor wounded to the savage fury of the Cossacks!!

Arrival at Kowno (Kaunas), 12th December, 1812

Providence continued to protect me in those terrible days, and allowed me to conserve my moral and physical energy. I stayed, with very few others near our eagle, alas! whose shaft had only a shred of material left, and which, deprived of one of its wings, carried off by a cannon ball at Eylau, nevertheless hovered over these disasters, as our sacred rallying sign. We arrived at Kowno. The crowd was without discipline, soldiers of all arms were without commanders, commanders were without soldiers, and there were *cantinières* and military employees. All who had hitherto escaped death rushed to cross the glacis and barriers. Marshal Ney, who was immediately following us, was able to halt the pursuit of the Russian regular battalions and Cossacks for a few hours. As in Smolensk and Wilna, the stores of food and clothing had been looted by those who preceded us. There were few or no inhabitants. In the streets there were only hungry people, with haggard eyes, asking each other where to find food.

I met one eating bread. 'Oh!' I said to him, 'tell me in which quarter you found it.' He answered me coldly, 'Look for yourself.' At a street corner I saw a queue in front of a house. Some came out, carrying bottles of brandy or potatoes. They are immediately assaulted. I left them to deal with the result of their recklessness, and I entered, pushed and jostled by the crowd, into a courtyard where there was a strong smell of alcohol. I was carried to the steps of a staircase leading down to a cellar, where the current of which I was a part was repelled by those who wanted to go up. I was beginning to regret very much finding myself in this crush when, despite myself, I reached the cellar floor. Smashed barrels let wine, rum and brandy flow into it, and we trampled up to our ankles in this liquid. This cellar was soon more than full. In the sinister darkness cries of distress are heard. Those who fell could no longer get up, and were suffocated by the alcohol, and no one could move forward or backward. Not wanting to perish miserably in this underground, I gathered all my strength, to bring myself into light at all costs, and without pity for the unhappy crushed people, whose cries could no longer even be heard. But I soon acquired the conviction that it was no longer possible to exit by the staircase. Seeing a window near me, I realised that this was the only way out. I told a *maréchal de logis-chef* of artillery of my plan, he being the only one near me who seemed capable of carrying it out. As a first thank you he shook my hand strongly. Then, we crossed the piled-up corpses together, and arrived at the foot of the window. I climbed it first; all my muscles were tense, and all my willpower was at stake to achieve it. Finally, after desperate efforts, I reached it, crossed it, and found myself in a courtyard, on the snow. Immediately I held out my hand to the *maréchal de logis-chef*, and, when we saw each other safe and sound, we kissed repeatedly without being able to speak, thanking God for our deliverance. Before leaving the enclosure where we were, we looked into the window in order to help any comrades who had the same idea as us. We heard nothing but cries of despair, which grew weaker, and soon followed by a gloomy silence. Finally, seeing our help useless, we shook hands, suppressing our emotion and, after exchanging our names and the numbers of our regiments, we each returned to our posts.

I returned to the place where the remains of the *1er Corps* was, and there I found a dear friend, Briançon, the regiment's *adjudant sous-officier*.[39] He was sick, his hands frozen, and he was losing courage. 'You haven't brought anything back?' he moaned.' No, nothing. 'Oh! my God, my God!' he said. Seeing him so slumped, crouching near a fire, I tried to cheer up his morale and for that, promised him to search again. On the same square was a house with many bivouacs and fires, in the courtyard, stable, and rooms, high and low. A soldier from the regiment came out, eating potatoes. Having asked him, he led me to a stable at the bottom of which I found personnel wearing the Emperor's livery, seated around a large pot full of nearly cooked potatoes. Sabre in hand, I demanded they to give me some. Without letting me finish my threat, they answered, 'Yes, you will have some, but shut up, otherwise we will be overrun.' I fell silent, but realizing their unwillingness, I told them, still sword in hand, that I was going to call if they didn't immediately let me take a share. I was then able to pick as many potatoes as needed to fill my pockets and my knapsack, which, for a month, had never left me day or night. I took great care to put them in my greatcoat, so as not to be robbed on the way. I returned safely to my unhappy friend. In response to his gaze, full of anguish, for he felt himself dying of hunger and cold, I handed him a steaming potato. Then, to avoid unwelcome visitors, we went to settle down near an abandoned bivouac. There was an abandoned wagon, on which was written 'Treasury of the Imperial Guard.' After having recovered a little, we waited for the signal to leave.

The wagon had had its padlocks broken, and all its fittings torn off. I climbed onto the wheel, and lifting the cover with my musket, I saw bags of all sizes. I burst several, from which escaped 5-franc and 20-franc coins. 'Well,' asked my friend, 'what is it?'

'Silver, gold.'

'Better,' he replied, 'if it was flour.' With that reflection, I closed the lid without taking anything. This wagon had already been visited and part of this treasure removed. Those of my comrades who had made space to carry this silver and this gold regretted it, because on leaving Kowno they had to throw away a large part of it to lighten their knapsacks. Those who did not do so, weighed down by the burden, could not follow and so remained in the hands of the Cossacks. However, Marshal Ney, with a handful of brave men, having kept the

Russians at bay for some time at the entrance of the town, was forced to re-enter it by closing the barriers. The wounded, frost-bitten, sick and other stragglers were immediately warned to get ahead of us to cross the bridge across the Niemen river, but a very small number responded to this call, the others, still numb around the fires, were taken by the enemies after our departure. While the heroic Marshal Ney disputed foot by foot the crossing of the city, all who had retained their weapons from generals to regimental officers and soldiers, assembled to move towards the bridge. It was crowded with the non-combatants who had preceded us, and who, seeing the Cossacks on the other bank, had flowed back and crowded there. The sidewalks were almost covered with those with frozen feet. I thought I saw the horrors of Bérézina again, but fortunately it did not happen. We had stayed, a few men from the regiment and I, around *Général* Gérard and our *Colonel* at the entrance to the bridge. Marshal Ney joined us there, and, continued to set the noblest example, not crossing over until after the last fighting soldier.

We had great difficulty in reaching the end of the bridge, and despite all our precautions we could not avoid trampling on these unfortunate people who covered it, and who, very probably, did not see their country again. Beyond that, about thirty men, with a few officers, were enough to disperse the Cossacks who, having crossed the Niemen upstream, dared to dispute our passage.[40]

The Russians, seeing us on the territory of Prussian Poland, stopped at Kowno, and we headed for Gumbinen. The road, near the bridge, was littered with 5-franc pieces, probably looted by the Cossacks whom we had chased from a treasure wagon. We remained strong, being indifferent to this money, since it was bread that we needed. The temperature had improved, and the column of soldiers of all arms which had been able to escape from

The Evening after Jena (14 October, 1806), by Édouard Detaille. Napoleon and his headquarters pass by French infantry as they display the battle standards captured from the defeated Prussian army.

Napoléon on the Battlefield of Eylau (7–8 February, 1807), by Antoine Jean Gros. Photo courtesy of the Toledo Museum of Art, Ohio, USA. Bertrand was part of the *7ème Corps d'armée* whose attack strayed into the firing arcs of the Russian massed artillery.

French Soldiers Plundering a Farm by Peter Heinrich Lambert von Hess (1792-1871)
Photo courtesy of Milwaukee Art Museum (M1962.138)
Gift of the René von Schleinitz Foundation

During the peace negotiations at Tilsit in 1807, Bertrand joined a large marauding party which plundered a farm. Having left their weapons at the camp, they were surrounded by armed Prussian locals and unable to defend themselves properly. Only the arrival of a French detachment, marching under arms and commanded by a surgeon, saved the marauders from being massacred. Note the light infantry voltigeur and chasseur in service dress in the foreground, and the voltigeur in grey greatcoat, behind. Bertrand had to make his own out of captured Russian material just before the battle of Eylau.

Corporal of a French light infantry regiment (chasseur company), 1807-1812.
From the illustrated plates published by Aaron Martinet (1762-1841)

Carabinier of a French Light infantry regiment (Carabinier company), 1813-15.
From the illustrated plates published by Aaron Martinet (1762-1841)

Death of Général Gudin at the battle of Valontina, (19 August, 1812), by Zvonimir Grbasic. Photo courtesy of the artist. This scene depicts *Général* Charles-Etienne Gudin leading the *7ème Régiment d'Infanterie Légerè* and the *12ème de Régiment d'Infanterie de Ligne* against the Russians just before he was struck by a cannon ball. Bertrand participated in the attack.

Marshal Ney supporting the Rear-Guard during the Retreat from Moscow, (1812), by Adolphe Yvon (1817-1893) Photo courtesy of the Manchester Art Gallery, Manchester, UK.

Earlier during the Russian campaign, at Smolensk, Marshal Ney rested his telescope on Bertrand's shoulder. During the retreat from Moscow, Bertrand remained in the ranks of the *7ème Léger* and was an eyewitness to Ney's personal example.

Charge of the Russian Cuirassiers at Kulm, (30 August, 1813), by Vasiliy Fiodorovich Timm (1820-1895) Outnumbered and defeated by the advancing Russian army, Bertrand would be wounded and taken prisoner soon after.

Officers of a French light infantry regiment in walking-out dress and service dress, 1813–15.
From the 1812 Manuscript by Carl Vernet (1758–1835)

Carabiniers of a French light infantry regiment (Carabinier company), 1813–15.
From the 1812 Manuscript by Carl Vernet (1758–1835)

Kowno marched without order, with the generals and officers in front. Many had frostbitten noses and ears, whitened with snow. I could allow myself to laugh at their unusual appearance, as I was virtually the only one unharmed.

Towards the middle of the night we arrived in a large village and were informed that we were stopping there until daylight. Everything had been devastated by those who had already been there. However, we got into a miserable cabaret, paying dearly for milk and potatoes, which we thought was a delicious meal. With some difficulty we managed to place ourselves on some straw near the first occupants of a room in this hovel. It was the first time since Moscow that we went to sleep under a heated roof. As soon as they lay down, each one fell asleep with a beneficial sleep. For me, the sudden transition from the most profound misery to this relative well-being kept me awake, which allowed me to see large-bodied peasants with suspicious faces enter. I made up my mind to watch them and, getting up, I approached the stove. A few moments later, having gone out into the yard, my foot struck an obstacle. I bent down, and my hand met an icy face. I went inside and woke up my comrades. We took up our weapons and some torches, and immediately we found two of our comrades in the dung, murdered with pitchforks. We were on our guard the rest of the night. At daybreak, the cornet sounded, and we assembled ourselves around our commanders, and we counted our numbers, because some time had passed and many people had not responded to the call. I immediately informed the *Colonel* of our sinister discovery. He took note of my report, but, as it was necessary to leave in haste, the punishment of the crime remained in the hands of divine justice. As always, those who remained deaf to the call of the cornet most probably paid for their lack of energy and their forgetfulness of duty with their lives.

Arrival at Gumbinen (Gusev), mid to late December, 1812

In the evening we arrived at Gumbinen, where, despite the crowds, we found, for the first time, inhabitants, inns, and distributions of food. We were finally able to eat, which seemed like a dream. Unfortunately several of us, not having spared our stomachs, which had weakened from prolonged suffering, died of indigestion. It was a great sorrow for us to see these brave men, having escaped so many perils, succumb like this. The *Colonel* obtained a piece of land for our poor comrades from the civil authorities.[41] Not only were we able to satisfy our hunger and stock up on provisions, but we also took care of the repairs and cleaning of our rags, as well as the most necessary personal hygiene. For my part, I had worn the same shirt since Smolensk and had not been able to shave since leaving this city. I also succeeded in completely getting rid of the vermin that was eating us all, by undressing at night, and putting all my belongings in the baker's oven where I was staying.[42] The next day we were walking on the road to Thorn. More Russians pursued us. Having some money between us, we resolved, six in number, to procure provisions for the following days. To this end, we asked our commander, as had been granted to others, to leave the route, on condition that we rejoin the next morning, at the meeting point fixed by the *Colonel*, along the road from Thorn to Strasbourg.

In our group I was the only one who kept all my weapons, two others, slightly wounded, had only their sabres, whilst the other three, with their hands frozen, were not armed. One of them not only had two fingers of the right hand badly frostbitten, but also partly frostbitten feet. His frozen fingers had to be amputated later. So we walked through fields in the snow, and after an hour of walking we saw a steeple point, and then we reached a village. The smoke from the chimneys indicated that it had not been abandoned by its inhabitants. We found a large number of comrades there who, having had a day's march on us, had settled there since the day before. After a meagre meal, paid for very dearly, we also bought some provisions at exorbitant prices. We were delighted at having reached our goal when, suddenly, one of us was seized with an overwhelming fever, which deprived him of all strength to walk. We had to reconcile our desire to join the flag at all costs, with our firm desire not to abandon our patient for a moment. The inhabitant with whom we had eaten having refused to rent us a harnessed sledge, we had to buy a vehicle and horse and in addition pay the peasant who had offered to serve as our guide to as far as the road from Thorn. Having satisfied all these requirements, we placed our comrade, frozen and feverish, on the sled, protecting him from the cold with straw and shreds of blankets, our provisions half in the sleigh, half in our knapsacks. Then the five or so able-bodied men preceded the carriage, led by the guide. The latter made us take a dirt road, and after two long hours of walking, when darkness was already falling, we found ourselves in front of a band of Prussian peasants. They rushed at us and the sleigh, the guide disappeared, and our patient was thrown onto the snow. We were surrounded, assailed, searched and completely robbed. Having wanted to defend myself with my musket, this weapon was torn from me, and one of these brigands held above my head the sabre taken from one of my comrades. Satisfied with their booty, these infamous thieves took away horse and sleigh, and were willing, doubtless fearing to compromise themselves, to return my musket, sabre and cartridges.

Here we were on the snow, far from any habitation, the daylight quickly fading and the cold increasing; being the only able-bodied and armed, I gave my musket to one of the wounded, and my knapsack to another, so that I could lend my arm to assist the weakest. We tried to get going, but despite all their efforts, all their goodwill, two of them couldn't move forward. The cold numbed them and I began to feel the disastrous effects myself. As for the poor, feverish, valiant soldier who had faced death on so many battlefields, I saw him pass away. He sank into my arms, the shadows of death already on his face. 'I see,' he said in a barely perceptible voice, 'that I'm going to leave you, why have the Russian bullets spared me? If I die here you will tell my dear mother that I thought of her.' Then he wanted to shake my hand but didn't have the strength. I cried and felt my courage give up on me. However, with a burst of energy, I sent the most stalwart of our sad group to reconnoitre around us, within sight. At the end of thirty to forty minutes of unspeakable anguish, I heard myself call several times, and, for a few moments afterwards our comrade joined us with a priest driving a sleigh. This ecclesiastic told us that having learned of the ambush of which we had just been victims, he hastened to come to our aid. We placed our patients in the sleigh, and in forty minutes of walking we arrived at a village inhabited by Catholics.

This parish priest, French by birth, had emigrated in 1792, and was naturalized as Polish.[43] He was our saviour. As soon as we entered the presbytery, the feverish man, first warmed up in front of a large fire, was placed in a comfortable bed between two eiderdowns, and an old maid boiled some beer with sugar for him. Then, as our host, while crossing the village, knocked on all the doors to warn the inhabitants, women arrived who helped the worthy priest to dress our wounded, to whom we gave all the linen they needed. Finally we were offered a solid meal; omelette, potatoes, bacon, beer, brandy. We were half in the dream. It was, after a display of human ferocity, an act of charity of the most touching and noble expression. After having eaten moderately for fear of an accident, around 0300 hours I gave the signal to leave. All these good people, the priest at their head, opposed it, reminding me of my imprudence, and adding that, the next day, a sleigh and a guide would be made available to us. But I had no difficulty in making them understand, that our imperative duty was to join the flag, and I was sure that my comrades felt like me that this obligation was sacred; so I was not surprised to hear our feverish comrade cry out: 'I alone have a lot to fear, but whatever happens I want to leave.' Seeing this energetic resolution, the priest had a good sledge harnessed, furnished with straw, hay, and blankets, the cold still being 20 degrees. Wanting to leave a memento for this venerable priest, I gave him the badge of my cartridge pouch (a hunting horn with the *7ème Léger* inscribed).[44] 'I offer you,' I said to him, 'a very modest object to thank you for the blessings you have showered, upon us. I have worn this badge in all the great battles, and I would be grateful if you would accept it of my compatriots who have been helped by you in their misery.'

'I accept it', he replied, 'this object will be all the more special, reminding me that after twenty years of exile I was able to do something for my beloved homeland in the person of its noble and brave defenders. I embrace your comrades at the same time as you. Always be brave in the service of France and the Emperor. Better health, have a safe journey, be happy, God will be with you.' Moved, we hugged this worthy priest and the generous inhabitants, our saviours, in our arms, and after expressing our deep gratitude to them, we took our places in the sleigh. I have, very unfortunately, lost the notes with which I recorded the name of this noble and charitable ecclesiastic and his village. I only remember it was four or five leagues from Gumbinen, walking parallel to the Prege river.

Two hours later we heard, with delight, our battalion's cornet sounding the call to rally. I reported our adventure to the *Colonel*. Our feverish man and the two wounded remained in the care of the ambulances sent from Thorn to meet us.

End of the retreat from Russia, 31 December, 1812

On 31st December, 1812, we returned to Thorn, which we had passed through nine months before.[45] We found this town encumbered with the remains of the *Grande Armée*, as well as a fairly large number of officers, *sous-officiers* and soldiers, coming from the depots, or leaving hospitals, which had joined their regiments. Although the inhabitants of this city, the second of Poland, were full of sadness and fear, as a result of the probable invasion of the Russians at short notice, they received us, in agreement with their civil authorities, as devoted friends. We found everything in abundance, food, clothing, comfortable lodgings. I had just been appointed *sergent-major*. Having left my *caporal-fourrier* with our host while I went to the *Captaine*'s lodging, I found, on my return, this *sous-officier* in agony. He died an hour later. The unfortunate man had indulged in eating and drinking more than his stomach could bear, and like so many others paid with his life for this imprudence.

Chapter 7

1813: Dresden, Kulm and Peterswald

On 2nd January, 1813, *Général* Gérard presented the remains of each regiment of the *1er Corps d'armée* to Marshal Davout, Prince of Eckmühl. 'Monseigneur,' said the *Général*, 'I have the honour to present to you the *7ème Régiment d'Infanterie Légère*. It has 47 officers out of 146; 34 *sous-officiers* out of 196; 111 soldiers out of 4,000. Here is what remains of this fine regiment which entered the campaign with five complete battalions. I do not need to recommend to you these brave men whom you have always seen around you since Moscow.'[1]

'I shall be able, on all occasions,' replied the Marshal, 'to remind myself of the merits of all them, and of which the Emperor is informed. All have always been worthy soldiers of a great nation.' Then, laughing, and alluding to the number of soldiers who escaped the disaster (111). 'The figure of 110 would have been better suited to the *7ème Léger*.'[2]

A few days after our entry into Thorn, our condition was restored, and we abandoned the rags we were wearing. We were designated to form part of a column directed towards Bromberg, a town on the Vistula Canal, eight leagues from Thorn.[3] The Russians had seized it, hoping to cut our way to Saxony. At night, we had driven them out of this locality, but they returned with reinforcements. Despite our small numbers, we fought inch by inch in the streets, against these fresh, well organized troops, who outnumbered us. It was nevertheless necessary, despite this fierce fight in the middle of the night, to give way, leaving our dead and our wounded in the hands of our adversaries and to retreat towards Saxony.[4] On the third day of walking, I was seized with a violent fever and painful headaches. It was impossible for me to follow. Many officers and soldiers were similarly affected. The *Colonel* put his sleigh at my disposal and I reached Torgau, a small fortified town on the Elbe. It was entered by a covered bridge, the only one I have ever seen. This place had a fairly strong garrison, which was armed as well as possible. Its Governor was the Count of Narbonne, an aide-de-camp of the Emperor. The only officer present in the company to which I belonged, *Lieutenant* de Falcoux, took me, accompanied by my comrades, to the hospital, and the column of which my regiment was a part continued its route to Erfurt. Three days after I entered the hospital, the Russians appeared in front of the city, the bridge was destroyed by order of the Governor, and a few cannon balls reached the outskirts. A blockade was imminent. All the sick who could walk to Erfurt were called to arms.

Despite my extreme weakness, I jumped off my camp bed, put on my equipment, and, not having the strength to carry my musket to my shoulder, I dragged it by the sling. Many other sick or wounded wanted to follow my example, but had to give it up in despair. The small detachment that left, under the orders of two officers, crossed the glacis. We turned around to see for the last time this city which our forebodings advised us to flee, and which, in fact, a few months later, became the tomb of almost all its defenders, killed on the ramparts or dead from an epidemic. The Count of Narbonne was among the victims. It was cold, with a clear sun; at a quarter of a league from Torgau my legs refused to carry me, my head was heavy. Forced to stop, I lost sight of the detachment. For a moment I thought of going back to the hospital, but, regaining courage, I dragged myself a few steps farther. Forced to stop again, I lightened my equipment, throwing my knapsack into a ditch, but determined never to part with my weapons. I was walking very painfully to a farm not far away when my strength betrayed me. Night was falling! Fortunately, an ambulance convoy passed, escorted by infantrymen, which had left Thorn like us, but along another route. The officer in charge of the convoy ordered my knapsack to be taken and I got into a wagon, the jolts of which were very painful to me. Arriving the same evening, in a small town and overwhelmed with suffering, I thanked the officer and left the ambulance to enter the first house I saw. I found some comrades who comforted me with some bouillon soup. With them was an artillery *maréchal de logis* from our detachment from Torgau. Thanks to him I was able to set off on a cart the next day. It was with this group that I found some happiness.

After several long days of walking we arrived, around 2100, at Erfurt.[5] The cart which I was on was forgotten in the square. I climbed off it and went to the police station to sleep there, but the head of this post made me enter a neighbouring house instead. I found help and assistance from the inhabitants and the many comrades who were there. They were part of a regularly organized detachment of the sick which left the city the next morning, in good order. I could not follow them because my fever had worsened, and confined me to the straw I lay upon. Having offered the little money that the artillery *maréchal-des-logis* had given me, to be taken to the hospital, I saw, shortly after, a sedan chair appear, in which the good people of the house installed me, and which allowed me to make an unusual entrance to the hospital. Once I lay in a clean and comfortable bed, broken with pain, I lost the feeling of reality. A venerable clergyman attached to the army came to console me after the visit.[6] I saw him again, in the middle of the night, at my bedside, to help me endure a violent attack. At dawn he had returned and held my hand in his, telling me about the Emperor, about France, about my family, about all our miseries in Russia. Relieved and calmed by this ardent charity, I felt better and could tell him the story of the horrible scenes to which I had been a witness. What affection one finds in the heart of a good priest!! At the time of the visit I recognized a *sergent-major* standing behind the doctor, who was acting as an orderly. He was one of my good friends from my regiment, who had accompanied me to the hospital in Torgau. I called him, he threw himself around my neck, and he told me, to my great surprise, that the *7ème Léger* was in Erfurt. A few moments later I saw the *Colonel* arrive at the head of my comrades, and I could not hold back tears of gratitude for so much kindness. The enchantment I felt seemed all the more complete, because I was very happy to find myself near the flag and my military family. The *Colonel* sent me the only doctor in the regiment to see if I was in a condition to be moved.

His opinion being favourable, I left with the regiment two days later, on 7th February, 1813, not cured, but with a happiness which improved my condition. I took my place, with two officers and the warden, on a cart as well equipped as possible to avoid the bumps and the cold. But in the evening, fatigue and the harshness of the temperature had brought back the fever. The next day, during a stage of six leagues, my sufferings were horrible. Also, when I arrived at the lodge, *Colonel* Rome had me transported to the hospital, and recommended me to the head doctor. Our unit's doctor came to wish me good luck, as did my comrades. The latter, knowing that I had been robbed, gave me some money too. The next morning, when I heard the regiment marching into the distance, I felt a terrible heartbreak. This happy and proud music, which I had heard so often the day before or in the morning of a battle, twisted my heart. Feeling unable to answer the call, it seemed to me that my strength was gone forever. However, I did not lose heart. Two days later, my condition worsened, following a violent haemorrhage. The doctor was opposed to my taking to the baths at Brünn, given my state of weakness. I was lost, when, after fourteen hours of this sad situation, a reaction took place in me. I felt a strong heat in my limbs and the blood stopped. I had been cared for, with the most absolute dedication, by a nurse called Mayer. But I remained so weak that the slightest touch made me cry out in pain. Four days later I became deaf and blind, then recovered my sight and hearing after two days. Feeling better, I thanked God. My ordeal, however, was not over. Even the hospital's corridors were crowded, and in our room of twelve there was a single nurse. This was not enough for our care, and two of my two neighbours died during one of his very brief absences. To make matters worse, a terrible epidemic fell upon this heap of sick and wounded. Not having the strength to leave my bed, I watched the parade of corpses that were carried through the room where I was, day and night. Having asked the surgeon to change rooms, the latter replied that I would not be more safe from the plague in another. I had, therefore, to continue to see these incessant and dismal processions. However, I was happy enough, despite my cruel anxieties, to keep a calm and clear head. Finally the epidemic ceased, and we were told that there were thirty-nine dead. We had no difficulty in believing it. I must say that all the doctors, surgeons, and other employees did not shrink from their duty and used all their zeal and their courage to fight the disease. Only one of them succumbed. Soon the fever left me, but I dared not sleep, thinking I could feel blood in my mouth and fearing another haemorrhage. I quickly lost this apprehension and, thanks to the doctor's good care, I was able, a few days later, to eat, get up, and go down to the courtyard, where I could and use my little nest egg to buy some sweets.

I was in full recovery. Thirty-five days after my entry into this tomb, I set out, in charge of a detachment of twenty-seven convalescents. A map of the route and transport were provided for us. I said farewell to the good doctor and to my remaining comrades, and being out of danger, I also gave a gift to my nurse, who was astonished to see me still of this world. On 15th March, 1813, on a beautiful sunny day, we took the road to Mainz. We stayed at Frankfurt-on-the-Mein, a large and beautiful city where the Imperial Guard was being reorganized. I left four men there in the hospital. When I arrived in Mainz, my detachment was put on subsistence and attached to one of the garrison regiments, as was done for all isolated detachments. This garrison was 20,000 men strong at this time, with Marshal Kellerman, Duke of Valmy, as its Governor. No one could leave the place without a pass, the heavily guarded doors of which were always closed, and the drawbridges only lowered on an order from the Governor. As soon as they retired, the patrols and police officers visited the furnished houses and conducted any soldiers they found in them straight to prison, without listening to their reasons.

As soon as I entered Mainz I saw the streets crowded with the sick and wounded who could not find room in the hospitals, and many of whom died on the pavement, despite the zeal of the military and civil authorities. I had made up my mind to get out of this abyss of misery at all costs, and to leave these walls which had already cost so much French blood. The commissioner of war whom I asked to be directed to my regiment's depot refused me outright. I presented myself at the Marshal's palace, with weapons and baggage and asked a *Capitaine* serving as an aide-de-camp for an audience with the Duke of Valmy. This *Capitaine* wanted to know the object of my approach. I refused to tell him, which led to me being politely but firmly rejected. Having in my pocket an indemnity for traveling from Frankfurt to Mainz, I was able to afford a modest dinner. There remained the question of where to sleep. I could not at any cost join the regiment to which I had been assigned for subsistence, nor I could not spend the night in a hotel, or in the street, for fear of being taken by a patrol. Still carrying my arms and baggage, and not knowing what to do, I prowled around the Marshal's palace and made up my mind to take up residence on a stone bench, near the post of honour. But we were approaching the end of March and the night was cold. Needing to take shelter under some roof, I made the desperate decision to enter this post. The *Capitaine* who commanded it, a brave man who had returned from Moscow, was greatly astonished that I had not been discovered by a patrol. He roughed me up for not rejoining the *corps* which had been assigned to me as soon as I had recovered, and even threatened to take me to prison. As I felt the benevolence beneath his abruptness, I frankly explained to him, in the following terms, the motive for my disobedience. In view of the shortage of officers, the depot of my regiment, in Huningué, must also be in need of senior *sous-officers*, to instruct the recruits and organize the new army to oppose the invasion. Moreover, it was the moment when the promotions were being made. I was afraid, staying in Mainz, of not being promoted myself, and thus seeing my future compromised. Knowing that the Marshal was to mount his horse the next morning at 0800 to review the troops and inspect the fortress, I wanted to report to him, at this time and for this purpose, and so I spent the night at the post.

The *Capitaine* agreed to receive me. I was treated as a friend by the men of the post, old and young soldiers alike, and shared their meal. They eagerly helped me with my weapons and kit. After speaking for a long time with them of the Emperor, of our battles, and of traitors, I slept heartily. The next morning, after having thanked the *Capitaine* and the comrades of the station, for their hospitality, I went to the vestibule, full of anxiety. From the palace, I saw the escort arrive, then the aide-de-camp who had received me the day before. 'You here again,' he said to me, 'why?' But at this moment the Marshal appeared. I carried and presented arms and, without leaving time for the aide-de-camp to speak, I explain my reasons to him, and my desire to join my flag.

'What you ask of me is impossible,' replied the Duc de Valmy, 'you must obey the Emperor's orders. If I granted your request, I would have to do the same for all those in your case.' Desperate, I allowed myself to remind him of an old passage from the *Moniteur*, prescribing that isolated *sous-officiers* whose depots were nearby should be sent there without delay. There was no answer. The Marshal was already setting his foot in the stirrup when, looking at the plate of my shako: 'You are from the *7ème Léger*, *Colonel* Rome commanding.'

'Yes *Monseigneur*.'

'Very well, the dedication of your regiment counts for something.' A few moments later, I joyfully held in my hands, an order of departure, and carried it as fast as I could to the commissioner of war. This individual was very surprised, but established my route map and told me to go to the paymaster, to collect my travel expenses. I guarded it carefully, fearing some unforeseen obstacle. I ran to the French gate, and after signing a registration roster at the post there, I saw the drawbridge lower. In two jumps I crossed the glacis and the outworks and set off happily on the road to Strasbourg. I cheerfully walked five leagues in one go to the first stop. There was an artillery park with an infantry detachment. After a hasty meal I left, having decided to sleep at Worms. After an hour's walk I was joined by a pay wagon headed for Strasbourg, and driven by two soldiers and a *sergent* of the train. I was kindly offered a ride in this vehicle, and I took advantage of this as far as Strasbourg.

There, after having had my route map stamped and receiving a ticket for lodging, I drew my travel expenses from the paymaster. I happened to be lodged at the house of a brewer, a former cuirassier, who had been retired with a pension of 300 francs following a serious injury received at Wagram. He and his wife offered me the most affectionate hospitality. After dinner, one of their friends came to spend the evening, who had also carried the sabre, and sported two beautiful and noble scars from the battle of La Moskowa. At 1pm the next day my two new friends took me as far as Bâle, carrying my musket and knapsack. At 10am the day after I was dropped off on the glacis of Huningué, where I entered by the French gate. My joy at finding myself before the regimental flag was immense, but it was soon mixed with bitterness. On the drawbridge I saw a *sergent*, who had been one of my former voltigeurs, whilst the post itself was commanded by a *Sous-lieutenant* who was none other than the *sergent-major* orderly at the Erfurt hospital. Among my comrades, two *sergent-majors* and two *sergents* had also been promoted to officers. They had all earned their epaulettes on the battlefields and I loved them no less, but felt that my star, hitherto brilliant, had died out, and concluded with sadness that those who are absent are always wronged. At the time, I didn't have time to let myself be discouraged.

The commander of the post embraced me, and we cried silently with joy. The other veterans of Moscow arrived, and I found myself instantly relieved of my knapsack and musket, and met with questions and embraced on all sides. What emotion! What deep happiness! I arrived, thus surrounded, on the *place d'armes* in front of the officers' cafe. All of them, several of whom had been my colleagues as *sous-officiers*, ran to shake my hand. *Colonel* Rome followed by my *Chef de bataillon* in congratulating me, and, with his extreme kindness, invited me to dinner. They all showed me their pain and their deep regret at not seeing me as an officer, and assured me that I will remain their comrade and friend. *Colonel* Rome's dinner was attended by all the senior and subordinate officers, and two *sergent-majors*. The *Colonel* was kind enough to tell me his sadness at the delay I was suffering and promised me some compensation soon. To prove his interest to me, he announced that he was placing me as *sergent-major* in the company of carabiniers of a battalion which would leave two days later for Hamburg. He added that its commander, *Capitaine* Cosso, would appreciate me all the more as he had been with the regiment in Russia. Cosso had been, in fact, a *caporal* in my section, when we entered Russia. I was all the more exact in my duties towards him, and I had only to praise myself for his attitude towards me. Apart from the cadre, this battalion was composed of young soldiers, dressed and equipped to the nines.

I also received my replacement articles, clothing and headgear.[7] There was a farewell party the day before we left. The next morning we left Huningué by the Rhine gate and embarked on large boats each containing two companies. The rest of the regiment, officers, *sous-officiers* and soldiers, along with the inhabitants, followed us along the river bank, as far as the advanced works. Departing to cries of 'Long live France, long live the Emperor', we sailed along the Rhine. Every evening we disembarked to spend the night on land. On the fourth day, we passed under the walls of Mainz. Early the next day we arrived in Cologne. We stayed there and were reviewed by the *Général* commanding the place, and by the commissioner of war. I was billeted upon a French architect, who welcomed me as though I was a child of the household. It is true that Cologne was in France at the time and I was able to visit the city and admire the Cathedral at leisure. When we left my kind host accompanied me as far as the boat. I continued to write to this family.

Having resumed our navigation along the Rhine, we arrived at Wesel after two days, which ended our journey on the Rhine. We stopped for a few hours to receive food, then we were piled up, standing, crowded like herrings, onto large carts. This was called traveling '*en poste*', and the Imperial Guard was always transported like this from Paris to the border. But great God! What a detestable means of locomotion! Shaken by a hard and rhythmic trot and by continual jolts, it was necessary, moreover, every four or six leagues, to change the cart, like a relay. One of our poor young soldiers lost his bayonet, another his *sabre-briquet* scabbard, and another the pompom of his shako. The trousers and the greatcoats were torn, the muskets had their woodwork, dogheads and frizzens damaged.

It was at the end of three days and three nights of this diabolical race that we arrived, crushed and stiff, in a small town on the Elbe, a league from Hamburg. We entered it in the most perfect disorder.

June, 1813

Marshal Davout was the governor of Hamburg, which contained a numerous garrison, and later sustained a long and glorious siege. We were actively working on the fortifications, which had already become very important. We spent the first two weeks of our stay at this fort repairing our clothing and armament, after our cursed trip in the carts. In addition, we had five to six hours of training per day. Then we could have our Sundays and enjoy this great city, rich in its trade with the whole world, well built, intersected by many canals, adorned with numerous public gardens and brilliant dance halls. We were able to indulge ourselves often in the pleasures of the waltz, except for leaving the ball in the morning to go out into the field for four hours of exercises.

July, 1813

Forty days after our arrival at Hamburg, my *Chef de bataillon* informed me in a report, of my appointment to the rank of *adjudant sous-officier*.[8] I gladly exchanged my woollen epaulettes for those of an *adjudant sous-officier*, and my *sabre-briquet* for an *épée*.[9] A few days later, one Sunday, we received the order for Saxony the day after. We were all pleased about it, because we felt that it was better to attack the enemy in the open countryside than to wait for him behind walls. That Sunday evening the *sergent-majors* gathered to celebrate my promotion and our departure. We had an excellent dinner at a good restaurant, where we drank toasts to the Emperor, the Empress, the King of Rome, and our commanders, then we went to the ball to say our farewells to our dancers. I was told by a young girl among the local German population, that they were touched by this uncommon courtesy. In Magdeburg, where I had had such burlesque adventures three years before, we found the other three battalions of our regiment, now reorganized. We then entered Saxony, where our young soldiers had just covered themselves with glory at Lützen and Bautzen.

August, 1813

We learnt that we were assigned to the *1er Corps d'armée*, commanded by *Général* Vandamme. The *7ème Léger* then went into excessively restrictive cantonments.[10] On 15th August, 1813, our young soldiers celebrated the birthday of Emperor Napoléon with joy and exclamations. Then, after a series of marches and counter-marches, we passed Dresden to occupy the entrenched camp of the suburb of Neustadt, on the road to Berlin. The town, where the Emperor had arrived the day before, was encumbered with troops of all arms, some coming from Pirna, and others crossing the Elbe to take the road to Berlin (Marshal Davout's *corps d'armée*). Fifteen days of marching day and night had severely tested our young soldiers. I was worn out myself, being always on the move when others were resting. The *Colonel* instructed me to go to the army headquarters at Dresden, to find the regiment's paying officer, in order to distribute supplies. I was fortunate enough to have the bread, meat, rice and brandy rations issued before all others, under the care of the *7ème Léger*'s captain of the week.[11]

We were back at camp by the middle of the night. Immediately the fires were lit and the pots started cooking their contents. As for me, since I had dined in Dresden with two *Gardes d'Honneur*, my colleagues and I only wanted sleep, so I immediately threw myself on a bundle of straw and fell asleep under the stars. However, I had barely begun to dream when the *Colonel*'s sapper, to whom I had indicated where I was bivouacking, pulled me by the feet.[12] I woke up with difficulty, cursing my fate. The *Colonel* sent me back to Dresden to receive four days of food. My task was difficult because, although I arrived first, I could not receive anything, as the fatigue detail of the regiment had not arrived, and those of the other regiments claimed precedence. When the *Capitaine* and his men, who had lost their way in the crowd, finally arrived, I was able, thanks to an employee of the stores to whom I had rendered a service in 1809, to open a back door and draw our bread, meat, rice, brandy. Regarding the meat, we had two oxen that were so tired that we had great difficulty in getting them to arrive at the regiment's location. Finally we returned to the camp, the butchers slaughtered them, and the distributions were made. I hurried to snuggle up again in my straw, to find the rest that I had been deprived of for three days and four nights. Vain hope! An hour later the regiment was under arms and set out without drums or trumpets, in the vanguard. Two hours of walking and we passed through, still at night, a town whose name I could not know, not having met a living soul. Two field pieces and a squadron of Polish lancers joined us at this place, where *Général de brigade* Pouchelon took command of the column. I heard him tell the *Colonel* that we were going to force march into Bohemia.

After four or five hours of march, an aide-de-camp arrived with a broken bridle, and gave a despatch to the *Général*. The regiment was halted and formed in line on the edge of a wood, with the main guards and small posts being established. We did not make soup. I immediately lay down at the foot of an old oak tree, my head on a bag and I was able to take two good hours of sleep which made me refreshed and ready. On 24th August, we returned to Dresden and resumed our place of battle with the *1er Corps d'armée*, at the head of the first division. The day of the 25th was spent performing changes in our position, with large movements by the artillery. During the night of the 25th and 26th we remained on alert, with our arms at our feet, and without lighting camp fires.

Battle of Dresden, 27 to 28 August, 1813

On the 26th, at dawn, we approached the Elbe, towards a bridgehead. In the afternoon there was a strong cannonade and rolling musket fire from the infantry. The *1er Corps d'armée* was not engaged in this action, which ended at night. But the next day of the 27th, the *7ème Léger* took its share of glory in the great battle of Dresden. Our young soldiers, who had only been with the regiment's flag for eight months, were full of the most superb spirit and courage. The regiment suffered greatly from the cannon, but we had on the other hand, the consolation of learning that a French cannon ball had punished the crime of *lèse-patrie* of the traitor Moreau.[13] I received, from the hands of the Emperor, on the battlefield, the Knight's Cross of the Legion d'Honneur.[14]

In the evening, the *1er Corps d'armée* crossed the Elbe in front of Königstein, where there was a fort isolated on a rock. We continued, *l'épee dans les reins*, against the rearguard of a Russian corps, in the gorges leading to Külm and Toëplitz.[15] We took two cannons and some prisoners. At nightfall we let the Russians continue their retreat, the *Général* leaving a company of voltigeurs behind and bringing the rest of the regiment back towards Königstein. The main body of the divisional column had remained there. Continuing our pursuit of the Russians the following day, we crossed a fairly wide river upstream of a mill, with water up to our knees. But on our return, in the same place, we found this stream changed into a rushing torrent by a storm, widened even further by floods, and carrying multiple branches.

We had to run from right to left, in the dark, to cross these many currents. The ranks were in disorder, with part of the regiment losing its way. We were shouting and calling to each other, causing a real uproar, and close to the enemy. The *Général* made the rallying beat with a single drum and soon almost all of the *7ème Léger* was gathered at the edge of the torrent. It was forbidden to try to pass it; some reckless individuals were carried away by the current for their disobedience. The miller was questioned, and confirmed the impossibility of reaching the other bank. However, the *Général* sent staff officers, to whom I was attached, to find a ford. The search being unsuccessful, we had to spend the rest of the night soaked to the skin and without lighting fires. Fortunately we had been issued biscuits and eau de vie. For the old soldiers accustomed to these miseries, this situation was acceptable, but our young soldiers suffered. In the daytime, we could build a footbridge with planks and various materials. An *Adjudant-major* crossed over with his horse to go and warn *Général* Vandamme, and soon a detachment of engineers arrived with their caissons, but they were not used, because we managed to pass, without accidents, over our makeshift bridge. Once over, we received the order to wait on the spot for the main part of the division, and we made the company of voltigeurs return. Then we resumed the march forward, crossing the torrent, much reduced, on our bridge. The beautiful August sun dried us up, a neighbouring village provided us with food, and this painful night was quickly forgotten.[16]

Disaster at Kulm, 30th August, 1813

The *1er Corps* arrived in Kulm on 29th August, 1813. At daybreak on the 30th, we were vigorously attacked by the Russians, Austrians and Prussians.[17] At first, the battalions of the *7ème Léger* were formed in close column by division, in an orchard. The shock was fierce and terrible because we were outnumbered ten to one. We charged and bayoneted an artillery battery which had done us great harm, but we were unable to gain ground in the gorges where the enemy waited for us, entrenched in very strong positions.

Around 1600 hours, a Prussian battery was unmasked on our right flank, at half-range, and in a short time the four battalions of the *7ème Léger* disappeared under the volleys of canister. Only one senior officer, *Chef de bataillon* Reyniac, remained with us, with three quarters of the other officers being killed, wounded, or made prisoner. Reyniac rallied all those who had escaped the carnage on a hillock, and we faced the enemy.[18] After a short time we found ourselves overwhelmed and about to be overrun. At a given signal we ran in order to reach the edge of a nearby forest. Our adversaries followed us, killing or taking a large number of us prisoner. *Chef de Bataillon* Reyniac was short, and stocky, so could not run easily. Two Prussians were after him. I turned around and came to his aid, encouraging him to gain ground. Armed with a superb sabre which I had taken on the 28th in pursuit of a Russian officer, I ran to the nearest Prussian. Avoiding his bayonet strike, I gave him a cuff that knocked his musket out of his hands. A sapper from my regiment, who had also turned around, fatally wounded the other Prussian, and the three of us entered the forest. We had great difficulty in progressing there because the ground was steep and the trees very tightly packed. Once we were safe from pursuit, we stopped so that our poor, exhausted *Chef de bataillon* could breathe. An hour later we emerged from the opposite edge, along with many small groups of our comrades. We shook hands, kissed each other, and asked for news of the absent. We had emerged onto a plateau, where we could see a column of infantry in the distance. Our anguish was short-lived because these troops belonged to the *Corps d'armée* of Marshal Gouvion Saint-Cyr.[19]

Why hadn't he appeared forty-eight hours earlier!! The *Chef de battalion* and an *Adjutant-major* went to meet the Marshal. The latter already knew the sad result of this battle and the capture of *Général* Vandamme, but he did not believe the disaster to be so great. We gathered everyone who had come out of the forest, and we thus obtained a force of 3,000 to 4,000 men, who had remained from a strong *corps d'armée* of 40,000 men about a few hours earlier. Corbineau, our *Général*, left us,[20] and we established our bivouacs near Péterswald for the night of 31st August to 1st September, 1813.[21]

On 1st September, we continued our march to Dresden via Pirna. The remnants of the various regiments comprising the *1er Corps d'armée* were immediately reorganized with detachments which had arrived from the depots the day before. After a few days, we were ready to march again. *Général* Vandamme was replaced by *Général* Mouton, Count of Lobau. Our *corps* returned to Pirna, and from thence to Kulm.[22] We arrived in sight of the heights where, a few days before, we had left so many comrades and commanders on the field of battle on that fatal day. We saw the Emperor appear at our head. He went forward, returned, and in accordance to his orders, we retraced our steps towards Pirna.

Rearguard action at Peterswald – Wounded and prisoner, 14th September, 1813

On the evening of 13th September we took up position on the edge of a wood. As usual, grand guards and small posts were established. In the middle of the night, the *Adjudant-major* on duty ordered me to accompany him on his visit to the outposts. We found the first grand guard under arms, after a strong Russian patrol forced a small post back. The *Adjudant-major* continued his tour to see two of the small posts he had placed himself, but we did not come across any more of them. I knew the name of one of the *caporaux* who commanded these posts. I called him, but the only answer we received was musket shots from the enemy. Our posts and patrols on our right fired back, and those who behind did the same. The bullets and splinters of branches whistled in our ears. With great difficulty we left the wood where our position had become critical, and found the bivouacs alerted, all the troops under arms, at their head *Générals* Philippon and Mouton, the Count of Lobau. The *Adjudant-Major* made his report, and at the same time we were vigorously attacked on our wings by musket fire. *Général* Philippon formed us into an attack column, then into a square, and sent the voltigeurs forward onto the wood. These, after several very vigorous attempts to hold back the enemy, saw themselves overwhelmed, and fell back on our square.

The regiment retreated in the greatest order. I saw the other battalions disappear while ours did not move. I hear *Général* Philippon order our *Chef de bataillon*, Brocq, to follow the line of retreat, but to execute it at the usual pace, so that the enemy knows very well that we are not falling back as fugitives. Our small square of 300 men marched for several hours, stopping from time to time to repel the Russian cavalry, hussars and lancers who harassed us and charged us more than twenty times with deafening cries. They were always repulsed, thanks to the courage and coolness of our young soldiers. At each of our halts, our voltigeurs, who flanked the square, shot down the most daring. Others fell on the bayonets of the first rank. These cavalrymen, and the 'urrahs' they cried out had not yet succeeded breaking us when, around 1400 hours, two artillery pieces lined up on our left flank. We had none to oppose them, and in a few moments canister rounds cruelly thinned out our broken ranks, and the ground was covered with the mutilated dead and dying. As soon as the cannon had ceased their carnage, the cavalry, which followed us closely, rushed upon us, with lance points or sabres, and all those who were not wounded fell into the power of the enemy. As for me, not wanting to surrender, and having spotted a ravine about fifty paces away, I ran there at full speed, hoping to escape from the horsemen. But turning around, I saw that I was pursued by three lancers or hussars, shouting like savages. I redoubled my speed, and, thanks to my vigour, the horses gained little on me. Unfortunately, after a few steps into the ravine, I was overtaken by my adversaries. I stopped then, relying on the loyalty of any victor to a prisoner. What a sad delusion! The first who came on me put his pistol an inch from my eye, I thought I would not have to suffer long, but as a result of a movement of the horse the shot deviated, the bullet struck me obliquely in the forehead and the whole left part of my face, from the ear, received the charge of powder.

I fell down, stunned, the blood blinded me, and I had a weakness. My would be murderer dismounted, snatched my *Legion d'Honneur* from me, and disappeared. At the moment when I gained my composure, I painfully sat up and, two other horsemen arrived. The first delivered three lance thrusts to my neck, the second gave three sabre strokes to the head. I received these, parrying, with my left arm. Then they left me to finish off two wounded officers nearby. I leave this act of ignoble cowardice to the meditation of any soldier concerned about the honour of his uniform, whatever nation he belongs to. Whilst in this sad state, I saw a column of cavalry cantering at the charge. This time it indeed seemed like death, and I commended my soul to God. I curled up on myself, showing only my back, in order to protect my head, already badly treated. The whole column passed over me. The horses, foaming, animated by the ardour of the chase, passed over me with their two feet held out in in front, but it was not the same with those behind. The back of their horseshoes struck me harshly, and I received deep bruises. When this whirlwind had passed, I sat down again, at which point a straggler wanted to give me a lance thrust, but his horse decided otherwise. He came back to me and tried to have me trampled by his mount, but the poor beast, more human than his master, always avoided me. However, by use of his spurs, this wild and fierce rider managed to make him put both hooves onto on my left knee. I then felt a pain so excruciating that I could not suppress a cry, the only one that escaped me during these assassination attempts. I fell back stretched, my face in a terrible state, my knee swelling visibly, and, as I could no longer move; my abominable executioner was going to finish me off. Luckily a young Russian officer, at the head of some cavalry, came up to me and said in good French: 'Get up, we're gathering the wounded and the prisoners two steps from here.'

'That is impossible for me, I replied, look at my knee.' On my assertion that I was French, he helped me to the assembly point. I found my *Chef de bataillon* there (Brocq) two *Capitaines*, six *Lieutenants* or *Sous-Lieutenants* and a certain number of *sous-officiers* and soldiers. Prince Constantin, brother of Emperor Alexander I, was there with his staff. He asked, in an absolutely improper tone: 'Where is your Bonaparte?

'Not far from here,' Commandant Brocq answered harshly.

He had to state our names and ranks so that we could establish some kind of control. It was, in fact, difficult to recognize our rank in the hierarchy, for we had been utterly despoiled by our victors. Meanwhile I sat, suffering horribly and feeling a fever coming, while strong columns of all arms passed by us, of Austria, Prussia and Russia. They were marching on Dresden and shouting 'Paris! Paris!' Our column of prisoners, escorted by Cossacks from the Don, was directed towards Toeplitz. Much has been made of the humanity of Tsar Alexander I, and yet the greatest number of French prisoners hardly felt its effects. He must have known very well that by having us led by Cossacks or Bashkirs, he would have forced us to endure the rude and barbaric whims of these savages, the humiliations and beatings. I was the only one injured who could not walk, and I despaired because there was no chance to find transportation in the village. However, *Capitaine* Lépine declared that would not abandon me. This officer had been a *sergent* in the regiment when I first arrived there, and had instructed me in how to handle my arms. As he was built like Hercules, he could carry me on his back to the village. I endured great suffering, because of my dangling leg, the slightest movement of which made me call in pain, in spite of myself. Arriving at the village, we found neither inhabitants, nor carriages. There were still two leagues to go before reaching Toëplitz, and the brave captain could not carry me all the way. The Russian officer, commanding the detachment, informed of my situation, had me mounted behind a Cossack. The road seemed very long to me because my knee continued to swell and the fever shook me. In the evening we reached this town where the reserves of the allied armies were, as well as a large number of wounded and French prisoners. We were parked in a meadow, like sheep, without care for the wounded, without food, the Cossacks forming a circle around us. However, in the middle of the night, a Russian officer had bread distributed to us, and eau de vie, of which I took a few drops in a glass of water, which did me good. Our guards received a heavy distribution of this same liquid. They took such advantage of it that almost all of them fell drunk at the feet of their horses and began to snore loudly. Many of my comrades, after wishing good luck and more happiness to those who remained, took advantage of this grotesque concert to throw ourselves into a nearby wood. I saw them leave with sadness, unable, alas! to follow them. The officer of the Cossacks had gotten drunk like his soldiers. When he woke up and noticed that a large part of his prisoners had escaped, he flew into a rage, fell on his men with great blows of the knout, striking from right and left, from top to bottom, accompanying this Muscovite correction with words which seemed most violent. Then, seeing that the evil was without remedy, he turned his rage against us, and, as far as Prague, well seconded by his Kalmucks, he made us suffer a thousand miseries.

At daybreak, a young Russian surgeon came to treat us, at the request of Commandant Brocq, who had been unable to escape due to a violent fever. He spoke perfect French, like all the officers of this nation. On 17th October, we took the road to Prague, with the wounded piled up in carts drawn by oxen. The slow march of these animals and the jerking caused by rutted roads made me suffer atrociously. Those who were fortunate enough to walk did so ahead of the carts. On the third day of the march, a Sunday, we arrived at the relay where we had to change carts, when the Catholic population from the town was coming out of mass. The new wagons having been delayed, the women of this locality, charitable as always to misfortune and suffering, crowded around us. Although they were repulsed by our Cossacks, they managed to give us bread, wine, meat, broth, linen and clothes. One of these noble creatures cleaned and washed our wounds, and put bandages and compresses on us. It was already late in the day when we had to separate from our benefactresses. On the battlefield of Peterswald, they had torn from me not only my cross, but my coat, and I had lost my shako there. I was able to obtain from one of the Cossacks in the escort a long Russian infantry greatcoat, made of thick cloth, as well as a kind of forage cap (képi).

Arrival in Prague

It was in this outfit that I arrived in Prague at 2100. Those who were neither sick nor injured were taken to an island in Moldau, the others to the castle of the former kings of Bohemia. This castle dominates the city, and was already encumbered with wounded of all nations. We were told us that they could not receive us, but that the next day we would be staying with the locals. All who could walk went in search of shelter for the night, and our carts remained isolated in the middle of a huge courtyard, where the cold could be felt.

Having seen a little straw in the corner of a turret, I dragged myself over there and was about to take off my greatcoat to use it as a blanket, when I saw a man and two women coming towards me. The man carried bread and tins of broth in a basket, the women carried lanterns. Stopping in front of me and seeing me moving, they asked me in German if I was French and an officer. On my affirmative answer in the same language, and seeing me covered in blood, they offered me broth and wine, which I happily accepted. Then they invited me to come to their house where there were already several wounded French officers. I thanked them warmly but pointed out to them that, being a prisoner, I could not leave without authorization. 'We will get it,' they replied, 'from the general commanding the castle.' At this moment I saw a *sergent-major* of my regiment approach. 'Foulquier,' I called out to him. Taken prisoner at the battle of Dresden, he had been instructed by the Governor to establish control of the French prisoners. He immediately offered to share his apartment at the chateau, but when I told him of the offer of charity of these ladies, he advised me to accept. He knew them enough to trust in their devotion to all the arrivals of French wounded, and they had the authorization of the Governor. Accepting their offer, I climbed onto a servant's back and the young person who had spoken to me led the way with her lantern.

A quarter of an hour later, they knocked loudly at a door, in front of which the young girl exclaimed: 'Come, Fritz is carrying a wounded French officer'. At once the whole family and staff rushed towards us. They carried me to the living room to a large armchair and everyone took care of me. In an instant I was stripped of my rags, and found myself, to my great shame, quite naked in front of the mother and the daughter. However, the charity of these admirable women silenced their modesty. The mother passed me a shirt, the son covered my hair with a cotton cap, and Fritz made a bed in a corner of the living room. After taking a little broth, I saw a surgeon arrive who, to my delight, spoke French. He bandaged my arm and my head, and after rubbing my knees, he supported them with splints. I was then carried to bed and everyone retired. I thought I was dreaming, feeling such great well-being. In the night, being unable to sleep, I saw the son and a servant bring me infusions of mallow. The surgeon came to visit again, and told me that he was treating many wounded French officers who had been taken in, like me, into private houses. I begged him to pass on my heartfelt thanks to my generous and kind hosts. At the end of nine days, the care with which I was surrounded returned me to happiness, to hope, and I moved towards a prompt convalescence.

Unfortunately, some of our comrades, forgetting the respect which misfortune owes to the hospitality accorded with such loyal devotion, pushed French gallantry so far as to cruelly offend the affection of husbands. Duels resulted from the insult done to the families, with several being caught in the act. We had to bear the consequences of this sad reply to the noble conduct of the inhabitants of Prague. The Governor, the Comte de Melval or de Belval, a French emigrant who had passed into the service of Austria, immediately ordered that all wounded French officers, without distinction of rank, who were in town, would go back to the hospital the same day. Exceptions were asked in vain for those who, like me, could not walk. My respectable hostess and her daughter saw their remonstrances on this subject rejected.

An Austrian *unteroffizier* came to fetch me. I was placed on a stretcher with a mattress and a pillow, and Fritz accompanied me to the hospital. The Russian officer in command of the entrance station politely told me that none of the objects used to transport me should enter the hospital. I regretted it all the more since barely being deposited by two kinds of orderlies on the only available bed in a large room, I was attacked by vermin which swarmed onto the miserable pallet, and particularly on the blanket. This establishment had served as an ambulance for the wounded Russians, Austrians and Prussians who had just been evacuated to make room for us. During the night I saw all those who could walk go for a walk rather than remain prey to these insects. The next day, at the visit, we presented our complaints to the doctor on this uncleanliness and on the quality of the meals, which was very bad. He promised to pass on our observations to whom it may concern. During the day, the Comte de Melval (or Belval), in the uniform of a senior Austrian officer, entered our room: 'I am,' he told us insolently, 'astonished by your complaints, in any case you have only what you deserve, the soldiers of the Corsican Bonaparte must understand that the end of their bloodthirsty attacks has come, you must be happy with the hospitality you are granted, whatever it is. I will not grant any of your complaints.' He pushed his insults so far that those who were on their feet wanted to make him pay dearly for his cowardice. But a *Chef d'escadron* of lancers spoke in the name of all and replied to this count who had deserted his homeland. 'If you have only come to add insult to our misfortune, it would have been more honourable to dispense with your visit. We will do without it in the future, and above all never come back here'. Finally, this wretch was thrown out. By mutual agreement we took the resolution to endure everything without ever complaining.

The German doctors and surgeons who treated us, although absolutely devoted, could not save any of the wounded who were amputated there, either through lack of knowledge or practice. On the other hand, the French surgeons who were prisoners of war, and in charge of the numerous field hospitals in the town, where there were French soldiers and *sous-officiers*, did not lose any on whom they operated. They obtained such a resounding success in their amputations that they were called to the field hospitals of other nations. As for me, I had nothing but praise for the care of Dr Christmann, who was in charge of the part of the hospital where I was. My knee, on which they expended a bag of flax flour and several litres of camphor brandy, was getting better and better, but one of the sabre thrusts I had on my left arm was getting worse. One morning the doctor found increased swelling and inflammation there. During the day the disease progressed such that by the next day the onset of gangrene was observed. The head doctor came to ask me to consent to the amputation of my arm. On my formal refusal, he did not hesitate to warn me that I ran the risk of dying soon. As all those I saw amputated died of haemorrhage after two or three days, I vigorously maintained my refusal, and with conviction! The wound was dusted with cinchona powder and lemon juice, which made me grimace, but I had a better night, and, at the next day's visit, the appliance was lifted, showing a red wound and, even better, the absence of gangrene. This is how, thank God, I kept my arm, which I still use perfectly today (48 years later) except in very wet weather. The perfect harmony which never ceased to reign between officers of all ranks contributed greatly to making us bear our troubles with dignity. I was registered on the prisoner records as a lieutenant, a situation which, in the Russian army, would correspond to my rank of *adjudant sous-officier*. Although being the most junior in rank and the youngest, I was always treated with the greatest benevolence by all my superiors, my companions in misery. They called me 'Cadet'. Being in contact with these strong and elevated souls, I understood the greatness of the role of the leader, and the salutary examples they gave me served as a guide for the rest of my life.

From Prague to Pest (December, 1813)

In the first days of December we were directed to Pest, and left that house of sorrow where we had suffered so much, with feelings of joy. A single detachment had been formed of all senior and junior officers, of all arms, with an escort of Austrian troops. Our first day of walking was unpleasant. With it pouring with rain and being cold, I could not walk despite all my efforts, and had to stay in a cart pulled by oxen. The day's stage ended in a village where we are very coldly received. We were divided into hostels, each with a bed for two. We had agreed to meet for half of our meals, so to stay united and keep our spirits up. When our modest dinner was over, we cheerfully spent the evening recalling our glorious memories, talking about France, the Emperor, and singing our sprightly bivouac ditties. It was like this every evening until we arrived at Pest.[23] The inhabitants remained very surprised by this gaiety in a situation which, for others, would have engendered despair. But that is the great strength of our nation, laughing at suffering and death. The next day offered fine sunshine and bitter cold, and we passed Vienna on our left and slept at Parsdorf.[24] We then passed by Pressburg, a glorious memory of 1809.[25] In Szored, a large town, the inhabitants were kind and benevolent to us. From there we went to Raab (Gyor), then to Comorn, a curious fortified town which we were able to visit, and which was reputed to be impregnable, the Danube being able to flood its ditches. The day we arrived in Tirnau Nagy Szombath (in Hungarian), I was able to walk a little, which did me a lot of good. As we had received a month's pay the evening before, we were able to invite the innkeeper and his son, a *sous-officier* in the Hungarian hussars. They both talked to us about Napoleon with enthusiasm. We were able to procure a flute for an artillery *Lieutenant* in our party, and violin for a *Capitaine* of the Young Guard. With this orchestra we were able to encourage the pleasant young women to accept our invitation to dance.

The next day, upon our arrival at Mürr, my arm had swollen up due to the cold. The inflammation was dark in colour. A doctor, as good as he was devoted, took care of me, and the next morning at the start of our march, he provided me with everything that was necessary. He took care that I was carefully placed into the cart, ensured I was as warm as possible, and gave me a letter for his colleague from Neundorf. The latter, on receipt of this envelope, came to see me on our arrival in this locality. He had studied in Paris, spoke perfect French, and lavished his care on me. The next day we entered Pest. We received a very good welcome from the inhabitants and were very surprised to see the portrait of our Emperor on many signs. After visiting the prisoners' depot, I had to enter the hospital. I felt a deep sorrow to leave my leaders and comrades who, since Prague, had surrounded me with so much affection and care.

At least I had the consolation of seeing one of them devote himself to staying close to me, in my pain. *Capitaine* Lussac, from Agen, had been a *sergent* in the *7ème Léger* when I first joined it in 1805. An old soldier who had served at Zurich and Genoa, he had received an musket of honour as a *sergent* in Italy. This was replaced in 1804 with a cross of the Legion d'Honneur, at the camp of Boulogne. At the battle of Eylau, all the officers of his company were killed and he alone survived among the *sous-officiers*. The Emperor appointed him *Sous-lieutenant* the next day, and two years later he became a *Capitaine* at Wagram. He had been one of my first instructors and we had marched together for 7 years as companions in glory or misfortune. This brave heart was able to make a case for accompanying me to the hospital, which we entered the next day, having said goodbye to our dear detachment as it continued on its way, with tears in our eyes. What a hospital!! It was a barracks for disabled soldiers, already occupied by wounded or sick French officers. The rooms were messy, the beds were filthy, and no one attended to us. A doctor made rare visits to us, although no one, it is true, was seriously injured. Here, as always, adversity made us feel the need to help each other, and the French character, cheerful to the point of lightness, allowed us to accept this situation without sadness.

We therefore established a mess, of which I was the director, being the most junior.[26] Two others went to buy provisions each day, in turn. We were able to live healthily, although very modestly. The *Capitaines* received 72 florins a month, the *Lieutenants*, 21 florins, and the *Sous-lieutenants*, including myself 16 florins. A florin was the equivalent of a franc, but as our allowance as prisoners was paid in paper money, we had just enough to avoid starvation, pay for medicine, and upkeep. Fortunately for me, *Capitaine* Lussac had generously decided that we would make a joint purse. At the end of a fortnight, my arm was cured, my knee in good condition and I was able to take advantage of the freedom to visit the town, for which we had been granted parole, with the only condition being that we returned by night. We were looked upon very favourably by the locals, the Hungarians being more French than Austrian, if anything. With the permission of the Commandant of our Barracks-Hospital, Lussac and I even went to the theatre twice. But our purse and especially our situation did not allow us to return there a third time. I wore, in fact, a frock coat which I had received from the hospitable family in Prague, which replaced my Russian greatcoat. However, this garment was threadbare, and moreover, having burned the bottom of the skirt when I came too close to the stove, I had to trim it, so that it changed from a frock coat to a jacket. Lussac was in about the same state as me. In addition, also, due to the cold and the snow, we were forced to keep to our room.

Chapter 8

1814: Return to France and Garrison Duty at Huningue

January

Between the towns of Pest and Buda, in the middle of the Danube, is the island of Sainte-Marguerite, where we saw the ruins of a convent, a place of pilgrimage. Nature and art had made it a delightful spot, and it became the frequent object of my walks. I was able to visit the superb castle of Buda, thanks to the kindness of a respectable old man, M. Schultz, an Alsatian. This good man often came to see us and comforted Lussac, who was quite ill at the time. Upon learning that Lussac used tobacco, he brought him a snuff box filled with copious amounts of the substance. As thanks, the *Capitaine* offered him a medal which the Russians had missed when they despoiled us. It bore the effigy of the Emperor on one side, and France on the other. Mr. Schultz happily accepted this jewel, which he swore to hold onto preciously.

A detachment of French prisoners arrived in the month of March, including officers and soldiers, and our room took on two wounded officers. We learned about the disaster at Leipzig from them, and the betrayal of the Saxons. The Austrian government systematically kept us in ignorance of such events. These accounts gave us added sadness, and rage against the wretched cowards who had turned their weapons against us on the battlefield. Every Sunday, we went to mass at the church closest to our barracks. In spite of the poverty and the variegation of our appearance, they showed us a great deal of respect, since they were aware of our situation. The priest even made, without telling us, a collection among his parishioners, and urged us to accept the money he had thus collected. While warmly thanking this worthy priest for his charity and his noble benevolence, we refused, giving him reasons which he fully understood. On Ash Day, I went to mass alone, and I arrived there drenched from the pouring rain. On leaving the Church, I found myself surrounded by a whole family; the father, mother, and two children. After being assured of my status as a French officer, they begged me earnestly to come to their home and then share their dinner. They were called Boissin, were originally from Grenoble, and ran a glove factory here. I declined their very affectionate offer, fearing to compromise them, since, for some days past, the Military Governor had been keeping us under surveillance and had withdrawn some of our freedoms. In vain I put forward the severity of the military authority and my melancholic behaviour. I had to yield to their gracious and pressing entreaties. After an excellent dinner, upon their affectionate solicitations, I reluctantly told them all our misfortunes since the retreat from Moscow. At 9 o'clock I went back to my room, returning the next day to thank our kind hosts. A few days later I introduced Lussac to them, and instantly we had a small circle of charming acquaintances. We were, moreover, highly regarded in this district, and as we wore the ribbon of the *Légion d'Honneur*, our crosses having been torn from us at Peterswald, we were only called 'The two French knights'. Thanks to the intervention of the Boissin family, we obtained permission not to return until 2 o'clock in the evening. We practically deserted our barracks-hospital and especially our mess, since that of our new friends was much superior, and was offered to us wholeheartedly.

Departure for the Banat of Temeswar

Our happiness was short-lived. Prince Eugène, viceroy of Italy, had resolved to join the Emperor, and despite his weak army, he had just defeated Murat, King of Naples. This latter individual, forgetting his past as a soldier and a Frenchman, had wanted to block his march. At this time, under the pretext of a so-called conspiracy, we were consigned to our hospital on the 19th March, and we were told that we would be leaving the next day. We had no baggage to pack, because almost all of our belongings could easily fit into a handkerchief. Our only concern was to go and say goodbye to the Boissin family, which we were refused, despite several entreaties. At daybreak we crossed the streets of Pest, escorted by a platoon of veteran soldiers, and without knowing where we were going. The newspapers had doubtless announced our departure, for the whole part of the city that we had to go through was crowded with curious people who lavished on us the signs of a fraternal sympathy. We responded as best we could. I looked everywhere for the Boissin family, and only saw them on leaving the faubourg. I jumped out of the ranks to jump on M. Boissin's neck, but immediately a veteran wanted me to return to the detachment. As I resisted him, the officer commanding the escort came to point out to me that I had forgotten my situation as prisoner and that I had to leave. Monsieur Boissin, holding his youngest son in his arms, then intervened and explained the reason for my forgetfulness with such warmth that the old and honourable soldier gave me, as well as Lussac, permission to walk close to our benefactors for a few minutes. Our farewells were very sad. I felt my heart sink, and my eyes were full of tears.

Our first stage was sad and long, with rain from noon onwards. We took shelter in a small, dirty and badly built town. It was the first time that we were staying with the locals, in pairs, and of course, I was with Lussac, as well for the remainder of the trip. The next day we were in Groswardein, a small fortified but very poorly maintained town, near the Turkish border.[1] Our host, a former non-commissioned officer in the Austrian army, had been wounded and taken prisoner at the combat at Regensburg in 1809. He had spent most of his captivity in the departments of the Midi in France, and he spoke to us as if it was the country of the gods! His hospitality was most affectionate. Three days later we were at Peterswardein, a stronghold situated to its advantage. We stayed there and gave our laundry to be cleaned. We were only given it back on the morning of departure, when we were setting off, so that we all considered it more or less stolen. For my part, despite my complaints and threats, I could not get my only spare shirt. This misfortune, unimportant by itself, was nevertheless very unpleasant, since I was now wearing all the undergarments I had. Arriving two days later in Temeswar, a frontier town, we stayed there for forty-eight hours. The lodging was at prices commensurate with our meagre budgets, and we enjoyed the excellent hospitality of several French families.

Four days later we were nearing the end of our journey, which was Kakowa, a small frontier town in the Banat region, which we saw after constantly walking across a plain as far as the eye could see.[2] Kakowa is poorly built, the streets unpaved, the houses, or rather the shacks, very sparse. We were taken to the end of this locality, and lodged in a house consisting of a ground floor and surrounded by a large courtyard enclosed by a wall three meters high. The officer commanding our escort informed us that this place was to serve as our barracks and that we were under the orders of a civil functionary. The house had only four walls, no furniture, and no cooking utensils. When the official in question came to see us, we politely made our complaints to him, but he replied that he had received no order to furnish the house, and that he could only give us straw. He was then asked to deprive us of his visit henceforth. We then received enough straw and a blanket for two.

As we were all masters of constructing bivouacs, we felt no embarrassment in establishing each of ours. After having been discontented and grumpy for a few days, we resumed our good and healthy gaiety. I slept on my pallet of straw side by side with my dear companion *Capitaine* Lussac, sometimes dreaming of my Flag, frayed by canister rounds, sometimes of my mother, and of Nismes. As in Pest, we set up a mess comprising nineteen people, and bought the necessities for the table and the kitchen. I was appointed director unanimously, and it was agreed that each would be on kitchen duty in accordance with a board displayed in the dining room. Only *Colonel* de Reynaud was excepted from this measure as we had, in fact, too much respect for the age and rank of this superior officer.[3] He was a Pole belonging to a very old and wealthy family in Warsaw. Having entered the service of France for a long time, he had commanded the *15ème Régiment de Ligne* during almost the entire duration of the Spanish wars.

Thanks to our organization, we were not too unhappy with regard to material life. The civil functionary, the governor of that region, had had the idea to invite us to frequent his house. We let him know that none of us would set foot in his house, in view of his miserable conduct towards us when we arrived. To satisfy our need for activity we had the idea of making replica foils with hazel sticks, furnished with a sort of guard (we had been forbidden to have real foils). So we enthusiastically began to make these weapons which, with long excursions and swimming, made the days of June seem short. Near our house ran a little river in which we did our own laundry, and took baths while our laundry was drying. I was able, with my savings, to buy a second shirt. On Sundays I went to a ball with an artillery *Lieutenant*, the youngest of the group, and the most energetic of dancers. We found families of the middling class there, and everyone showed us a lot of goodwill. The men had long hair, kept greasy and shiny by the use of tallow or oil, and they wore a kind of jerkin with very wide breeches, of canvas or cloth trimmed with rich embroidery. The women had a kind of tight-fitting cuirass that made them stand very straight, and a skirt that did not exceed the ankle. These garments were richly embroidered with gold and silver. Their beautiful, neatly plaited hair was adorned with long, round-headed pins of fine workmanship, silver, gold, and some embellished with precious stones. Without being of great beauty, they showed a most graceful suppleness and agility. The men and women both wore light boots.

Their dance was a kind of Mazurka, the women were arranged in a circle, and a male dancer came forward and grabbed one of the fingers of a female dancer, others did the same, so that the same woman could have as many dancers as fingers. The group thus formed began to move, then each knight ran quickly from one female dancer to another. There was no ballroom, the ball being held outdoors. After conquering the good graces of men and studying this bizarre and original mazurka, we could also pinch the dancers' fingers, and turn until the last stroke of the bow. Then, thanks to the abundance of food and its cheapness, we had the satisfaction of succeeding in inviting male and female dancers to join us, keeping ourselves, in relation to them, within the limits of gallant respect. We even managed, although not speaking the Banat language, to make ourselves sufficiently understood by our guests.

Colonel de Reynaud, that worthy old soldier, frank, loyal, and very agreeable, had taken me in friendship. He called me 'Cadet' or 'the dancer'. We took long walks together and he kept showing me signs of his kindness. As he received monthly funds from a banker in Vienna, he wanted at all costs to make me profit from his resources. Having obtained linen and knowing that I lacked some, he also had some made for me. It was impossible for me to refuse, because everything he gave me was offered with such noble delicacy that I would have feared to hurt him. An offer of a completely different kind was made to us by the Austrian government, that of taking service in its army. This rash proposal which was inflicted on us in our misfortune made us deeply indignant and was rejected with contempt. Our hearts and our thoughts, although Szrakowa had become a pleasant enough prison, were entirely with France, with the flag, and with the hope of seeing them again.

In the course of September our governor informed us that the allied armies had entered Paris; a few days later he informed us of the Emperor's abdication at Fontainebleau and the conclusion of peace. We must have expected a treaty to be negotiated, but we refused to believe in the abdication. However, we had to face the facts.[4] This fatal news broke our hearts, it was a day of mourning and tears, our cheerfulness disappeared, and our barracks became a cloister from which we only left to go to the provisions. Shortly after, this same governor informed us, in arrogant terms, that the usurper was replaced by the elder branch of the Bourbons. We responded with disgust to his communication. Very few of us had known our new sovereign, and this change of dynasty saddened us all the more because we thought we would bear the consequences and disastrous effects of it. However, I affirm on my honour that, despite our fury, no unseemly word was spoken against this family. The honest and dutiful soldier must conform to the force of events and circumstances, and to serve under another flag provided that it is indeed that of the Fatherland.

Return to France, 4 October, 1814

On 4th October, we were still making swords with our hazel sticks under an old oak tree, when our comrade in the kitchen ran up and told us that the Governor had something to tell us. As we were returning, in a very bad mood against this old official, he told us that we were leaving the next day. Immediately an explosion of cries. 'Vive l'Empereur, Vive la France', and, seeing his figure reflect his displeasure, we repeated 'Vive, Vive Napoleon, on our way tomorrow to our beautiful France'.

We left Szakowa, still carrying our baggage in a handkerchief placed on the end of a stick over our shoulder. I had, in addition, an old shepherd's bag, which Lussac and I carried in turn to Strasbourg. Having obtained permission to double and even triple the stages, we quickly crossed Banat, Hungary, and Austria, returning to Bavaria one Sunday. Our stopover was in a pretty little town where we stayed at the hotel. We had hardly settled down when we saw a regiment of Bavarian dragoons arriving, returning from France. Several officers came to our hotel. Three of them, including a squadron leader, asked in very good French to introduce themselves to us. Having been received, they declared themselves proud to have been under the orders of Marshal Macdonald, at Wagram and at Smolensk, to have been decorated with the *Legion d'Honneur* by the Emperor, and finally invited us to dine on behalf of the corps of officers, assuring us that we would speak absolutely only of the great things accomplished together as comrades-in-arms. We paid them a visit and accepted, apologizing for our poor prisoner clothes, whereupon they made us offers of good fellowship which we refused while thanking them warmly. The dinner was excellent; it had been a long time since we had such a feast. The evening was animated by cordial gaiety. We took coffee in another room, where we offered, in turn, some punch, out of our meagre resources. Heads were naturally warmed a little by all these drinks, which I used moderately for my part, having a proportionate taste for alcohol. I was nevertheless afraid of seeing some incident set fire to the powder keg, which did not fail to arrive, around three o'clock in the morning.

At this moment, a Bavarian Captain arrived who, having been to dinner with his family two leagues away, came to apologize, shake his glass against ours and wish us a good trip. He sat down next to one of our comrades, a staff officer named *Capitaine* Beaupoil, and the conversation unfortunately turned to the late French campaign. The Bavarian Captain related that, being part of the forces besieging Besançon, he had taken an aide-de-camp of *Général* Marulaz prisoner during a sortie. Now this prisoner was none other than *Capitaine* Beaupoil. This officer immediately stood up and said 'I recognize you, you were four against me, and if my horse hadn't received a shot in the head, you would have caused me no concern. Although I was only one on foot against four of you on horseback, I parried your sabre thrusts for a long time, and even a thrust whose mark you must still have on your chest. But in the end I succumbed and you behaved like a coward, striking me with your sabre when I was unarmed.'

And for a moment, everyone is on their feet, the most lively words are exchanged and the duel is decided for the same morning. *Capitaine* Beaupoil having left the choice of weapons to his adversary, the latter decided on the pistol. These were supplied by the Bavarians; the witnesses were on one side two Bavarian officers, on the other Lussac and myself. At daybreak we left the hotel. After useless efforts to prevent the affair we measured the distance of twenty paces which was to separate the combatants. The procedure was to designate the one who fired first, with the second having the right to walk ten paces near before firing at his opponent. Luck favoured the Bavarian, who had a rather pitiful attitude, as he seemed barely able to stand. He shot his pistol, and his ball lodged into a tree behind Beaupoil. Our comrade, with a frightening calm, immediately marched on his adversary, his finger on the trigger of his pistol. I shuddered to think that he was going to blow the brains out of the Bavarian, and that we would pay dearly for this death, being among a people who though once our ally was now our enemy.

But, having come within ten paces, Beaupoil fired his pistol in the air and said, 'You will remember that you owe your life to a French officer whom you had dishonestly mistreated on the field of honour, and who asks you to forget everything and be his friend'. Combatants and witnesses squeezed hands and exchanged embraces. Both Frenchmen and Bavarians, delivered from a cruel anguish, manifested their joy at seeing honour satisfied and blood spared. Again our hosts raise their glasses to us, and the trumpet call 'boute-selle' was heard. The Bavarian dragoons left the city by one gate and we by another.

A few days later we arrived at the small town of Grosberdorff, in Württemberg. It was the lodging that was assigned to us as we completed our stage. Almost at the same time, there entered a strong detachment of Württemburg hussars, returning to garrison after having taken part in the campaign of France. After locating our lodgings, six of us went to a brewery whose beer had been recommended to us as being the best of the city. Hardly had we been seated at a table, after having placed our caps on a neighbouring table, when seven or eight officers of the hussars arrived. One of them, in order to put down his shako and other objects, using his sabre like a broom, made our poor hats fly to the ground without saying a word. At this insult we jumped up. *Capitaine* Beaupoil said to the Würtemburger officer: 'You insult the misfortune of French officers, you who wear on your chest the cross of the *Légion d'Honneur* received from Napoléon, our Emperor. In the name of my fellow prisoners of war present here or in town, I slap you, and ask you for a weapon to fight with you.'

The wretches respond to this honourable request by hitting us with their scabbards. We armed ourselves with beer mugs, chairs, sticks, anything that came to hand, whilst the hussars draw their sabres. It was a free-for-all of hand-to-hand combat, with mugs, and glasses shattered. I climbed onto a table and, armed with a chair, I swung like a deaf man. One of us was wounded by a sabre blow, two hussars fell, entangled. Beaupoil and Lussac seized their weapons, which they used vigorously. Blood flowed, and finally we remained masters of the ground. But it was a short-lived victory, because the guards soon arrived, we were disarmed and taken to prison. Our comrades, informed of this unfortunate affair, immediately approached the authorities. The burgomaster made us undergo an interrogation, which we answered frankly. The master of the brewery and his servants were heard as witnesses in the presence of our comrades, who also deposed in our favour. This worthy burgomaster had served at our side, as a captain of Württemberg artillery during the campaign of 1809. He showed himself to be kind and benevolent. He had food brought to us and came himself to tell us that at nightfall we would leave by carriage with our comrades. We left him at 10 o'clock in the evening, after having received proofs of his sympathy and accompanied by his affectionate good wishes. At daybreak we had travelled two stages, and arrived in a small town where the orders of our dear burgomaster had preceded us for our accommodation.

Arrival in France: To Strasbourg, August, 1814

Four days later we saw the masts of some large boats: it was the Rhine! Many of us had not seen this river for ten years! What joy! Everything we saw on the other side was French! On reaching the Kehl bridge, we had barely taken a few steps when we were surrounded by French officers and *sous-officiers*, who had come to meet us although on enemy territory. A veritable dizziness seized us. We kissed and embraced each other, crying out France! France! Then we set off. In the middle of the bridge we saw with sadness two outpost boxes, each bearing an escutcheon, one of France and one of Baden, near two sentries from the two countries! A few of us threw ourselves at the French post and embraced it frantically. At the head of the bridge, on the left bank, we found *Lieutenant-Colonel* Butard, a former *vélite* of the Imperial Guard. He had been a *Sous-lieutenant* in the *7ème Léger* after Eylau, and I had served under him later when he was a *Chef de bataillon*. He was in charge of receiving prisoners of war and giving them all kinds of assistance that they urgently needed. He commanded a camp established on the bank of the Rhine. The *sous-officiers* and soldiers were kept in tents there on their arrival, while the officers were given tickets for lodging at Strasbourg. This excellent *Lieutenant-Colonel* invited me to dinner, and the next day we asked for an indemnity proportionate to our rank from the paymaster. I took the opportunity to buy myself boots and underwear. To celebrate our arrival in Strasbourg and to bid farewell to each other, since we were about to be sent back to our respective units, we met one last time as companions in captivity.

The dinner took place at the Hôtel de la Maison Rouge, on the Place d'Armes, and was happy and wild. We had forgotten all our miseries! We ended our evening at the theatre, where they were playing Le Marriage de Figaro.[5] Finally, around one o'clock in the morning, we parted, our hearts heavy to leave our comrades in misfortune. We exchanged handshakes, embraces, promises to write to each other and exchanged addresses, and each one went to his destiny.

Two days later *Capitaine* Lussac and I arrived at Huningue, in the proximity of Basel.[6] I still think of the a warm welcome that we received from our friends and commanders of the *7ème* when we returned to the flag. In accordance with the terms of the peace treaty the French army was to be considerably reduced. The *2ème Léger* and the *26ème Léger* were integrated into the *7ème Léger*. These troops formed three battalions, but the progress of this reorganization was very slow, because of the many early retirements pronounced by the Government of Louis XVIII. I got to know *Capitaine* Perrot, coming from the *26ème Léger*, who is a *Général de division* today, and who, in 1848, commanded the National Guard for a while.

In the barracks, after evening roll call, the men of the three light regiments enjoyed telling each other of the great things they had accomplished under the orders of the greatest Captain in the modern world. We remembered Austerlitz, Jena, Friedland, Moskowa, Champaubert, Montereau, and each showed the noble scars of wounds received in the field of honour. It would be the same during our retirement, all of us had seen or heard the Emperor do or say such and such a thing, hand over the cross of the *Légion d'Honneur* on the battlefield to a drummer for having beaten the charge of his own volition at the opportune moment, or to a soldier for his fury with the bayonet, etc. I was proud, for my part, to be able to say that I had been decorated, by his hand, in Dresden. Yes, the Emperor remained our flag, our rallying point. The memory of our glorious past made us forget for a moment the misfortunes of our country, and we felt that our heart, with all our soul, went towards it, although discipline made us obey the white flag of the Bourbons.

Our organization was almost complete and earned us a review from our *Général*. Immediately after the parade one of his aides-de-camp came to me, he was, as far as I can remember, a Monsieur de Croy. He reminded me that we had been companions in misfortune and suffering in the sad hospital in Prague. Having invited me to lunch the next day, he spoke to me at length about this painful past.

'I will never forget,' he said to me, 'that you were near my bed, consoling me and raising my completely dejected courage; one day when I felt very bad, I thought I was near the end. Thanks to your good heart, to your fortitude, I reacted, the next day I was better, and this improvement then only continued. Your leaving the hospital before me was a very painful blow to me, but your goodbye, so cheerful and so confident, made me overcome my weakness. Sixteen days after your departure for Hungary I was also discharged from the hospital, and at the declaration of peace I was directed to Mainz. From there I wrote to my mother, and you were the first whose name came to my pen, telling her of my miseries. I deeply regret to see you still in this rank and promise you to tell the *Général* all about you.'

I was deeply touched by his testimony of affectionate gratitude, and saw him off in his carriage the same evening, for he was returning to Colmar with his *Général*. Circumstances made his support useless to me. Eight days later he wrote to me to announce his return to Huningue on account of the arrival of the

Duc de Berry, who was to review us and put a definitive end to our organization.

Review of the Regiment by the Duc de Berry, November, 1814, in Huningue

The three battalions of the regiment were formed in line on the glacis of the square when the Duc de Berry arrived. He was given all honours due to him, and after a few words to the *Général* and the *Colonel* (Croizard), he passed in front of each battalion. As the *adjutant sous-officer* on duty, bearing the records and other documents, I did not leave the *Colonel* and could therefore hear everything this Prince said. He asked inopportune and awkward questions to soldiers, who still had the tricolour flag in front of their eyes and the eagle in their hearts. He completely forgot that, to rally them to the White Flag, gentleness and benevolence were needed. Also, since the answers were not to his liking, he continued to take the wrong road in asking them, and I saw on his face the violence of his character taking over.

After he had inspected the three ranks of each battalion, the regiment formed into a column to parade. Although this movement had been made calmly and with precision, the Prince did not seem satisfied with several *pelotons* in executing it. He showed his displeasure in a tone and by words that were not very moderate, from which I could, moreover, see that he was not a good judge in the matter. He thus showed that, in his anger, he took into account neither his capacity as a commander, nor his situation as a Prince of the blood. Everyone, officers and soldiers, looked at each other in dead silence. The inhabitants who were present at the review, mute with astonishment, withdrew immediately.

After the parade, with which the Prince also declared himself dissatisfied, the three battalions formed a square and he distributed ten crosses of the *Légion d'Honneur* to officers, *sous-officiers* and soldiers.

At this moment, Monsieur Aspeli, *Major* of the regiment, and an old soldier who had been forgotten among the proposals for the *Légion d'Honneur*, presented himself to the Duc de Berry complaining very respectfully of this oversight, and asking for the reasons. He had not finished when the Prince, mad with anger, rushed at this superior officer and tried to tear off his sword, then his epaulettes, saying 'It is time that these kinds of complaints stop, they can no longer be admitted. I have the order of the King my master to grant ten decorations and I will not give eleven, etc'. Finally, turning to the *Colonel*, he ordered that *Major* Aspeli be taken immediately to the covered bridge, a military prison at Strasbourg.

The attitude of the Prince since the beginning of the review had made a painful impression on us, but this scandalous scene was the height of our indignation. All of Huningue, where *Major* Aspeli had the esteem and consideration of the inhabitants, joined the regiment in deploring and stigmatizing this Prince's neglect of his dignity, self-discipline and of the high mission of a chief. I remain persuaded that he had hatefully interpreted the King's orders, and exceeded the powers entrusted to him.

Nevertheless, the *Colonel* had to obey, and the *Major* was taken to Strasbourg a few hours after the review, by a *Chef de bataillon*. He returned, two months later, on 3 January, 1815, to resume his service with the regiment at Huningue. In February, his claim received the satisfaction it sought, as a royal order appointed him a *Chevalier* of the *Légion d'Honneur*. This is how King Louis XVIII repaired the fatal levity of the Duc de Berry.

The fortress of Huningue was essentially a large barracks. Apart from the military establishments there were only 40 to 50 bourgeois houses and these houses were for the most part only hotels, cafés, or more or less comfortable inns. So as soon as our organization completed, we resumed garrison service. As the exercises were almost suspended at this time of winter, we easily obtained permissions to go to Switzerland via Basel and Schaflouse, or into the Black Forest by crossing the Rhine at Huningue. We were generally well received everywhere. The inhabitants liked to talk to us about the wars of the Republic, Masséna, Moreau and other generals for whom they showed great esteem. It is true to say that their good reception derived from the satisfaction of their interests, because they did a great trade, especially of milk, butter and eggs with the left bank, and principally with Huningue where the garrison was always numerous. In addition, as in Switzerland, Sundays and holidays are rigorously observed and all public places closed, especially during services, so that young men and young women came to France for the balls held in Huningue or neighbouring villages. We found ourselves very happy with this gracious invasion of Swiss women in their seductive costumes, which presented the most charming sight when seen with our uniforms. Inevitably, the rivalry between Alsatian and Swiss women sometimes caused trouble between the dancers, but the brawls were never serious and the police watched over them strictly.

One Saturday, two comrades and I went to Basel to pass the day and dine at the Hotel des Trois-Rois. As there was no monument worthy of attention in this city, we went into a café to play billiards while waiting for the hour of the meal. Two individuals who were already there offered us wine, which we refused. We continued to refuse their requests, until finally we stopped responding to their unpleasant insistence. Taking our silence as an insult they

1814: Return to France and Garrison Duty at Huningue

become insolent. We stopped our game and we were about to retire when we heard them insulting the Emperor in crude terms, saying 'Bonaparte's soldiers were only the instruments of a leader of a band of looters'.

Despite our desire to avoid a collision, we fought back, and the most impertinent of these filibusters was rash enough to offer us a duel with pistols, adding that we were three cowards. To this insult, one of us, Dumoulin, whose son-in-law is today *Colonel* of the *4ème Ligne*, replied 'whoever you are we accept the duel, but first, I will make you feel the weight of the hand of a Bonaparte's soldier'. So saying, he grabs the duellist by the collar, and corrects him whilst we hold the other. The guard, summoned by the proprietor of the café, led the two provocateurs to prison. As for us, we were invited to leave the city, which we did immediately. A report was sent addressed to the burgomaster of Basel, and to the commander of the Huningue garrison. Also, although the wrongs of our aggressors had been noted, the *Colonel* placed us under arrest for 48 hours, while recognizing that we had the moral high ground.

I had been introduced to the family of *Major* Chausel, Commandant of the Place, an old brave man who had lost an arm at Marengo. It was his nephew who had introduced me to him. I had often practiced skill-at-arms with this young man. The commandant had a daughter, young and beautiful, with whom the nephew was madly in love. He admitted it to me and asked me to deliver love letters for his cousin. I refused indignantly, and some time later the Commandant, having discovered his nephew's rashness, threw him out. In his fury, this young man imagined that I was the author of his disgrace and that I wanted to supplant him. He pushed his jealousy to the point of insult and we fought a duel, on the other side of the Rhine, and in Swiss territory. The swords were measured and returned to our hands.

'Guard yourself', I told him, 'and above all be brave.' I saw him, indeed, agitated like a madman. He fenced in so utterly disorderly a manner and displayed such extraordinary wrist strength that I feared he might succeed in disarming me. The third time I was hit with a long tear at the bottom of the ribs, the point of his sword having slipped on the buckle of my suspender following an engagement.

The *Colonel*, having learned the causes and the details of the duel, congratulated me on my moderation, and I was placed under arrest. As for this young man, his crazy escapade barred him from the houses where he was received and his uncle sent him back to his parents. Before leaving Huningue my adversary came to acknowledge his faults, to ask my friendship, and to shake my hand. He entered the military academy at Saint-Cyr soon after, and in 1825 I met him during a review at the Champ de Mars, serving as a *Lieutenant* in the *25ème de Ligne*. He was killed, as *Capitaine*, on the breach of Constantine. I also had the misfortune, as a result of my foolish jealousy for another person, to fight a duel and seriously wound one of my old comrades of Berlin, Vienna and Moscow, who had received a bullet in the right arm at Smolensk in 1812. I cursed my destiny and my detestable brutality; but my friend recovered, forgave me, and we remained as heartfelt as before. His name was Odon, and he was, like me, from Nismes. Volunteering for the war of independence in Morea, he was killed in an combat in the advance-guard.

Shortly after this incident the year of 1814 ended, in which the Great Captain, at the head of the glorious remnants of our army, had made that immortal campaign within France herself. Defending the sacred soil of *la Patrie* step by step, he had struck foreign columns everywhere. But the traitors, the party men who were called royalists, whose infamous intrigues were aided by foreign bayonets, witnessed the humiliation of the name of France with a cold and satisfied eye. Eternal shame to those who committed this demeaning cowardice.

Towards the end of the year, muffled prejudices and disconcerting rumbling could be felt against us; I asked God to continue his protection of our beautiful country of France.

Chapter 9

1815: Service with the Army of the Rhine, Disbandment, and Home to Nîsmes

The year 1815 began with a duel between two comrades, one of whom was my friend. An altercation, the cause of which was not serious, but which had been followed by swear words and insults, had taken place during a dinner, where we were receiving an officer of the regiment returning from captivity. At dawn on 1st January, 1815, the inhabitants and soldiers were on their feet, music was playing, the drums gave drum rolls in salute to the officers, and visits to each other took place. I escaped this grotesque and importunate din, because the witnesses and combatants of the duel left by the Basel gate. Ten minutes later we descended into a ditch, the opponents removed their outer clothes despite the harshness of the temperature, and they received their foils. The fight began fiercely, with the blows being made with extreme violence. Seeing this, the witnesses, by mutual agreement, intervened and stopped the fight. It was well done, because the two enraged antagonists immediately shook hands. The *Colonel* sent for me a few moments later, and when I had told him the causes and the circumstances of the meeting he said to me simply, smiling: 'In future choose another day.' To further darken this beginning of the year, I received a letter from my sister informing me that my dear mother was seriously ill. I was sad beyond expression, and I shut myself up at home and only went out when on duty. Fortunately, fourteen days later, in response to a letter full of anguish written to my sister, I received from her the news that she was feeling better, and later that she was recovering.

Then the horizon cleared up. I remained in my rank of *adjudant sous-officier* under the reorganization, and was more fortunate than many other *sous-officiers* who were dismissed or retired before they reached the usual age. I maintained the most affectionate relationship with many of the officers of the regiment with whom I had served when I was a *sous-officier*. I went with them some time later to a large town in the Duchy of Baden to take part in a ball. Our dance partners, Bavarian or Swiss ladies, all graciously accepted all our invitations, which did not seem to be to the taste of the male dancers there. From their hateful and derogatory remarks, I thought they were taking their share of the general dislike we felt we were surrounded by, but it may also have been mere jealousy. In any, case they were looking to start a quarrel with us. I had the good fortune to know one of the Swiss dancers, a man named Beaumann who had been a *sergent* in the *126ème de Régiment de Ligne*. Thanks to his intervention everyone calmed down and we were able to spend the evening happily.

Return from the Isle of Elba (20 March, 1815)

On one of the first days of March, the three battalions of the regiment had just arrived on the exercise ground, outside the French gate, when the rumour of the Emperor's landing at Fréjus circulated through the ranks.[1] Officers and soldiers looked each other in the face, some fearing false news, others with the joy of certainty. The two hours spent on manoeuvring in the field seemed very long and did not pass without many comments. Once back in the barracks, *sous-officiers* and soldiers went from one room to another, trying to mutually persuade each other that the newspapers were going to confirm this great and happy news. The next day, the regiment having been confined to barracks, each room became a club and the name of the Emperor came on everyone's lips.

The commander of the garrison put up posters encouraging the garrison and the inhabitants not to act disruptively. Our *Colonel* upheld this order by directing that the officers and soldiers remain calm and loyal to the government of Louis XVIII. The residents and soldiers obeyed, nothing more. We remained confined to barracks, even as the Emperor entered the city of Grenoble, following his triumphal entry through the departments of Var and Isère. In spite of the absolute official ignorance in which we were left, unofficial news reached us every day, serving to reassure and increase our hope.

Finally, one Sunday, while the *Colonel* was reviewing the regiment on the Place d'Armes, a buzzing sound was heard in the distance, outside the square, on the side of the Porte de France. Shortly after the inhabitants of a neighbouring village entered the town in crowds, announcing the arrival of the mail. The commander of the place, frightened by this tumult, began to make his arrangements for defence, but it was too late. The courier crossed the drawbridges and entered the city to cries of 'Vive l'Empereur'. Around the postilion's hat floated tricolour ribbons, and the horses were literally covered with them.

The courier announced the Emperor's entry into Lyons.[2] Then this mass of inhabitants and peasants, all having on their hats or buttonholes the three colours, shouting 'Vive Napoleon, long live the Emperor,' with an enthusiasm difficult to describe. Our officers could not then hold us back; we broke ranks and fraternized with the inhabitants. The unfortunate courier, stunned by questions, was escorted to the post office by a procession made up of soldiers, residents with wives and children, all shouting 'Vive la France, Vive l'Empereur'. The Postmaster, seeing the crowd demanding, albeit with calm and moderation, the reading of the dispatch, went out with the *Colonel* and confirmed the entry of the Emperor in Lyons.

At this official news the enthusiasm had no bounds, we ran in the streets, we kissed everyone, and all faces were beaming with joy. However, at the voice of our commanders, we resumed our ranks to return to the barracks. A few moments later everyone came out, and, as if by magic, everyone, officers and soldiers, had replaced the white cockade with the tricolour. A whole day of celebration followed, then came the night, which was as calm in the streets as at the barracks. The next day we were unconfined to barracks. Like the day before, the courier's horses, arriving in the afternoon, were covered with tricolour ribbons, and moreover, tri-coloured flags floated at the corners of the mail coach. Soldiers and bourgeois unhitched the horses and drew the carriage to the post office themselves. The dispatches informed everyone of the magnificent reception given to the Emperor by the people of Lyon. The following days, residents and soldiers went to meet the mail coach to escort it to the office, always with the same enthusiasm. It was a truly extraordinary and touching spectacle to see these enthusiastic people walking beside the car, overwhelming the courier with questions. The questions intersected in the following manner: 'Have you seen the Emperor?' 'Does he still have his little hat and his grey frock coat?' 'It was he who gave me the cross of the *Légion d'Honneur*, see, the eagle is always at his post.'

When we finally learned of the Emperor's entry into Fontainebleau, then into Paris, it was delirium.[3] Shakos and hats flew in the air and everyone sang the famous song 'Where is better than in the bosom of our family?'⁴ In the evening all the houses were illuminated. At the barracks each soldier wanted to have his candle on the window of his room and we had to run to Basel to get some, our stocks being quickly exhausted. The call for the 'retreat' was delayed, and after this day of joy everyone returned peacefully to their quarters, happy to have seen the white flag of the Bourbons disappear.

Distribution of the Eagles at the Champ de Mars, 1 June, 1815

I was part of the deputation of the *7ème Régiment d'Infanterie Légère* which went to Paris for the distribution of the Eagles along the Champ de Mars, on 1st June, 1815. This deputation included the *Colonel*, an officer from each rank, a *sous-officier*, a *caporal*, and a soldier. The ceremony was grandiose and the splendour of religion shone there with all its brilliance. After the blessing of the Eagles, each *Colonel* received his flag and we took the road to Huningue the next day. On our return to the regiment, the reception of the new Flag took place. The inhabitants of all the villages within six leagues around came to take part in this national solemnity. I find no expression to convey the intensity of the feelings of joy and enthusiasm which gripped hearts when the Standard Bearer, after he had been acknowledged, came to take his place in the order of battle. The regiment then broke up into *pelotons* to take our Eagle back to the *Colonel*, with the regimental musicians at its head. Inhabitants of the fortress and the surrounding countryside, as well as women and children, followed us pell-mell, uttering cries of joy and happiness. Then, with the music of the band in our minds and escorted by this crowd, the regiment returned to quarters. It was an unforgettable day that lasted well into the night without any incident disturbing order and discipline.

The campaign of 1815

Terrified by the return of Napoleon, all of Europe was now in arms, being united under the pressure of the English. The general feeling in France was to strike the foreigner straight to the heart. Preparations for war had advanced with incredible rapidity. Divisions and *corps d'armée*, led by the Emperor, crossed the frontier. The victory at Ligny opened the campaign, but betrayal soon awaited us. During the night of 17th and 18th June, *Général* de Bourmont and many others went over to the enemy! Curses to the perjurers who have betrayed *la Patrie*! Then came the next day, the battle of Waterloo!!

The Army of the Rhine was commanded by *Général* Rapp, a true friend of the Emperor.[5] Its headquarters was at Strasbourg and it manoeuvred on the left bank of the Rhine, from Strasbourg to Haguenau, relying on Saverne.[6] My regiment was part of it and had taken position in front of Haguenau. In front of it, within cannon range were Bavarians and Württemberger troops. During the night of the 20th to the 21st of June, during a frightful storm, our small posts and large guards were vigorously attacked by them, and the firing became very heavy in a short time. The *Colonel* had the outposts supported by voltigeurs, and the three battalions followed the movement, but, towards one o'clock in the morning, the fire slowed down and then ceased. We had about forty men *hors de combat*, five of whom were killed, including an officer, an old friend of mine. The rest of the night was spent in observation, with our arms by our feet. The next day, *Général* Estève arrived with the *10ème Régiment d'Infanterie Légerè*.[7] He sent out a reconnaissance and ordered the *Colonel* to capture the village where the enemy was entrenched with two battalions. An hour later we had chased the Bavarians without too many losses, but towards midday they, having received cavalry and artillery reinforcements, set the village in flames with incendiary shells and counter-attacked. We were about to be overwhelmed when we received the general's order to fall back on the *10ème Léger*. In the evening, the masses of the enemy having shown themselves, the *Général*, either out of prudence or by superior order, ordered a retreat, leaving my battalion in the rearguard. We marched in square unmolested as far as the division, where we resumed our position in the battle order.

From then on, until King Louis XVIII had already returned to Paris, we had affairs or outpost skirmishes without yielding an inch of ground, and remained four or five leagues from Strasbourg. We were helped by a free corps of about 1,200 men, made up of former soldiers from the department, commanded by retired officers. They rendered us great services by their knowledge of the country and did a lot of harm to the enemy.[8] Our last combat took place on 10th July and was rather serious. The enemy caused great losses, and we were told that a Prince of the royal family of Württemberg was wounded there.

In the evening the *corps d'armée* took up position in front of the outworks of Strasbourg and, from that moment, not a single cartridge was burned. The National Guard was in charge of the interior service of the city, and discharged their duty with zeal and courage. They often went out with our battalions to watch the enemy. On all occasions they gave proof of their patriotism and their attachment to the national flag. Finally, an order from Paris came to suspend all hostility, and the Army of the Rhine returned to the city. A party occupied the Faubourg de la Robertsau and the citadel, the drawbridges were raised, the gates closed, all the important points guarded militarily, and all communication suppressed with the outside world. The commissioners of the allied armies, who came to confer with *Général* Rapp were introduced and re-appointed as negotiators. In a word, all the precautions of a state of siege were scrupulously observed. These measures did not surprise us, for there was a persistent rumour of the Allies' desire to enter the place and not leave. It was understood that, without this posture, Strasbourg would be lost for France, and that, consequently, the King and his Government made a point of honour to reject all proposals of entry of the allies, even partial. It was for this reason that the Army of the Rhine was kept in arms while that of the Loire was in full dissolution. But we had the deep sadness to see the arms removed from the arsenal. There was a dangerous fermentation of public opinion, with the inhabitants and the garrison wishing to oppose this measure, which was considered an outrage. *Général* Rapp, informed of this effervescence of spirits, let it be known that he had no right to disobey the King's orders, although he was heartbroken, since this removal of arms was one of the articles of the Treaty of Peace recently signed in Paris. Consequently, he invited everyone to remain calm. It was with despair that we therefore saw the wagons, filled with those arms which we had so well defended, leave the Rhine gate in broad daylight, cross the bridge, and disappear forever.[9]

The Dalouzy Incident (September, 1815)

From that moment, spirits were tense and discontented. A few days later a general order informed us that the Army of the Rhine was going to be disarmed and dissolved, which brought tensions to a climax and led the way for the most extraordinary incident in the annals of military history. At that time, the army was owed two months in arrears, and yet we needed funds to meet our travel expenses, since we were going to be directed to our respective departments. No matter how much we were led to hope that this pay would be sent to us after we returned to our homes, we did not believe it. All of us, officers and soldiers, remained determined to demand it before having laid down the arms with which we had repelled the allies, and thus preserved the beautiful fortress of Strasbourg for France and Louis XVIII. In the barracks, in the streets, we only talked about this question. A deputation of officers of all arms and employees of various administrative bodies went together to *Général* Rapp. When they arrived in the courtyard of his hotel, they asked for an audience, stating the reason. The *Général* refused at first, then granted an audience. A *Capitaine* of my regiment, Monsieur Cossot, speaking on behalf of all, asked if it was possible to settle the arrears before the dismissal, and explained the urgent need for everyone at this time to receive this money. The *Général* replied in a bad mood and dismissed the deputation with unseemly procedures, so that tempers were only the more embittered.

When the *sous-officiers* learned of this step and its unfortunate result, they immediately decided to present the same complaint, despite the efforts of the commanding officers. Indeed, given the circumstances, they could not succeed in stopping them from taking this action, despite it being so contrary to discipline. Two hours after the failure of the officers, there was general agreement between the *sous-officiers* of all the regiments and the administrative councils. A deputation was elected, composed of twelve of them, taken in from all units and branches of service. This deputation immediately presented itself to *Général* Rapp in the same manner as that of the officers. The *Général*, who went down to the courtyard to receive them, refused to hear anything and ordered them to retire immediately. He was obeyed without a word, or murmur. I had just been appointed *Sous-lieutenant* and was serving in one of the regiment's companies but the *Colonel*, accustomed to my service as a *adjutant sous-officer*, instructed me to follow the delegation of the *sous-officiers*, to observe and not lose sight of anything. I was thus able to witness the unheard-of event which was about to take place. First I saw the deputation, made up solely of *sergent-majors*, *sergents*, and *brigadiers-fourriers*, without any *adjutants sous-officiers* (so as not to jeopardize their earning an officer's epaulette), go from the hotel of the *Général* to the Place d'Armes. There they formed the circle and began to discuss ways of obtaining satisfaction. Dalouzy, a *sergent* of my regiment, the *7ème Léger*, began to speak. He was from Reims, and had been my bed-mate in 1806 and 1807 (during the Prussian and Poland campaigns). He was a brave soldier, a man of action, a difficult character, but with a high heart.

'We must', he said, 'overlook our discipline for a while, and forget that we have leaders. My proposal is violent and blameworthy, I know that, but, since our leaders can do nothing for a few days, which I understand, I am going to propose to you the means of making them pay us. Will you assist me?'

The cry was an unanimous 'Yes! We will assist you, propose your plan.' After laying out his plan, Dalouzy requested that, first, a Chief be appointed to take command of the Army of the Rhine. On the proposal of Dalouzy by the drum major of the *53ème de Ligne*, Dalouzy was elected unanimously and accepted as its chief.

Before breaking the circle of attendees, he identified those reputed for their intelligence and their energy from among the most senior of the *sous-officiers*. From them, he appointed those who were *sergents-majors* and *maréchaux de logis-chef* to command the regiments, and the *sergeants* and *maréchaux de logis* to command those of the battalions, squadrons and artillery batteries. No other denomination for them was used than that of their current rank, and no other distinguishing marks than their *sous-officier* stripes. The drum major of the *53ème de Ligne* was appointed commander of the garrison, and immediately took possession of the offices, accompanied by the *brigadier-fourriers*, to process the paperwork. At the same time, Dalouzy gave the order to take up arms in all the barracks. He assigned each *corps* a position to occupy, such as the arsenal or stores, had the drawbridges raised, the doors closed, in a word, put in place all the measures of a state of siege. At the same time, *sous-officiers* were given the task of informing the generals, the intendants, the colonels, the paymaster of the army, the receiver-general of the department, the treasurers of each *corps*, that they were not to leave their homes, with respectful firmness. These *sous-officiers* had to take care that these forced arrests were not violated.

As for *Général* Rapp, Dalouzy sent two elite companies and two pieces of cannon, to the palace, with lit fuses. All these arrangements were made with incredible precision and promptness. Thus master of the place, Dalouzy called a *sergent-major* acting as a *Colonel* and four *sergents-fourriers*. He instructed them to accompany him and lend him their assistance to whatever he was about to do, pointing out that he alone was responsible.

Then, escorted by this extraordinary General Staff, he went to the Mayor and reassured him about the events already known and those to come. He invited him, with all the respect due to this magistrate, to come to an agreement with the Receiver-General or any other competent authority so that we can settle what was due to the Army of the Rhine within 24 hours. The Mayor formally refused to do so, declaring that, in such a serious circumstance, and for a matter of great interest to public safety and perhaps even the salvation of *la Patrie*, he must seek the advice of the Strasbourg municipal council. Dalouzy replied that the actions taken were indeed contrary to discipline, but that it was not an insurrection against public order. He declared that he was counting on the loyal support of the municipality, so that it would agree with whom it may concern so that the treasurers of all the units of the Army of the Rhine can, the next day, receive the sums due, against the statements of balance legally drawn up and signed.

'It is the only way,' he added, 'to bring the troops under the authority of their commanders, which is set aside for a moment by the force of circumstances. I will be the first to give example in his regard. The inhabitant has nothing to fear from the soldier, I will answer on my head for order and tranquillity. I am giving you, moreover, a copy of the agenda that I have just posted on the city walls.'

This agenda was written as follows:

> My brave Comrades of the Army of the Rhine, you and I have been able, up to this day, in peacetime as on the battlefield, to recognize the first duty of the soldier: passive obedience to our chiefs. I am aware that we are digressing from this duty today. However, it is out of necessity and need, but I hope, we will get to that soon.
>
> Let us remember that we are on the soil of *la Patrie*, in the midst of our fellow citizens who owe us nothing, and from whom, therefore, we can demand nothing, except their assistance, if necessary, to enforce the glorious name of the French. When you placed me at your head, I only accepted this heavy task for the good of all, and I will do the impossible

to prove myself worthy of your choice. However, I must warn you that I will punish severe examples those of you who would forget themselves to the point of drunkenness, insult or abuse of the inhabitants.

Strasbourg, September 1815. Signed: GARRISON.

The whole Army of the Rhine remained under arms while Dalouzy waited at the Town Hall for the answer to his request. He didn't wait long. The Paymaster-General consulted with the *Général* Rapp and the Mayor, and the latter told Dalouzy to inform him of the figure of the arrears that the Paymaster-General and the City would face. Dalouzy immediately begged the *Colonels*, regimental commanders of all arms, and senior employees of the Army of the Rhine to kindly have their accounting officers draw up regular pay statements, he not having them and so that his actions would not be in vain. He asked only to receive his pay as a *sergent*. The *sergents-majors*, under the direction of the Captain-paymasters, worked all night, and the next day the statements were brought to the approval of the Intendant and *Général* Rapp. In the afternoon of the same day the regimental paymasters received the amount stated on their pay slips from the Paymaster-General. *Généraux*, *Colonels*, staff officers and troops, down to the last soldier of the Army of the Rhine, received what was due to them from the hands of the accounting officers.

Immediately afterwards, *sergent* Dalouzy went to ask the Mayor to make white flags available as soon as possible, for distribution to each regiment, this flag having become the national emblem, since King Louis XVIII had long since returned to Paris. Two hours later he distributed them to all the *corps*. Then he assembled the greater part of the army on the Place d'Armes, taking great care to leave the exterior and interior posts in place, for he did not forget that foreign forces were at the gates of the city, and that they had to be watched, and if necessary pushed back. Having formed the square, he placed himself in the middle, in the presence of a crowd composed of inhabitants and officers of all arms of the Army of the Rhine. He gave the following address in a firm and assured voice:

> My dear and brave Comrades, As I told you in my agenda, we have all come out of the obedience that we had so long and so religiously observed. The time has come to return to duty and discipline. I am happy to be able to address you, on behalf of the Mayor and the inhabitants of Strasbourg the most sincere thanks for your honourable conduct and your admirable discipline during the two days and the two nights which have just passed. Allow me to be your interpreter with them to express our gratitude to them for the loyal and fraternal assistance they have lent us.

Many cries of 'yes! yes!' could be heard.

> Now all is over, let us return to our barracks, resume our ranks, and say to our Chiefs: Command us; we want, as before these two days, to obey you for the sake of service and discipline. You can count on us, to life, to death, for the maintenance of order and the glory of our dear *Patrie*. I will show you the example, follow me.

'Vive la France, Vive l'Armée!' This cry was repeated with enthusiasm. Dalouzy dismissed the square, which formed into divisions. Each column then marched to the rear of the square

and deployed into battle order, drummers and musicians playing. Then taking the lead, he commanded the procession which was carried out with the greatest correctness, in front of all the officers and the inhabitants. At the various exits from the square, each regiment, battalion, or detachment departed to go to its barracks. Dalouzy led the *7ème Léger* to the Saverne Gate, where the *Colonel* and all the officers were. He approached the commanding officer, sheathed his sabre, and said to him: 'If I am found guilty, I place myself at your disposal.'

'Go back to your company,' replied the *Colonel*, simply. All the officers immediately resumed their command and the most perfect order was immediately established. All the other commanding officers received the same submissions. It should be noted that, on the one hand, Dalouzy had held that all who belonged to the Army of the Rhine, from the General in Chief to the last soldier, received his pay, so that, if necessary, each one had his share of responsibility. On the other hand, he had assumed sole responsibility so that, in the future, no one else would be implicated. In fact, the authorities were later were able to humiliate him, but never bring him before a military tribunal. A few days later, all the personnel that had belonged to the Army of the Rhine were directed, on a map, to their homes, to contribute to the organization of the new departmental legions. Only the valiant and fine battalions of the Alsatian National Guard remained to defend Strasbourg. *Sergent* Dalouzy obtained permission to stay some time in Strasbourg.

The Austrian general had come to deal with the execution of various articles of the peace treaty, and was present during the events that had just taken place. He loudly declared that what he had just seen was only possible with the French. Having summoned Dalouzy to his home, he first made observations on his neglect of discipline, but then congratulated him on the firmness of character with which he had maintained order in such a dangerous crisis. He ended by offering him the rank of Captain in the Austrian army, guaranteeing the confirmation of his appointment, by commission. 'General,' replied Dalouzy indignantly, 'a soldier of the *7ème Léger*, who beat your armies at Eckmühl and Wagram, must scornfully reject this strange and despicable proposition, coming from the mouth of an old soldier like you. My life belongs to France, it is she alone that I want to serve.'

Immediately after dismissing this offer, Louis XVIII sent *Maréchal de Camp* le Comte de Quinsonas to Strasbourg, as the garrison's *Commandant d'Armes*. He had been an émigré, serving as a general in the Russian army, and returned to France along with the senior branch of the royal family. The Comte de Quinsonas formed his staff only from émigrés who did not hesitate to say that Bonaparte's soldiers had been nothing but buccaneers. According to them, they alone represented our past and even future glories. They naturally hastened to throw *sergent* Dalouzy in prison. The latter, by applying for a residence permit for Strasbourg, intended to settle there, and the city authorities and the inhabitants having accepted him there, promised him aid and protection. In spite of his protests, in spite of the certificate of the Mayor and of the former municipal council all in his favour, he obtained only silence on the part of the civil and military authorities. After quite a long stay at Strasbourg prison, he was transferred to Paris, then to Nantes, then to Brest, without being able to obtain a trial, civil or military, despite the request he made at each of these stages of his captivity. The Legion of Morbihan was stationed at Brest, commanded by *Colonel* de Cadoudal. He was a relative of the famous Breton chef, known for his ardent royalism and his boundless devotion to the Bourbons. One day he visited the military prison. The prisoners were in the courtyard when Dalouzy went straight to him and, with a respectful calm, said to him: 'I am *sergent* Dalouzy from the case of Strasbourg, I have been dragged from prison to prison for a long time, I beg you to put me on trial. If I am found guilty, and if the law strikes me, I will bow respectfully before the decision of the judges.'

'I know only imperfectly of your case,' replied the *Colonel*, 'but I give you my word that I will take care of it.' A few days later, *Colonel* de Cadoudal, informed of Dalouzy's conduct and made aware that the incessant complaints of this brave soldier had never reached the King, obtained the immediate release of my former comrade from the Minister of War, as well as his reinstatement with his rank in the legion of his department. This is how the misfortunes of this *sous-officier* who had commanded the Army of the Rhine for two days ended, thanks to the intervention of a lofty and generous heart.

We had left Strasbourg in detachments commanded by officers. The one to which I belonged, directed towards the department of Gard, marched in stages to Lyons, through the towns occupied by the allies. I had hastily written to my mother, after ten years of absence, to embrace her and all my family and had asked her to answer me *poste restante* in Lyons. As soon as I arrived in this town I found a letter from my brother who had just been discharged as a result of a wound received during the siege of Zaragoza. He told me to do the impossible and obtain a residence permit in Lyons. In any case, he wanted me to stay there until he wrote to me again. We stayed and the next day I got the head of the detachment to stay another two days, on the condition of returning to Vienne.[10] I had given as a pretext that I had family in Lyon. A *sergent-major*, one of my friends, like me, a child of Nîsmes, had obtained the same authorization. An Austrian division had occupied Lyons for a few days. Although victorious, they did not seem reassured and had taken very rigorous police measures against travellers and especially against the soldiers. We had hardly settled into a hotel when we saw a policeman arrive, sent by the Austrian general commanding the place. This agent read a large poster to the manager of the hotel, prescribing that anyone passing through must have a passport, a road map, or a residence permit issued by the Austrian military authority. We, my friend and I, had no documents to present, since the road map of the detachment was in the hands of the commanding officer. We could not therefore put ourselves in order, for to present ourselves at the Place was to deliver us up to Austrian bayonets. However, we ventured to go out to do some shopping and see what was going on, in uniform. Barely had we been a hundred paces when we found ourselves opposite an Austrian patrol which, fortunately, paid no attention to us. We returned immediately, determined not to leave the hotel except to rejoin our detachment. In the meantime I received a second letter from my brother, letting me know of the atrocities that were being committed at Nîsmes, under the direction of the horrible, filthy and bloodthirsty brute Trestaillon.[11] Not wanting to dwell on this dreadful memory, I refer to the story of this drama written by M. Madier de Montjau, whose son was the fierce *Montagnard* of the National Assembly in 1848. My brother ended his letter by begging me, on the behalf of God and my mother, to stay a few more days in Lyon, because the soldiers and especially the officers who approached the gates Nîsmes were at the very least attacked with stones, as soldiers of Bonaparte. The master of the hotel, who was also from Nîsmes, gave us, for his part, distressing details about what was going on there. But we considered, my comrade and I, that our duty was to follow our detachment to the end, whatever happened to us. Consequently we set out early in the morning, in order to reach Vienne before departure. At the head of the Guillotière bridge, a sentry forced us to enter the Austrian post. The officer asked us, in fairly good French, for our road map. I tried to explain our situation to him, but he would not listen and gave the order to put us in prison. If his order was carried out our situation would have become very perilous. We would indeed have been escorted to the headquarters of the place where we could be taken, despite our protests, for spies, and we know that, in this case, military justice is summary and rapid. We were therefore very anxious when, at the same moment, a wagon loaded with wine and brandy arrived alongside the guardhouse, The Austrian soldiers from the post and others who were there demanded a drink from the driver of the wagon. The latter vigorously refused and was threatened, then beaten. The Austrians pierced the barrels, drank excessively, and many fell to the ground drunk. The population rioted and came to the rescue of the driver. The officer to whom complaint had first been made, gave no answer. The crowd consequently threw themselves on the Austrians, a fight ensued, and the latter were struck with their own arms which were torn from them, and cries of 'A l'eau, au Rhône!' were heard. The officer lost his head, and ordered his post to take up their arms. They were immediately jostled and taken away. As for us, taking advantage of this disorder, we happily pumped our legs, blessing our lucky stars which were plucking us out of the danger. We were happy to arrive in Vienne so as to take our rank in the detachment.

Before our departure from Pont-Saint-Esprit we were warmly welcomed by the inhabitants, but at Uzès, the last stage before Nîsmes, the populace received us with the most vulgar insults. I could not help saying to one of these furious fools, misled by his royalist opinions, 'But if I am a soldier of Bonaparte, I am also a soldier of France, who for ten years, has been fighting for *la Patrie*, and not as a brigand as you say.' This fanatic answered me with expressions that I dispense with repeating. This reception, made us fear more serious violence, so we put on civilian clothing and left this town at once, for our safety's sake.

Return to Nîsmes, December, 1815

On 9th December, 1815 at 10 o'clock in the evening, we arrived at Nîsmes!! Arriving at a certain part of the city, we shook hands and each went towards their ancestral home. A deep emotion gripped me! Ten years away from home! In front of the arenas I stopped to contemplate these noble ruins, so beautiful and so majestic in the silence of the night, the sight of which awakened in me all my childhood memories.[12] A few steps further I found myself at the foot of the image of our Saviour and the sign of Redemption, placed in a recess, and which I had venerated from my earliest years. I knelt down and prayed a short, earnest prayer to God, then walked to my mother's house. It was half past ten when I knocked on the door. I was let in, and went up and found myself in the presence of my mother, my brother, my two sisters and two relatives. I announced myself as bringing news about a soldier (I looked like a bourgeois). All eyes were fixed on me and I could clearly see that ten years of war had changed me to the point of being unrecognizable. But my dear mother's eyes and heart could not be wrong. She gets up: 'My God,' she says, 'don't you see that he's my child, your brother!!' I threw myself into her arms and pressed her to my heart without being able to speak. All rose mute and weeping with joy, and for a moment there was real happiness on earth, that which loving hearts, so long separated, feel. Soon relatives, friends, and neighbours come running and crowded the home. I didn't know how to respond to their affection or to their questions. It was only around one o'clock in the morning that everyone was able to go back to their beds to enjoy a beneficial rest. After putting myself in order with the military authorities so as to ensure my position and to avoid any interruption in my service, I renewed my acquaintance with friends and sweethearts from a young age, many of whom were now married and had children. Others, belonging to different branches of service, had just returned, like me, after the disbandments. I happily divided my time between the former to talk about our youth, and the latter to proudly remind ourselves of our battles, our wounds and the great figure of our Emperor, whom we had so often seen face death at the height of the fray. One of my comrades, wounded and taken prisoner at the battle of Dresden, and who had been with me in the hospital in Prague, told me that on his arrival he had been ill-treated by madmen.

A few days later I was walking with him in the public garden, when we were accosted by three individuals. One of them said to me 'Who gave you this ribbon, was it your Bonaparte, your Corsican?'

'Yes, I replied, 'it was the Corsican Napoleon, 1st Emperor of the French.' This joker then had the audacity to ask me where my decoration came from. 'From the fields of honour,' I told him, 'where people of your kind are never to be found.' Furious, they were about to throw themselves on us when two passers-by and the keeper of the garden intervened. The latter having been insulted by one of these wretches, immediately took them to the guard house. Insults and attacks against everything that had belonged to the army were repeated constantly. The government and the local authorities could not put a stop to these deplorable disorders, despite their sincere desire to do so. It was only on the arrival of an Austrian division at Nîsmes, sent to police the city, that the civil and military authorities were able to begin to restore calm and security. The fury and abominable excesses of our adversaries had humiliating consequences in a city where political passions were coupled with religious hatred, although the Protestants were then only a very small minority. Nevertheless, not wanting to remain exposed to these insults and this violence, I begged my dear mother, as well as my brothers and sisters, to let me go away for a while, and to return only after the appeasement of inflamed spirits. Deeply saddened by this painful resolution, I left, after kissing my mother for the last time, because I never saw her again.

Having served ten years and being decorated, I could and should only continue to serve my country. My rank of *Sous-lieutenant*, which I held from the Hundred Days, was not recognized by the government of Louis XVIII. I had to reconquer my ranks up to that of *Capitaine*. I retired from this rank in 1839, after thirty-three years of service in the French army, without an hour of interruption.

END

Notes

Foreword

1. Chaland de la Guillanche was the editor of the original manuscript by Vincent Bertrand, published in French under the title *Mémoires du Capitaine Bertrand: Grande Armée 1805-1815* (Paris, 1909). The following work is a translation of this published work into English, with an original introduction and note on the French light infantry by the translator.

Introduction

1. Surviving service books show similar infractions to Bertrand's in their pages.
2. See Thomas Bugeaud, *Memoirs of Marshal Bugeaud, from his private correspondence and original documents* (London, 1884).

Brief History of the *7ème Régiment d'Infanterie Léger* 1805–1815: History, Training, and Identity

1. Its predecessor was created in 1788, as the *7ème Bataillon de Chasseurs d'Auvergne*, and later the *7ème Demi-Brigade d'Infanterie Léger*, but had been incorporated into the *3ème Demi-Brigade d'Infanterie Léger* in 1794. See M. Brahaut, *Histoire de l'Armée et tous les Régiments, depuis les premiers temps de la monarchie Française jusqu'à nos jours* (Paris, 1860), III vols, III, pp. 33–4.
2. Frédéric Berjaud, 'Le 7ème Régiment de 'Infanterie Légère de 1800 à 1815,' at http://frederic.berjaud.free.fr/Articles_de_Didier_Davin/07eLeger/07e_Leger.htm.
3. Clément La Jonquière, *L'éxpedition d'Égypte, 1798-1801* (Paris, 1899), IV vols, II, p. 276; III, p. 248.

4. For information on silver muskets, see Chapter 1, fn 4.
5. The fact that the coat's tails were 20cm too long suggests that the regiment had adopted the shorter tailed coat more suitable for the light infantry in the interim. See Terry Crowdy, *Napoleon's Infantry Handbook* (Barnsley, 2015), p. 68.
6. Arthur Chuquet, *Ordres et Apostilles de Napoléon* (Paris, 1911) IV vols, I, p. 585; eds François Houdecek and Gabriel Madec, *Napoléon Bonaparte: Correspondance Génerale* (Paris, 2007), XV vols, IV, no. 7931.
7. Correspondance de Napoléon I, publiée par l'ordre de Napoléon III, XXXII vols, IX, 328, no. 7566.
8. Ian Castle, *Austerlitz: Napoleon and the Eagles of Europe* (Barnsley, 2005), pp. 95, 115, 125.
9. See Charles Schneid, *Napoleon and the Conquest of Europe: The War of the Third Coalition* (Westport, 2005), p. 136.
10. In addition, the footnotes of his grandson, Chaland de la Guillanche, offer additional information on the routes, distances and other details specific to the *7ème Léger*.
11. Brent Nosworthy, *Battle Tactics of Napoleon and his Enemies* (London, 1995), pp. 27–9; and Chapter 2, 'The Elements of Victory: A theory of combat effectiveness', in John Lynn, *Bayonets of the Republic: Motivation and Tactics in the Army of Revolutionary France, 1791-1794* (Oxford, 1996), pp. 21–40.
12. For more information on the three methods of fighting by the French infantry, see Jean-Baptiste Marcellin Marbot, *Lieutenant-Général, Remarques Critiques sur l'Ouvrage de Lieutenant-Général Rogniat* (Paris, 1820), pp. 47–69. An English edition by the translator of *Fighting with Napoleon's Light Infantry* will appear in print shortly.
13. According to *Général* Duhesme, who served under Marshal Davout, 'The light infantry and the line infantry now seem to form but one arm; for, excepting the cut of clothing, everything is common and uniform among them: the same arms, same organization, same regulations, the same inspectors-general; they both have only a general rule of equipment, instruction, and manoeuvres.' Philippe Guillaume Duhesme, *Général de division, Essai sur l'Infanterie Légère, ou Traité des petites Opérations de la guerre* (Paris, 1814), p. 9.

14. In reality, a *compagnie* (company) was an administrative unit, whilst the *peloton* (company) was the actual fighting unit. Of the same size, the difference was that the personnel of the *compagnie* were permanent members, whilst the *peloton* was temporary, as on the day of battle members of a *compagnie* might be distributed elsewhere, to ensure that each *peloton* was of equal strength to the others. The term is interchangeable in the infantry manuals, probably to avoid confusion.
15. The best time for a regiment to practise the 'School of the Battalion' was during relative periods of peace, when the combat regiments were assembled and resting. Examples included the camps of the Army of the Ocean Coast along northern France 1803–05, the interim period between the 1805 and 1806 campaigns in Germany, and the armistice of Pläswitz in 1813.
16. This remains conjecture at present, but the discovery of any memoirs, treatises or journal articles discussing the practicality of the 'School of the Battalion' would be most interesting to the scholar of training and tactics of the French army.
17. Anon, *Règlement Concernant l'Exercise et les Manoeuvres de l'Infanterie* (Paris, 1791, 1792, 1807, 1812), II vols.
18. See Anon, *Manuel d'Infanterie, ou Résumé de tous les Réglements, Décrets, Usages, et Renseignements Propres aux Sous-officiers de cette Arme* (Paris, 1813). Unlike the 1813 edition, earlier editions did not include the 'School of the Soldier', or the 'School of the *Peloton.*' Interestingly, the 'School of the Battalion' was still omitted from the 1813 edition.
19. Duhesme, *Essai sur l'Infanterie*, pp. 175–462; Guyard, *Colonel, Instruction Pour Le Service Et Les Manoeuvres De l'Infanterie Légère en Campagne* (Paris, 1805); Charles Antonine Morand, *Général de division, Manoeuvres Pour Une Companie De Tirailleurs Ou De Flanquers* (Paris, 1807?). Marshal Davout was sufficiently impressed to have Morand's work circulated among the divisions of his *Corps d'armée*.
20. Nosworthy, *Battle Tactics of Napoleon and his Enemies*, pp. 93–5, 96–7.
21. Crowdy, *Napoleon's Infantry Handbook*, pp. 106–07.
22. John Elting, *Swords around a Throne: Napoleon's Grande Armée* (London, 1989), p. 346, fn 17.

Chapter 1

1. A commune (currently) in the Haut-Rhin department of northern France. The *7ème Regiment d'Infanterie Légère* was raised in 1788 as the *Chasseurs d'Auvergne*. In 1805 its *Colonel* was Joseph Boyer, in command since 1803. (Translator's note)
2. Augereau's *7ème Corps d'Armée* passed through Huningué on 23rd to 26th October, 1805, on its way to the Voralberg. It acted as a reserve corps, supporting Marshal Ney's operations in the Tyrol. On the day Betrand joined the *7ème Léger*'s depot, Augereau's corps had already forced the surrender of the Austrian commander Jellacic at Füssen, and was stationed around Augsburg. (Original editor's note)
3. When in garrison, French soldiers shared one bed among two soldiers, with only sergeants and above enjoying a bed to themselves. It was the custom for the most senior soldier to share with the newest recruit, thereby hopefully facilitating an exchange of experience. This was not always the case: when Marcelin Marbot's father enrolled him in the *1er régiment de Hussards* as a young boy, his first bedmate was a cobbler's assistant who used an apron coated in foul-smelling wax for a pillow. See *The Memoirs of Baron de Marbot, Late Lieutenant-General in the French Army* (London, 1892), II vols, I, p. 42. (Translator's note)
4. The silver musket was a reward for heroic conduct issued from December 1799 to the creation of the *Légion d'Honneur* in 1803. Issued to infantry, they bore a silver shield-shaped badge on the right side of the musket stock with the bearer's name and his deed inscribed. Cavalrymen were awarded with carbine versions of the musket or non-regulation sabres, but the musket was also awarded, especially to dragoons. Artillerymen received gold-plated grenade badges on a velvet background for their shoulderbelts, and drummers silver-edged drumsticks. Fellow memorialist Jean-Roch Coignet of the *96ème Regiment d'Infanterie de Ligne* won a silver musket at Montebello in 1800. See also Elting, *Swords around a Throne*, p. 598; M. Brauhaut, *Histoire de l'Armée et de tous les regiments* (Paris, 1860), IV vols, III, pp. 124–5. (Translator's note)

5. The 'School of the Soldier' (*École du soldat*) was the first of the three official courses for training an infantryman, as prescribed in the French infantry regulations of 1791 and the subsequent manuals based on it, that were in use during the Napoleonic Wars and beyond. It focussed on teaching the individual soldier marching and musket drill. The 'School of the *Peloton*' involved manoeuvring and volley fire as a *peloton* of about 90 soldiers and corporals until 1808, and 132 men after. Finally, the 'School of the Battalion' (*École du bataillon*) involved manoeuvring and firing as an entire *bataillon* of eight line companies up to 1808, and later six companies after 1808. Once all three schools were completed, the soldier was considered qualified to join the combat battalions of the parent regiment. See Anon, *Réglement concernant Exercise et les Manoeuvres d'Infanterie* (Paris, 1791). It is interesting that Bertrand makes no mention of light infantry training. (Translator's note)
6. The original name used is *Tudesque*, an archaic insult meaning boorish or coarse, derived from German and first used in France in the sixteenth century. (Translator's note)
7. Bertrand uses the term obol, which was one sixth of a drachma, an ancient Greek unit of currency. After 1795, a sous was slang for five centimes, or one twentieth of a franc. (Translator's note)
8. Augereau's *7ème Corps d'armée* missed the battle of Austerlitz, fought on 2nd December, 1805, remaining at Souabe to protect the communications of the *Grande Armée*. (Original editor's note)
9. The *7ème Corps d'armée* was sent at this time to the Msin, and its headquarters placed at Frankfort-on-the-Main. (Original editor's note)
10. It is likely that Bertrand meant the Edict of Fontainbleau of 1685, which caused an exodus of Huguenots from France through repressive legislation and forced billeting of troops. By contrast, the Edict of Nantes of 1598 guaranteed a degree of toleration for Huguenots. (Translator's note)
11. Augereau's *7ème Corps d'Armée* would be stationed around Ober-Hadamar on the river Elbe, itself a tributary of the Lahn, until 26 September, 1806. (Original editor's note)
12. Guindet earned the *Légion d'Honneur* for killing Prince Louis in mounted single combat. Charles Parquin of the *20ème Chasseurs à Cheval* recalled Napoleon saying he would have made Guindet an officer

if he had captured the Prince alive, but Guindet pointed out to Parquin that Prince Louis was in no mood to surrender. Whilst single combat between regimental officers and even generals of opposing armies was not uncommon, it was extremely rare for a high-ranking aristocrat to be slain by a non-commissioned officer like Guindet in such a manner. The incident was therefore much celebrated in multiple accounts and illustrations. (Translator's note)
13. Rossbach was a Prussian victory against French and Holy Roman Empire forces on 5th November 1757. (Translator's note)
14. After the long cantonment by the river Lahn, the *7ème Léger* remained with Augereau's *7ème Corps d'armée*, but the brigade commander was now *Général* François Amey, and the division commander, *Général* Etienne Heudelet. (Original editor's note)
15. These were in fact Saxon cavalry occupying Isserstadt and Schecke along the road past Jena to Weimar. General Heudelet's division, including the *7ème Léger*, left their bivouac at 0200, and marched through Jena at 0800, engaging the enemy at the outskirts of Mühlthall. By 1000, the *7ème Léger* had forced the Saxons to retreat. (Original editor's note)
16. The second division of Augereau's *7ème Corps d'armée* including the *7ème Léger*, stopped at Auerstadt on the night of the 17th October. (Original editor's note)
17. It is likely that this was a company marker flag, rather than the battalion's eagle, which would not be carried on a foraging expedition. (Translator's note)
18. On the 27th October, the *7ème Léger* was sent to Neubrück below the river Havel, with two 4-pounder cannon. They stayed there until the 4th of November, when they returned to Berlin. From the 6th November to the 30th, the *7ème Corps d'armée* marched through Custrin, Landsberg, Bromberg, Thorn, Plock, towards Varsouvie, and up to the left bank of the Vistula. (Original editor's note)
19. The *7ème Regiment d'Infanterie Léger* had three battalions during this campaign. (Translator's note)
20. This most likely meant an attack column, in which each battalion was two companies across and eight deep, less the voltigeur companies, which were in skirmish order. The carabinier companies probably formed a

separate reserve, as was the practice with the grenadier companies in a line regiment prior to 1808. (Translator's note)
21. The opposing Russian commander, General Barclay de Tolly, defended his side of the river Wkra with three battalions of infantry, three squadrons of cavalry and twelve cannon at Sochocin, and the same at Kolozab, with three battalions occupying a wood between the two villages. Francis-Loraine Petre, *Napoleon's Campaigns in Poland, 1806-1807* (London, 1901), p. 84. (Translator's note)
22. This detachment consisted of two companies of the *7ème Léger* and some light cavalry, under *Chef d'Escadron* Massy. See Robert Goertz, 'Action at Sochocin, 24 December, 1806,' https://www.napoleon-series.org/military-info/battles/1806/Sochocin/c_sochocin.html (Translator's note)
23. It is not clear how the detachment brought their weapons and ammunition across, unless it was by the boats. (Translator's note)
24. This appears to be the origin of historical confusion regarding the bridgehead, especially among French sources. Two crossings were attempted; the first by *Général* Heudelet's division at Sochocin, to which the *7ème Léger* belonged; the second by *Général* Desjardins at Kolozab, 3km south-east of Sochocin. Heudelet attacked twice and was repulsed each time with heavy casualties, whilst Desjardin's succeeded. Once Desjardin's two brigades were across the Wkra at Kolozab, Heudelet sent two brigades to Kolozab to follow Desjardin's across the Wkra. Once news reached the Russians at Sochochin that the French had crossed elsewhere, they withdrew, allowing some of Heudelet's infantry to cross and link up with Bertrand's detachment. Heudelet drew heavy criticism from Baron Marbot in his memoirs for what he considered to be an unnecessary crossing, causing additional bloodshed just to claim a success. However, Heudelet's orders were to establish a bridgehead. To not come to the assistance of Bertrand's detachment would have been negligent and dishonourable. See Petre, *Napoleon's Campaigns in Poland*, pp. 84–5; Goertz, 'Action at Sochocin, 24 December, 1806'. (Translator's note)
25. On his return from Egypt in 1799, Napoleon took a half-squadron of Mameluke cavalry with him. Mamelukes were the ruling warrior class of Egypt, excelling at individual horsemanship and swordsmanship.

Their ability to manoeuvre precisely in large formations, however, as required by European cavalry tactics, left much to be desired. Their sword of choice was the highly curved yatagan, capable of slashing reins and slicing off limbs. (Translator's note)
26. The Mamelukes were part of the Old Guard, comprising elite units of infantry, cavalry, and artillery, which usually followed Napoleon closely on campaign. The cavalry furnished escort squadrons for the Imperial household, whilst the Guard as a whole acted as the central reserve in battle. (Translator's note)

Chapter 2

1. The *7ème Corps d'armée*, for the moment, stayed at Nidenbourg and Hohenstein under Allenstein, where the Russians would most likely cross the river Pasleka (Passerge). On the 3rd of January, 1807, the headquarters of the *7ème Corps d'armée* was at Plousk. The division to which the *7ème Léger* belonged was on the right bank of the river Vistula, left of Plowna. (Original editor's note)
2. The Russians took the offensive on 18 January, passing between the majority of the French army and the sea. They were above Osterode and Lobau by the 1st February, 1807. Aware of Napoleon's outflanking movement to their rear, to sever their communications and pin them against the Baltic coast, the Russian General Bennigsen hastily withdrew northwards and sought to slow down the French through a series of rearguard actions. (Original editor's note)
3. The *7ème Corps d'armée* lost 929 dead, 4,271 wounded, and barely had, by the night of the 8th, 6,500 men present with their units. (Original editor's note)
4. The *7ème Léger* formed part of *Général* Petit's brigade, and went into cantonments on 23rd February, at Hohenstein, Merken and Kuncgengut. (Original editor's note)
5. According to Jean-Baptiste Barres, a velite in the *Chasseurs à Pied* of the Imperial Guard, the inhabitants around Tilsit also buried their food in their back gardens, especially bacon and hams. See (ed. Maurice Barrès), Jean Baptiste Barrès, *Memoirs of a French Napoleonic Officer* (Barnsley, 2017), p. 102. (Translator's note)

6. The ramrod was the thin metal rod used to ram the powder, ball and cartridge down the length of the musket barrel. In addition to probing the ground with ramrods, Jean-Roch Coignet, a soldier in the Grenadiers à Pied of the Imperial Guard, found provisions placed under the rotting corpses of cows, and boxes hidden up trees. See (ed. Lorédan Larchey) Jean-Roch Coignet, *The Narrative of Captain Coignet, 1776–1850* (New York, 1890), pp. 147–8. (Translator's note)
7. On the 10th March, 1807, the *7ème Léger* was at Aile. From the 11th to the 31st March, the *3ème Corps d'armée* was around Aile and the river Passerge. From the 1st to the 30th April, the *3ème Corps* was around the town of Osterode. (Original editor's note)
8. On 6th June, 1807, *Général de division* Gudin's division was at Allenstein, on the 7th at Podleickeim, on the 8th at Osterode, and on the 9th it bivouacked at Ockendorrf. (Original editor's note)
9. *Général de brigade* Pajol commanded a light cavalry brigade consisting of the *5ème Hussards, 7ème Hussards*, and *3ème Chasseurs à Cheval*. (Original editor's note)
10. For information on the *armes d'honneur*, see Chapter 1, fn. 4. (Translator's note)
11. As part of Marshal Augereau's ill-fated attack through a snowstorm into the Russian army's centre, the *14ème Regiment d'Infanterie de Ligne* drifted even further off course and became isolated between the two armies. Forced into squares by Russian cavalry and attacked by infantry, it was unable to withdraw despite several aides being sent to order them to do so, including Baron Marbot. The regiment was destroyed. (Translator's note)
12. The phrase Bertrand uses is *joue les jambes*. (Translator's note)
13. On the 15th June Gudin's division was at Gauleben. On the 16th, it crossed the river Pregel between Tapiau and Materau. On the 17th at Labiau with the forward posts on the route to Tilsit, and on the 18th towards Skaisgirren. On the 19th the division was at Paskalamen, until the 26th, and on the 27th it was at Draugowsky. On that that day the French army went into barracks. (Original editor's note)
14. Since there was no Kalmuck unit in the Russian Guard, it would seem that they disguised themselves as Kalmucks to avoid being traced by

their officers. Given the small ponies that Kalmucks rode, suited to their hit and run tactics, it seems unlikely that their riders would be as large as the first 'Kalmuck.' Russian guardsmen however, were known for their impressive height, especially the Guard infantry. (Translator's note)
15. The phrase Bertrand uses is *front de bandière*. (Translator's note)
16. Bertrand may have trained with the *demi-espadon* at the regimental fencing classes, but he was likely on this occasion to be armed with a *sabre-briquet*, since this was issued officially to the elite infantry companies and in some light infantry regiments, even the normal chasseurs companies as well. (Translator's note)
17. *Prévôts* were assistant instructors to the masters at arms, who were essentially the regimental fencing tutors. (Translator's note)
18. The French infantry's attack pace, of 100 paces a minute. (Translator's note)

Chapter 3

1. The word Bertrand used is *démoucheter*, or to remove the protective tip of a foil. (Translator's note)
2. The battle of Breslau, 1757, and the siege of Schweidnitz, 1762, were fought during the Seven Years War. Glogau was a fortress town captured by the French in 1806. (Translator's note)
3. The word used is *racoleur*, a type of military recruiter who paid money to soldiers to desert and join the army of another nation. They were shady characters, and their trade invited death by firing squad for all involved, as desertion was punishable by death in most armies of the Napoleonic period. (Translator's note)
4. *Mérope* is a tragedy that was first performed in 1743. (Translator's note)
5. The drummer may have been a company drummer, that is, a combat soldier, whilst the musician was most likely part of the regimental band, and probably a civilian virtuoso hired at the Colonel's expense. (Translator's note)

Chapter 4

1. Betrand's knowledge of British politics is somewhat flawed, as Prime Minister William Pitt had died on 23rd January, 1806. (Translator's note)

2. It is reasonable to assume that the first lesson Bertrand refers to was during the War of the First Coalition, in particular the victories of Jemappes in 1792 and Fleurus in 1794. The second lesson may have been during the War of the Second Coalition, with notable victories in 1800, at Hohenlinden and Marengo. The third lesson was definitely that of the Ulm and Austerlitz campaigns in 1805. (Translator's note)
3. As Napoleon's younger brother, Jérôme was made King of Westphalia in 1807. It was a conglomeration of German states and territories created after the dissolution of the Holy Roman Empire in 1806. (Translator's note)
4. The phrase Bertrand uses here is '*que les soldats français savaient très bien se servir de l'arme blanche*'. (Translator's note)
5. The headquarters of Marshal Davout's *3ème Corps d'armée* was in Hanover at the beginning of March, including *Général* Gudin's division. Of the division's brigades, the 1st under *Général* Petit was at Hamelu. Of the brigade's regiments, the *7ème Léger* was at Halberstadt, numbering 2,897 men in three battalions. The *12ème de Ligne* and *21ème de Ligne* were at Blankenbourg and Halmen, and the 2nd brigade under *Général* de Lorencez was at Celle and the city of Hanover. Since 1714, British monarchs were also rulers of the state of Hanover, until the electorate was overrun by French troops in 1803 and became part of Westphalia in 1807. (Original editor's note)
6. King Richard I of England, Duke of Normandy, Aquitaine and Gascony (1157–99), was captured near Vienna in 1192, on his return from the Third Crusade. His captor, Leopold of Austria, did so because he accused Richard I of orchestrating the murder of his brother, among other personal affronts. He was held at Dürnstein until 1193, and ransomed in 1194. The act of imprisoning a crusader was illegal throughout participating European states, resulting in Leopold's excommunication by Pope Celestine III. (Translator's note)
7. Also known as the battle of Dürnstein, where on 11th November, 1805, a 5,000-strong infantry division of Marshal Mortier's newly formed corps was engaged by 40,000 Russians of Marshal Kutuzov's army. This division, commanded by Gazan de la Peyrière and led by Mortier in person, was attacked and counter-attacked multiple times over difficult

terrain, until reinforced by Dupont's division. The Russian encirclement was halted by the onset of darkness and the need for Russian troops to look to their own rest and shelter. During the night, the two divisions broke out of the Russian cordon, although the rearguard, consisting of the *4ème Léger*, was captured. See Ian Castle, *Austerlitz: Napoleon and the Eagles of Europe* (Barnsley, 2005), pp. 108–11. (Translator's note)

8. On the 10th May the *7ème Léger* resumed the former post that it left after 25th April, along with Montbrun's light cavalry division. (Original editor's note)

9. This was the first siege of Mantua during the Revolutionary War, and took place from 4th July, 1796 to 2nd February, 1797. The Austrian army in northern Italy attempted to relieve the garrison on three occasions. Napoleon based his strategy around this, inflicting multiple defeats on the Austrian field forces. The garrison surrendered to the French two weeks after the Austrian defeat at the battle of Rivoli. (Translator's note)

10. The Angelus is a Catholic prayer marking the immaculate conception of Jesus Christ. (Translator's note)

11. On the 5th June, Eugène's forces joined with cavalry of Montbrun and Lauriston, fought the battle of Raab on the 14th June, and began a bombardment of that town on the 15th. The Austrian forces there capitulated on the 23rd, and Lauriston entered on the 24th. The army of Archduke John was expelled from Hungary. (Original editor's note)

12. This is the island of Gross-Scüttt. On the 31st May Davout attempted to establish a bridgehead from Pressburg, but was unable to maintain it. Davout threatened to bombard the garrison on the 23rd and 24th June, unless they withdrew to the left bank. On the 30th Napoleon wrote to Davout to continue his operations against the bridge. When the armistice was signed, the French left a single division in front of Pressburg, whilst the Austrians evacuated the town. (Original editor's note)

13. Diogenes (412 or 404 BC–323 BC), the ancient Greek philosopher, who slept in a large wine jar, as part of his simple living. (Translator's note)

14. Having established a bridgehead across the Danube, Napoleon launched a series of attacks against the Austrian forces, to gain information on their strength and to prevent them from retreating. It was his intention to

force them to deploy and prepare for a pitched battle. See James Arnold, *Napoleon Conquers Austria: The 1809 Campaign for Vienna* (London, 1995), Chapter 7. (Translator's note)

15. The word Bertrand uses is *mitraille*, or grape shot. However, this was primarily used for naval service, consisting of a central iron column around which a canvas bag containing large iron balls was attached. It is more likely that Bertrand meant canister shot instead, consisting of a thin cylindrical metal case which contained 40–80 lead balls. Canister was standard issue among land-based artillery throughout Europe. Non-artillery memorialists (or perhaps their English translators) often confused the two. See Philip Haythornthwaite, *Weapons and Equipment of the Napoleonic Wars* (London, 1996), p. 61. (Translator's note)
16. Marshal Davout's corps, occupying the right flank of the French army, decided the battle in favour of the French, with full scale attack on the Austrian left flank. At 0700 Gudin's division was facing the tower in the village of Markgrafneusiedel. (Original editor's note)
17. This raises the question of whether the cooking-pot carriers actually fought in the ranks with these items strapped to their knapsacks. French infantry usually fought with their knapsacks on, but there is little information on the cooking pot (*la gamelle*) and hatchets that were assigned to each squad (*escouade*) of 12–15 men. Such an item would surely obstruct the man in the rank behind from loading and firing his musket, unless all cooking-pot carriers stood in the rearmost of the three ranks. See Elting, *Swords around a Throne*, pp. 216–17; Crowdy, *Napleon's Infantry Handbook*, pp. 91–2. (Translator's note)
18. Ettienne Tardif de Pommeroux de Bordesoulle (1771–1837), also spelt Bordesoult, was appointed commander of the 2nd Cuirassier Brigade of the 3rd Cuirassier Division. He had been wounded at the battle of Wagram. Charles Mullié, *Biographie des célébrités militaires des armées de terre et de mer de 1789 à 1850* (Paris, 1851). (Translator's note)
19. The phrase Bertrand uses is *gilets de bazin*. (Translator's note)
20. During a battle, French generals and their aides were often too busy on horseback and too far from their servants to look to their stomachs. Their memoirs often include anecdotes of starvation in the midst of victory, and a reliance on the willingness of passing troops to share their food.

The soldiers of a unit were not obligated to feed their own officers, let alone outsiders, of whatever rank. (Translator's note)
21. *Colonel* Lamaire, commander of the *7ème Léger*, was himself wounded at the battle of Wagram.
22. This was the affair at Znaïm, which took place on the 11th July, 1809, one day before the armistice. (Original editor's note)
23. Sinapism is the application of a poultice containing ground black mustard powder. (Translator's note)
24. In contrast to Napoleon's iconic and simple uniform of an off-duty colonel of the *Chasseurs à Cheval* of the Imperial Guard, a marshal's full dress consisted of a blue tailcoat embroidered with gold lace oak leaves and bullion epaulettes, a broad silk sash of gold with white stripes around the waist, white breeches with ornate gold lace on each thigh, and a large bicorne hat with gold trim and white feathers along the upper edge. Accessories included a ceremonial sword and swordbelt of personal choice, various orders and decorations awarded by France and allied nations, and a baton covered in blue velvet and with gold eagles. It would seem the inhabitants of Brünn had mistaken Davout for Napoleon. (Translator's note)
25. The Emperor reviewed the divisions of Friant and Gudin at Austerlitz on the 16th October, 1809. (Original editor's note)
26. William Pitt (1759–1806), was prime minister of the United Kingdom from 1804 to 1806. He was the driving force behind the Third Coalition of 1805, in which substantial subsidies were paid to Austria, Russia and various minor powers. They mobilized multiple armies that were to attack the France empire on several fronts, from Hanover, central Europe, and Naples. The coalition disintegrated after the defeat of the Austro-Russian army at Austerlitz on 2nd December, 1805. Pitt died on 23rd January, 1806. See Ian Castle, *Austerlitz: Napoleon and the Eagles of Europe* (Barnsley, 2005). (Translator's note)
27. Bertrand refers to the assailants as *Allemands*, despite the fact that they are Austrian. This could be a derogatory remark aimed at any German-speaker. (Translator's note)
28. This was the Treaty of Schönbrunn of 1809. Bavaria was an ally of France and contributed the largest contingent of troops out of all the

German states that comprised the Confederation of the Rhine. See John Gill, *With Eagles to Glory: Napoleon and His German Allies in the 1809 Campaign* (Barnsley 1992), p. 489. In addition to the dismantling of fortifications in Vienna, Austria was also required to cede Salzburg, birthplace of Mozart, to Bavaria. (Translator's note)

29. On 12th October, 1809, Frederich Staps approached Napoleon with the pretence of presenting a petition, but was stopped and arrested by Général Rapp, due to his hand being concealed in his coat pocket. A knife was found in his possession, and he admitted to the assassination attempt upon questioning by Napoleon. He insisted he was not insane but patriotic, and blamed Napoleon directly for the wars against Austria. He asserted he would continue to assault Napoleon if pardoned, and so was executed by firing squad five days later. (Translator's note)

Chapter 5

1. Marie-Louise married Napoléon by proxy in Vienna on 11 March, 1810. For an account of the Braunau leg of her journey to Paris, see Maurice de Tascher, *Campaigning for Napoleon* (Barnsley, 2006), p. 277. (Translator's note)
2. Magdeburg is a city located in central Germany along the river Elbe. It was notoriously sacked and burnt in 1631, during the Thirty Years War. More recently, it was briefly besieged by French forces under Marshals Murat and Ney from 25 October, 1806, to 8 November, 1806. Occurring after the French victory at Jena-Auerstadt, the 25,000 Prussian garrison surrendered to the remaining 18,000 French troops once a bombardment seemed likely. (Translator's note)
3. *Lieutenant* Moncey would transfer to the *2ème Régiment de Chasseurs à Pied as Capitaine* in 1812, returning to the hussar arm in 1813, this time as a *Major* in the *7ème Hussards*. He was awarded the *Légion d'Honneur* by Napoléon during the Russian campaign to the approval of all his comrades. It would be interesting to see how quickly Bertrand would have become an officer if he followed this well-connected patron. See ed. B.T. Jones, *Napoleon's Army: The Military Memoires of Charles Parquin*, (Wiltshire, 1969), p. 166. (Translator's note)

Chapter 6

1. The *7ème Léger* received a company of regimental artillery. (Translator's note)
2. There was a review of other units at the same time in Gumbinen. According to the report of 15th June, 1812, the *7ème Léger* had 5 battalions with an effective strength of 4,163 men. The other regiments of Gudin's division were the *12ème de Ligne* with 5 battalions and 4,142 men; the *21ème de Ligne* with 5 battalions and 4,744 men; and the *127ème de Ligne*, which was formed in 1811 of two battalions of German troops from Lübeck and Hamburg. (Original editor's note)
3. Jean-François Rome (1773–1826), was appointed *Colonel* of the *7ème Léger* on 15th April, 1811. He was wounded at the battle of Borodino, on 7th September, 1812. (Translator's note)
4. The original term is *la Diane*. This was a bright, staccato tune, measured by drum beats and intended to wake the sleeping soldiers. (Translator's note)
5. Five bridges were thrown upstream from Kowno, one near the confluence of the Lesza, 2 between this confluence and the village of Ponémouni, 150 toises from each other. (Original editor's note)
6. On 26th June, the Emperor placed two battalions of the *7ème Regiment d'Infanterie Légère* at the disposal of Montbrun, with a recommendation to spare them. (Original editor's note)
7. Presumably 28th June, 1812. (Original editor's note)
8. According to Count Philippe de Ségur, 'In these first marches, which were painful, order and discipline were maintained in Davout's corps, which suffered less from famine than the others.' The same author states that the infantry of Davout's *1er Corps d'armée* carried in their knapsack 'two shirts, two pairs of shoes with spare nails and soles, a pair of pantaloons, one pair of cloth half-gaiters, a few articles requisite to cleanliness, one bandage, a quantity of lint, and 60 cartridges. In the two sides of the bag were placed four loaves of biscuit bread of 16 ounces each. Under these were 10 pounds of flour in a long, narrow linen bag. The whole knapsack and its contents, together with the straps and the hood, rolled up and fastened at the top, weighed 33 pounds and 12 ounces. Each soldier also carried a linen bag, slung in the form of a shoulder-

belt, containing two loaves of three pounds each. This with his sabre, his shoulder belt and musket, he had to carry 58 pounds of weight, and was provided with bread for four days, biscuit bread for four, flour for seven, and 60 rounds of ammunition.' See Count Philip de Ségur, *History of the Expedition to Russia, undertaken by the Emperor Napoleon in the Year 1812* (London, 1825), II vols, I, pp. 285–6. If Bertrand had the discipline and strength to preserve these rations and kit, it certainly would have assisted him in remaining with the rearguard during the retreat, rather than becoming a straggler or marauder. (Translator's note)

9. It would seem that this order was to detonate the artillery ammunition, possibly because it was not possible to capture it. (Translator's note)
10. An abatis is a defensive structure made from trees. Their construction varies, but there are usually wooden spikes along the abatis prevent infantry and cavalry from climbing over. (Translator's note)
11. Gudin's body was recovered and returned to France by the Russian government in 2021, in a ceremony attended by a guard of honour in Napoleonic-era uniforms. His remains reveal that the cannonball injured a leg, which was amputated. His death was caused by gangrene. The division's new commander was *Général* Gérard. (Translator's note)
12. According to de Ségur, '. . . Gudin's division, deprived of their general, had drawn up there by the corpses of their companions and of the Russians, amidst the stumps of broken trees, on ground trampled by the feet of the combatants, furrowed with balls, strewn with the fragments of weapons, tattered garments, military utensils, carriages overthrown, and scattered limbs . . .'. De Ségur, *History of the Expedition to Russia*, p. 262. (Translator's note)
13. The *7ème Léger* had 32 decorations. Captain Moncey, Commander of the author's company and wounded, was decorated. He had been a page of the Emperor. (Original editor's note)
14. (14th Bulletin of the Grande Armée). At Valontina Gudin's division attacked with such intrepidity that the enemy had convinced themselves that it was the Imperial Guard. The passage to Wiasma occurred on the 29th August, 1812. (Original editor's note)
15. *Cantiniers* were sutlers authorized to sell additional supplies to the troops of the French army. Their female counterparts, *cantinières*, are celebrated

in various memoirs. *Gendarmerie* were the military police attached to the *Grande Armée*, most famously the *Gendarmes d'élite* of the Imperial Guard. *Gendarmes* also served inside France, maintaining law and order. (Translator's note)
16. Gérard's division was part of the French centre under the orders of Prince Eugene, and together with with Morand's division, took the Borodino redoubt. These two divisions had been detached from Davout's *1er Corps d'armée* for the battle and attached to the *4ème Corps*. (Original editor's note)
17. A Biscayan is a large-calibre musket. (Translator's note)
18. The *peloton* belonged to the dragoons of Siberia and Irkousk, commanded by General Korff, whose charge had been directed against *30ème Régiment d'Infanterie de Ligne*, of *Général* Morand's division. (Original editor's note)
19. This may seem to be a breach of the rules of war, but it was an accepted convention that, once the battle was over, those defeated or abandoned by their units should not take up arms. Furthermore, these three soldiers had not surrendered to the French, and the Russians were known for pretending to be dead, and then taking their arms and shooting once the enemy had passed. This practice led to French troops showing less quarter to Russian troops than those of other nations. (Translator's note)
20. I bequeathed this certificate to my two grandsons, orphans of father and mother, who following their success in their studies, will enter the military academy at Saint-Cyr, and will take their place in the ranks of our army. They will be proud to have it and to be able to say: 'This title of honour comes from our grandfather, an old soldier of Jena, Eylau, Friedland, Wagram, Smolensk, Moskowa, Dresden.' (Author's note)
21. At the rear of the back of the Dorogomilow suburb. (Original editor's note)
22. Partial fires had broken out from the first moments of the entry of the Grand Army into Moscow, but the city-wide fire spread by heavy winds took place on 16th, 17th and 18th September, 1812. (Original editor's note)
23. The term Bertrand uses is *feu de deux rangs*. (Translator's note)
24. It would seem that this was a 'duty' battalion furnished by the regiment, which foraged on behalf of the regiment, to prevent disorder and excesses.

As the regiment had five battalions for this campaign, it made sense for such a large unit to be organized prior to the retreat from Moscow. (Translator's note)

25. The evacuation of the wounded began on 15th October, 1812, the Emperor left the city on the 19th. (Original editor's note)
26. The total forces under Kutuzov's command numbered 90,000, but the numbers present at the battle of Malojaroslawetz were about 24,000 on either side. The battle was a tactical victory for the Franco-Italian army, but a strategic defeat for Napoléon, as the only path for retreat was over the same route of his advance, now devoid of supplies. (Translator's note)
27. The *Grande Armée* marched in four echelons: The Imperial Guard; Marshal Ney's *3éme Corps*; Prince Eugène's *4ème Corps*; and Marshal Davout's *1er Corps*. (Original editor's note)
28. Along with Grouchy's cavalry. (Original editor's note)
29. The battle of Vyazma was a bitter rearguard action in which Marshal Davout's *1er Corps* was almost surrounded and routed by General Miloradovich's Russian army. Whilst Napoléon's various *corps d'armée* were reordering their line of retreat on 2nd November, Miloradovich noticed a gap between the *1er corps* and those of Eugéne's Italian *4ème Corps d'armée* and Poniatowski's Polish *5ème Corps d'armée*. Initial Russian attacks captured the *4ème Corps*' baggage and threatened to isolate Davout's 14,000 men. However, an unsupported Russian cavalry advance enabled Eugéne to counter-attack, thereby stabilizing the situation. As the French continued their retreat, however, Miloradovich repositioned his troops and opened artillery fire, which caused heavy casaulties to Davout's men. By the time the Russian infantry arrived to support the cavalry, Davout's *Corps* had sheltered behind those of Eugene and Ney, which bore the brunt of the attacks. The *7ème Léger* was tasked with guarding Viazma as the last units of the *Grande Armée* retreated. See Edward Foord, *Napoleon's Russian Campaign of 1812* (London, 1914), pp. 316–18. (Translator's note)
30. 'Division' in this context means a frontage of two *pelotons*. The five battalions of the *7ème Léger* seem to have formed a single attack column with closed intervals between each division, a formation usually used by a single full-strength battalion. (Translator's note)

31. The *1er Corps* arrived at Orscha on the 19th November, 1812. (Original editor's note)
32. The *3ème Corps* left Orscha on the 21st at 0800, and the *1er Corps* soon after. (Original editor's note)
33. During the night of November 23rd to 24th, the Emperor sent *Général* Chasseloup-Laubat of the engineers and *Général* Éblé of the pontonniers from Bobr to Borisov, with wagons containing tools. They arrived at Borisov on the 25th, together with Marshal Mortier, Duke of Treviso. The main body of the army arrived at the Berezina on the 26th, and the *3ème Corps* only on the 27th. (Original editor's note)
34. The organization of the French army had been completely altered by the Restoration government. The regiments and divisions of the *Grande Armée* were replaced with *legions* with names corresponding to the their regions. (Translator's note)
35. If the candles were made of beef or mutton tallow, rather than more expensive beeswax, they would have been edible, and suitable for frying other foodstuffs in. (Translator's note)
36. 8th December, 1812. (Original editor's note)
37. This was most likely a cornet from a voltigeur company, since many light infantry regiments preferred the drums of the line infantry for their chasseur companies. Although the cornet produced a less effective sound for communicating signals than the drum, it was much more suited to the skirmishing role of voltigeur companies due its lighter, compact nature. See Elting, *Swords around a Throne*, pp. 337–8. (Translator's note)
38. The mountain of Ponari, 4km from Wilna. (Original editor's note)
39. Bertrand probably meant his battalion's *adjudant sous-officier*, since each battalion within a regiment had one. (Translator's note)
40. On the 13th December, 1812. (Original editor's note)
41. Presumably for their burial. (Translator's note)
42. The heat and smoke probably killed off the vermin, most likely lice. (Translator's note)
43. He was probably a non oath-swearing priest during the French Revolution. In 1790, the Catholic Church in France was subject to radical reform, with clergymen being required to swear an oath to the French nation, and to accept salaries from the French government. This placed

their loyalty in conflict with the Pope, resulting in those that accepted the new oath, and those who did not. This would explain his emigration to Poland in 1792. (Translator's note)
44. The phrase Bertand uses is *'je lui donnai la plaque de ma giberne (un cor de chasse avec la mention 7ème régiment d'infanterie légère).'* As the standard badge for light infantry was a hunting horn only, it would appear that *7ème Léger* used a regimental variant, most likely with a number 7 present, possibly inside the loop of the horn. (Translator's note)
45. When *1er Corps d'Armée* gathered at Thorn, it numbered 996 officers and 2,362 *sous-officiers* and soldiers, of which 729 officers and 1,807 *sous-officiers* and soldiers were fit for duty. When it entered Russia, the *1er Corps* had been 65,000 infantry strong. Such was the fate of the best controlled, the best supervised, the best governed of all *Corps d'armée*, under a leader whose intelligent severity was recognized to preserve men by discipline; but Davout was also the one who, in the first trials of the retreat, had suffered the most for the common good. (Original editor's note, citing *Camille Rousset*)

Chapter 7

1. The *7ème Léger* had, in fact, always held the extreme rear guard, with Marshals Davout and Ney. (Original editor's note)
2. This was in reference to a curse word originating from the region of Gasconny, from which a large number of the regiment were recruited, in particular, the department of Gard. (Author's note)
3. The Cossacks of Wittgenstein's army reached Marienwerder on 12th January, 1813. This skirmish was probably fought around 16th or 17th January. (Original editor's note)
4. On 17th January, Marshal Murat handed over command of the army to Prince Eugéne de Beauharnais. This force consisted of those men of the *1er*, *2ème*, *3ème*, *4ème* and *6ème Corps d'armée* still capable of fighting in the open countryside. Eugéne found 11,500 men, which he formed into three divisions, one of which was French, under Gérard, one Bavarian under Rechberg, and one Polish under Girard. His cavalry numbered 1,000 horses. Each *corps d'armée* had a depot, with that of the *1er* Corps fixed at Stettin. As each infantry regiment was

able to provide only one or two companies, on 23rd January, Napoléon reduced the infantry regiments to four battalion establishments. He ordered the cadres of the first battalion of each regiment to remain with the army, those of the second to go to Erfort, and the cadres of the remaining battalions to return to their regimental depots. (Original editor's note).

It is likely that the cadres of the second, third and fourth battalions, as well as the regimental staff were marching along the route referred to by Bertrand. (Translator's note)

5. Since the distance from Bromberg to Torgau is about 320km, we can estimate a rate of 30km per day, which no small distance for men who had already undergone such trials. Torgau was only reached after 10 or 11 days of walking, either around 26th or 28th January. On the other hand, Torgau is about 179km from Erfurt, so it takes about 5 days of walking. In total: 10 days of walking to Erfurt. Adding the 3 days spent in Torgau we see that Bertrand arrived in Erfurt on 5th February, 1813. (Original editor's note)

6. The French army had no chaplains on the official establishment, being officially a secular army. It is possible that this clergyman was a chaplain on the establishment of one of the allied contingents. (Translator's note)

7. These replacement articles were probably from the 1812 Bardin regulations, most notably the short-tailed, high-waisted habit-veste and pokalem undress cap. (Translator's note)

8. The *adjudant sous-officier* was the senior non-commissioned officer in an infantry battalion. According to the celebrated memorialist Baron Marbot, 'it is this warrant officer who has the lists of all the sous-officiers in the battalion, and it is he who assigns them in turn the daily tasks, the guard details, the detachments, etc. The adjutant sous-officier announces to the sergent-majors how many men their companies are to furnish, and puts an end to the disputes that often arise between them. After informing them of the time and place at which the guards are to meet each other, he gathers the contingents of each company, and punishes those sergent-majors who brought in their details too late or fewer than was required of them. The adjutant sous-officer has the battalion orders

copied and circulated to all its companies and gathers in their reports and situations; he supervises the guard house and other prisons, has the fires extinguished, leads the fatigue detail furnished by the whole battalion to the stores, and during the distribution of supplies he ensures that order reigns amongst the fourriers, and prescribes to each of them their turn. Finally, he is the chief of all the sous-officers of the battalion, and the linchpin of all that concerns their service to the battalion.' See Colonel Marcellin Marbot, *Remarques Critiques sur l'Ouvrage de Lieutenant-Général Rogniat* (Paris, 1820), pp. 103–04. (Translator's note)

9. According to the 1812 regulations, The *adjudant sous-officier*'s epaulettes consisted of a fringed epaulette on the right and a fringeless contre-epaulette, on the left. The fringe would consist of mixed red and gold lace. The shoulder boards had three red and two gold stripes running alternately along their length. Their sword knot would probably have a similar design, ie. mixed fringe tassel and alternate striped strap. (Translator's note)

10. The *7ème Léger* was, at this time, part of the 1st Brigade commanded by *Général* Pouchelon, of the 1st Division under Général Philippon, of the reorganized *1er Corps d'armée*. The other regiment of Pouchelon's brigade was the *12ème Régiment d'Infanterie de Ligne*. The *7ème Léger* was commanded by *Colonel* Jean-Vincent Autran. (Original editor's note)

11. The role of commanding the fatigue detail responsible for drawing and carrying the supplies fell to the *Capitaines*, who rotated through this duty on a weekly basis, hence the term *capitaine de semaine*. Consequently, it was a role, rather than a rank. It seems that they did this on behalf of the entire regiment, not just their battalion. (Translator's note)

12. Each infantry regiment had a small detachment of sappers attached to the regimental headquarters. They were officially in charge of small-scale engineering works, such as preparing camps or clearing obstacles from the route of march. In this instance, the sapper appears to have functioned as an orderly to the *Colonel*. (Translator's note)

13. *Général* Moreau was a successful French commander during the Revolutionary wars, and rival to Napoleon for the political loyalty of the army in 1800. He was exiled for suspected involvement in a plot to

overthrow the First Consul, and in 1813 he served as a military advisor to Tsar Alexander, until his death at Dresden. (Translator's note)
14. The Imperial Decree was dated 19th September, 1813; History of the *82ème*, former *7ème Léger*. (Translator's note)
15. This was a combat at Gieshübel (23rd August) against the Prince of Wurttemberg who, having assaulted the Kohlberg, was driven out by Vandamme and pursued as far as Peterswald. (Original editor's note)
16. Presumably Peterswald. That day, 29th August, 1813, Vandamme again overthrew the Russian rearguard between Hollendorf and Peterswald. (Original editor's note)
17. Following Napoleon's victory at Dresden on 26–27th August, 1813, Général Vandamme's 34,000 strong *1er Corps d'armée* pursued the allied corps of Ostermann-Tolstoy, 14,700 strong. On the 29th August, Vandamme attempted to seize the mountain passes through which the retreating allies were passing, but failed. On the 30th August, Vandamme was faced with 60,000 allied troops, with Friedrich Von Kleist's Prussian corps, Ostermann-Tolstoy's allied corps and the Austrian corps of von Colloredo-Mansfield. (Translator's note)
18. The word Bertrand uses is a *mamelon*, which is usually a breast-shaped hill. (Translator's note)
19. On 28th August, Gouvion Saint-Cyr had received the order from the Emperor to link up with Vandamme, and then take the *2ème Corps* to Gieshübel. However, he stopped at Maxen and the next day (29th August) he allowed Marmont's *6ème Corps* pass in front of him. On 30th August, Mortier's *2ème Corps* of the Young Guard) left Pirna to march on Kulm, Marmont was at Aetenberg, Murat's cavalry reserve was at Zétau, and Gouvion Saint-Cyr was at Lièbenau. (Original editor's note)
20. *Général* Corbineau commanded the *5ème* light cavalry division attached to the *1er Corps d'armée* on the march on Kulm. (Original editor's note)
21. To Liebenau. (Original editor's note)
22. The *1er Corps d'armée* stayed in Dresden from 1st September to 6th September, 1813. On the 7th it was reviewed there by the Emperor. On the 8th it returned to Bohemia, being at Bernersdorff on the 9th. It was around Frastenwald on the 10th, with the *11ème* division being at Péterswald, the *2ème* at Nallendorff, the *23ème* division at Hellendorff (being recently

assigned to the *1er Corps*). On the 14th, the Austrian general Colloredo attacked along the roads of Breitenau and Péterswald, leading to the retreat of the *1er Corps* on Gieshübel. (Original editor's note)

23. Buda and Pest would not be united as Budapest, the capital of Hungary, until 1867. (Translator's note)
24. It seems likely that Bertrand is referring to Parndorf, 47km south-east of Vienna, and 200km west-north-west of Pest. (Translator's note)
25. Modern-day Bratislava, capital of Slovakia. (Translator's note)
26. The term Bertrand uses is *ordinaire*. This was a group of 14–16 soldiers who, when in garrison, had weekly sums deducted from their pay, which contributed to a fund for purchasing food, drink, and other necessaries. It was run by a *caporal* or a trustworthy soldier. As an *adjudant sous-officier*, Bertrand would have been more familiar with the running of an *ordinaire* than the commissioned officers, who had different dining arrangements. See Crowdy, *Napoleon's Infantry Handbook*, pp. 121–2. (Translator's note)

Chapter 8

1. In Hungarian Nagy-Varad, on the Szébis river. (Original editor's note)
2. Probably Tshiklowa, about 30km from the Turkish border. If we follow the march from Prague to (Isakowa?) on a map, we see that Austria made its prisoners follow an astonishing itinerary well beyond a direct line from departure to destination. (Original editor's note)
3. *Colonel* Hilaire-Benoit Reynaud had commanded the *15ème de Ligne* since 1804. (Original editor's note)
4. The battle of Paris was on 30th March, 1814. The Military convention was signed on 31st March at 2 o'clock in the morning, with the entry of the allies into Paris later that morning. Napoléon abdicated in favour of his son on 4 April, before abdicating fully on 13 April. The peace treaty was signed on 30 May, 1814. This meant that Austria had taken five months to inform its prisoners of the abdication and four months to release them. (Original editor's note)
5. This appears to be the play by Beaumarchais, rather than the later opera by Mozart. (Translator's note)
6. French Huningue and Swiss Basel are adjacent towns on the left bank of the Rhine River. (Translator's note)

Chapter 9

1. The Emperor disembarked at Fréjus on 1st March, 1815. (Original editor's note)
2. 10th March, 1815. (Original editor's note)
3. At 0900, on the 20th March, 1815. (Original editor's note)
4. The original title of the song is '*Où peut-on être mieux qu'au sein de sa famille*'. (Translator's note)
5. (The Army of the Rhine (*1er Corps d'armée*), comprised the *15ème, 16ème* and *17ème* Infantry Divisions, the *7ème* Cavalry Division and 46 guns, in all approximately 22,000 men. The *7ème Régiment d'Infanterie Légère* was part of the *17ème* Division, along with the *55ème, 58ème* and *104ème Régiments d'Infanterie de Ligne*, under the command of *Général de Division* Grandjean. (Original editor's note).
6. Since Saverne lies 20km west of this Strasbourg/Haguenau line, Bertrand probably meant that it was a supply depot and line of communication. (Translator's note)
7. According to *Général* Rapp's memoirs, the *16ème* Infantry Division was commanded by *Général de Division* Albert, the *1er* Brigade of which included the *10ème Léger* and the *32ème de Ligne*, under *Général de Brigade* Beaumann. The *2ème* Brigade comprised the 18ème de Ligne and 57ème de Ligne. On the other hand, it seems that *Général* Estève was, at this time, employed in the Vendée region under the orders of *Général* Travot. However in the history of the *81ème de Ligne* (ex-*7ème Léger*), *Général* Estève is designated as commander of this brigade at this time. (Original editor's note).
8. 2,900 mobilized National Guardsmen were assigned to the *5ème Corps*. See *Memoirs of Général Rapp*. (Original editor's note.)
9. From 27th June to 26th August, *Général* Barbanègre, together with 30 men of the depot of the *7ème Léger*), 100 gunners and 3 gendarmes, sustained a glorious siege at Huningue, against an Austrian and Swiss army of 24,000 men. On 27th August, the day of the capitulation, the garrison, reduced to 50 men, paraded with the honours of war, in front of Archduke Jean and the enemy army, who were stupefied at the sight! (Original editor's note)

10. Vienne is a town 35km south of Lyons, and 220km north of Nîsmes, Bertrand's home town. (Original editor's note)
11. This was the White Terror, in which pro-Royalist gangs briefly terrorized those who had served the Napoleonic regime. (Translator's note)
12. Nîsmes is noted for the survival of many ancient Roman buildings and ruins. (Translator's note)

Index

1er Corps d'armée, 83, 117, 119, 120, 122
7ème Corps d'armée
    camp at Brest, xxi, 6
    Jena, 16
7ème Régiment d'Infanterie Légère
    Bertrand's reunion with, 148
    Dalouzy, see Dalouzy, *sergent*
    Dresden, battle of, 119
    flag/eagle, 43, 70, 89, 94–5, 113, 140, 142, 161
    history, xx–xxii
    Kulm, battle of, 120–1
Alexander I, Tsar of Russia, 24–5, 126
Army of the Rhine, xii, 161–4, 166, 167–8
Augereau, Marshal Charles Pierre François, Duc de Castiglione, 11

Bavarian dragoons, 143–5
Berlin, 9
Bertrand, Vincent
    capitivity, xii
    convalesence, xii, 128–33
    food, 9, 22, 24, 47–8, 50, 54–5
    hospitalisation, 45–6, 107–10, 130, 134
    Légion d'Honneur, 119

    marauding party, see French Army, foraging expeditions
    prisoner, 125–6
    promotion, 113
        caporal, xi, 54
        sergent, xi, 59
        sergent-major, xi
        Sous-lieutenant, xiii, 165
        adjudant sous-officer, xii, 116
        Lieutenant, xiii
        Capitaine, xiii
    wounding of, x, xii, 42–3, 45, 124–5
Bonaparte, Napoléon, 1st Emperor of the French, 21–2, 46–7, 117, 119, 148–9, 157, 158

Cossacks, 21, 78, 80–4, 88–9, 93, 94–5, 98, 126

Dalouzy (*sergent*), 163–72
Dresden, battle of, xii, 119
Duc de Berry (Beri), 150–1
duel, 31–3, 145, 153–4, 156

Emperor, the, see Bonaparte
Eckmühl, battle of (1809), x
Eylau, battle of (1807), 15–16

French Army
  flag/eagle, see *7ème Régiment d'Infanterie Légère*
  foraging expeditions, 6, 23–4, 43
  infantry, organisation of, xxii
  personnel, xiv–xv

Gard,
  department of, ix, 172
  legion of, xii
Grande Armée, xxi
Guillianche, *Colonel* Chaland, x–xiii

Hamburg, 115–16
Heilsberg, battle of (1807) 21–3
Huguenot communities, 3
Huningue, 1, 152

Jena, battle of, x, 7–8
  town, 6

Kellerman, Marshal François Christophe de, Duc de Valmy, 112
Kowno, 94–6
Kulm, battle of (1813), xii, 120–2

Lacour, comrade, 1, 2, 4, 43
Lépine, comrade, 126
Légion d'Honneur, xii, 119
  theft of, 124
Louis Ferdinand, Prince of Prussia (1772–1806), funeral bier, 5

Lussac, comrade, 134–5, 136, 137, 146, 148

Moreau, Général Jean-Victor Marie, 119
Moskowa, battle of (see Russia, 1812 campaign)

Pest, 132–3
Peterswald, xii, 122–3
Polish people, Bertrand's admiration of, 19
Prague, 128
Pressbourg, siege of, x, 133
prisoner (see Bertrand)
promotion (see Bertrand)

rations, 117–18, 120
Rapp, Jean, *Général*, 164–5, 168
Reynaud, *Colonel*, comrade, 140, 142
Russia, 1812 Campaign
  Berezina, battle of, x, 84–7
  evacuation of Moscow, 76–7
  invasion of, 59–75
  Krasnoë, battle of, 82–3
  Malojaroslawetz, battle of, 76
  Moscow
    occupation of, 70–6
    fire of (1812), xi, 72–3
  Moskowa, battle of, 68–9
  Niemen, crossing of
  Smolensk, battle of, 64–5

Valontina, battle of, 65–6
Wiasma, 80–1
Wilna (Vilnius), 90–1

Saalfield, battle of, x, 5
School of the soldier, 1
Strasbourg, Bavarian/Württemberg assault of, 161–2
swimming, 4, 140

theatre, 34–5, 135, 148

uniform, infantry, 2

Vienna
    demolition of fortifications, 48
    occupation of, 40, 50–1

Wagram, battle of (1809), x, 42–3
Waterloo, 161
White Terror, xii, 173
Wkra river, crossing of, 10
Würtemberg hussars, brawl, 146–7